9th edition

Long-Term Care

How to Plan and Pay for It

Joseph L. Matthews

NOLO
LAW for ALL

Ninth Edition	OCTOBER 2012
Editor	BETSY SIMMONS HANNIBAL
Cover Design	SUSAN PUTNEY
Production	SUSAN PUTNEY
Proofreading	SUSAN CARLSON GREENE
Index	MEDEA MINNICH
Printing	BANG PRINTING

Matthews, Joseph L.
 Long-term care : how to plan and pay for it / Joseph L. Matthews. --
9th ed.
     p. cm.
 Includes index.
 ISBN 978-1-4133-1751-0 (pbk)--ISBN 978-1-4133-1752-7 (epub/ebook)
1. Older people--Long-term care--Evaluation. 2. Long-term care of the
sick--Evaluation. 3. Older people--Long-term care--Finance. 4.
Long-term care of the sick--Finance. 5. Consumer education. I. Nolo
(Firm) II. Title.
 RA644.5.M38 2012
 362.16068'1--dc23

                            2012022807

Please note

We believe accurate, plain-English legal information should help you solve many of
your own legal problems. But this text is not a substitute for personalized advice from a
knowledgeable lawyer. If you want the help of a trained professional—and we'll always
point out situations in which we think that's a good idea—consult an attorney licensed
to practice in your state.

Acknowledgments

Many thanks go to Ralph Warner, who saw immediately the value of a book such as this and who gave the project its birth. And thanks also to Betsy Simmons Hannibal, who has carefully steered the book through its subsequent editions.

Special thanks go to Peter Yedidia, president of Geriatric Health Systems of San Francisco, who gave generously of his time and vast professional experience in matters of health care programs for the elderly. His corrective commentaries greatly strengthened the manuscript.

Special thanks also to Diane Arnold-Driver, coordinator of the Center on Aging at the University of California, Berkeley. She shared readily her great expertise in geriatric care matters and tactfully made a number of suggestions which redounded to the significant benefit of the text.

Thank you also to Lora Connolly and Sandra Pierce-Miller of the California Department of Health Services, who took the time to clarify a number of matters pertaining to state partnership long-term care insurance programs.

And many thanks to Stan Jacobsen, whose thorough research has not only helped keep this book up-to-date, but has also provided readers with valuable new information.

Also, my thanks to Spencer Sherman for updating the third edition.

A final and most exuberant thanks goes to editor Barbara Kate Repa, whose perspicacity and skill are matched only by her patience and good humor. She needed all of them with me. The quality of this book is in large measure due to her talents.

About the Author

Joseph Matthews has been an attorney since 1971. He has for many years been involved in matters relating to seniors, and is the author of *Social Security, Medicare & Government Pensions* as well as *How to Win Your Personal Injury Claim*, both published by Nolo.

Table of Contents

Your Long-Term Care Companion

Maybe you're trying to sort out how to find the best living situation for yourself as you age and begin to need regular help with the activities of daily life. Or, maybe you're helping someone else—your spouse, parent, grandparent—plan for or manage long-term care. In either case, you've no doubt already learned what a daunting task it can be, full of practical hurdles and emotional ups and downs.

At times, you may feel isolated and overwhelmed by all that you have to handle. But you're not alone. Almost three-fourths of all people needing assistance with daily living receive it, unpaid, from family and friends. But more than five million people pay for care they receive at home. And over three million people over age 65 live full-time in a nursing home, assisted living facility, or other type of residential care setting—at a cost of $30,000 to $150,000 per year.

Our society has developed a myriad of programs, places, and people to help elders through their final years more comfortably and more affordably. In particular, there has been an enormous growth of alternative care and living arrangements to replace the old two-choice system in which either the family took on the entire burden of care or an elder went into a nursing home. These new arrangements offer different levels of care to meet a wide range of needs. And almost as important, they do so at different levels of expense. There are also many avenues—local, state, and federal government programs and private insurance—to help pay for care.

While the recent mushrooming of long-term care choices is a great boon to many people, it also presents a new set of problems: How can I sort through the many, sometimes bewildering options in long-term care?

That's where this book comes in. It can help you make sense of the many types of care and residences, it explains financing options, and it can help you find local caregivers, agencies, and facilities.

For those in the planning stages for long-term care, the book explains the benefits and risks of long-term care insurance and helps you choose a policy if you decide such insurance is a good idea for you. It also explains eligibility rules and coverage of Medicare and Medicaid (Medi-Cal in California). This book also explains how to protect your medical and financial choices by preparing advance health care directives and power of attorney documents.

When it comes time to make actual arrangements for care, the book can help you:

- decide whether home care is possible, find and arrange that care, and introduce you to supplemental community-based assistance
- explore the many residential alternatives to nursing homes, including assisted living and multilevel residential facilities
- find and choose among nursing homes, if that turns out to be the best alternative, or
- find and hire a geriatric care manager who can personally help you find the care you need.

Once you or a family member is actually receiving care, this book can help with two more difficult matters. It explains how to protect yourself, or your elder loved one, against the various kinds of fraud that are too often attempted with the elderly. And it explains how hospice may become a sensible, comforting alternative to continued aggressive medical care during the final months of life.

We know that no book by itself can transform the difficult tasks and emotions of long-term care into a stroll in the park. But we do know—as we've heard from so many readers of previous editions—that explaining the options in simple, straightforward language can be of great help in making the transition to long-term care as smooth as possible for elders and for the people who care for them.

Get Updates and More Online

When there are important changes to the information in this book, we'll post updates online, on a page dedicated to this book: **www.nolo.com/back-of-book/ELD.html**. You'll find other useful information there, too, including author blogs, podcasts, and videos.

Making Decisions About Long-Term Care

Although the sudden onset of an illness or disability does not always permit much advanced planning for long-term care, this book encourages you to be the best comparison shopper possible. If you are able to explore alternatives before rushing to move into a nursing facility, you improve your chances of obtaining the level of care you need—and perhaps saving a great deal of money.

Being prepared and researching alternatives when choosing long-term care allows you to realistically assess what is needed, and to choose only the kind of care that is actually required. In this way, you can avoid the loss of independence and great cost that come with taking on more care than necessary. This is particularly true when some combination of home health care and personal assistance would be sufficient to permit a person to remain at home instead of entering a residential nursing facility. Or when an assisted living or residential care facility can provide sufficient care to allow a person to avoid entering a nursing facility. When time permits, doing some financial planning *before* residence in a long-term care facility becomes necessary may permit you to protect some of the value of your home or life's savings.

Finally, and importantly, the more thorough you are, the greater the opportunity for everyone concerned to participate—particularly if the person who needs care is not easily able to investigate and make decisions on his or her own. With more alternatives, everyone involved will have greater emotional room to come to terms with the decisions that have to be made.

Getting Started

If you need care, you may find it a hard topic to raise with others. It may feel like a blow to your self-esteem or that it means you are really "old." You may also be reluctant to begin a process of giving up some of your independence or surrendering full control over your life. And when you know you need the help of your family, you may be fearful of becoming a burden.

If you believe that someone else—a family member or other loved one—is in need of care, you may be reluctant to bring up the subject because it may seem like a challenge or an insult. And, within the family, there may be anxiety, guilt, and wide differences of opinion about what care is needed and who should provide it.

The first step in getting necessary care is to overcome your reluctance to talk about it. Once the discussion has begun, you can use the information in this book to organize and choose the right kinds of care.

Get Help From Others

To get the discussion underway and keep it on the right track, it is often best to look outside the family. An unrelated person can sometimes soothe ruffled family feathers, present a neutral opinion, and offer solutions the family might not know about. Also, you may find it easier to reveal fears and other feelings to an outsider than to an involved family member.

Here are some of the people you can turn to for help in beginning to evaluate long-term care needs:

- Your personal physician is often a good place to start, not necessarily to moderate discussions but to define your medical needs and refer you to others who may be helpful in making arrangements.

- Traditional word-of-mouth is still one of the best ways to begin tackling any new problem. Friends and neighbors whose opinions you trust, and who may have already faced similar situations, are often a good source of information. The people at your local senior center may know of sources for long-term care assistance. These word-of-mouth sources often let you know of "unofficial" personal care aides who would not be available through more formal channels.

- A clergy member may be able to help directly or to refer you and your family to professionals who can introduce alternatives and coordinate planning.

Area Agencies on Aging

Area Agencies on Aging operate federally funded programs that help older persons and persons with disabilities live with dignity and choices in their homes and communities. An Agency on Aging may be able to help you choose and find the kind of long-term care that's right for you.

Most states have their own Agencies on Aging—and there may be local offices of the state agency in your own community. To find your local agency, check the state government listings in the white pages, call the Eldercare Locator at 800-677-1116, or look online at www.eldercare.gov.

- County family service agencies, Area Agencies on Aging, or other senior information and referral services are experienced sources that can provide direct access to specific care providers and help you develop an overall care plan. These agencies can direct you to a counselor or social worker who specializes in long-term care for elders and can help you begin your discussions and planning. (See the Resource Directory in the appendix of this book.)

- If residence in a nursing facility is not absolutely necessary, many people make use of the services of a professional geriatric care manager to see what at-home and other supportive services are available and to organize care from different providers. (Geriatric care managers are discussed in detail later in this chapter.)

- If you or your loved one has Alzheimer's disease or a similar mental impairment, you can turn to organizations that specialize in providing information and referrals to people facing these difficult situations. (See "Alzheimer's Disease Organizations" in this book's appendix.)

> **Involve the Care Receiver**
>
> If you are a family member helping to plan for someone else's care, bear in mind that the most essential participant in planning long-term care is the person whose care is being considered.

Assess Medical Needs

Because a specific physical or mental condition often leads to the need for long-term care, one of the first things you should do is get professional advice both about the need for immediate care and about likely changes in the condition over time. Talk with your primary care physician first; he or she may refer you to a geriatric specialist for further consultation.

An additional resource to help you assess medical and personal care needs is a geriatric screening program. Local hospitals have them, as do community and county health centers. If you have trouble finding a geriatric screening program, check with your county social service agency or local or Area Agency on Aging, call the senior referral number in the white pages of the phone book, or on the Internet, search for "geriatric screening program" and the name of your city, county, or state.

Some important things to consider when assessing an older person's need for medical care are:

- **Specific medical requirements.** The doctor or other health screening personnel can discuss the elder's specific medical needs (such as monitoring and administering drugs or providing physical therapy), explain how they can be met, and let you know who can do it. The doctor or health care worker can also discuss the level of ongoing care that would be required to deliver those medical services: family members supplemented by occasional visits from home care aides, a more sophisticated home care program, or various levels of residential nursing facility care, for example.

- **Changes in care over time.** The doctor or other health care worker can also discuss the medical prognosis—that is, what the future is likely to hold: whether to anticipate a short or long recovery period, whether a condition is likely to stabilize, or whether it will become worse over time. Knowing about likely medical developments will help you plan the right level of care for these changes.

- **Mental impairment.** Thorough geriatric screening and evaluation are particularly important when the elder seems to have a mental impairment. An older person's physical problems may become much more difficult to manage because of added symptoms of forgetfulness, disorientation, or general listlessness.

  Such mental impairments may indicate the early stages of Alzheimer's disease or other forms of dementia, which will require careful long-term care planning. (See Chapter 5 for a detailed discussion of care options for those suffering from Alzheimer's disease or similar impairments.)

  Sometimes, though, what looks like an irreversible loss of mental facilities may really be the result of some specific and treatable problem, such as improper medications or overmedication, poor nutrition, depression over the loss of a spouse or a friend, or a subtle medical condition that has not been diagnosed and treated. It is very important not to mistake a temporary and treatable loss of mental capacities for a permanent condition.

  In determining the true nature and cause of any loss of mental faculties, family members and friends can be particularly helpful to physicians and other health workers. The people who see an older person frequently are in the best position to know what factors may be contributing to diminished mental capabilities.

Evaluate Personal Needs and Capabilities

You will also have to figure out what sort of personal, nonmedical care is needed and what aspects of daily life a person can still manage without outside assistance. The need and ability to care for oneself is not simply a matter of physical competence. Often, it depends just as much on personality and emotional state. So, don't just consider what kind of care is needed and whether providers are available and affordable. The ultimate decision should also depend on how important it is to the elder to remain in control of his or her own life.

Some people fiercely hold on to personal independence and privacy. For these people (if they also have the ability to organize, manage, and pay for individual programs to meet their specific needs), it may be possible—and important—to stay at home and receive only minimal outside assistance.

Others may be willing to have an outside agency organize more comprehensive care programs, as long as they or their family members remain in primary control of daily lives. For one of these people, an agency-directed program of home care in a family residence or in secured housing, perhaps combined with adult day care, may be the best option, especially if family members are willing to give additional assistance.

Still other people prefer the security and ease of complete care organized and provided by others. For such a person, a residential care facility may be best, even though he or she may not physically require the high level of care offered there.

Learn About Family Leave Laws

The days and weeks when a family member's need for long-term care becomes apparent can be extremely difficult and stressful. Balancing your work responsibilities with your efforts to understand, locate, and arrange care can be overwhelming.

In recent years, many states and the federal government have tried to help solve this problem by requiring employers to provide some unpaid leave when a family member needs attention because of a health crisis. The federal Family and Medical Leave Act (FMLA) provides some needed help by requiring the following:

- Companies with 50 or more employees must give workers up to 12 weeks per year of unpaid leave to care for a child, spouse, or parent with a serious health condition.

- Companies must allow employees to return to their old jobs, or equivalent jobs at the same pay, when they return to work.

- During the leave, companies must provide the same health benefits as when the employees are being paid.

However, the law does not apply to all employees—or to all caregiving situations. You are entitled to FMLA leave only if you have worked for your employer for at least a year and have worked at least 1,250 hours (about 25 hours per week) during that time. Also, you are entitled to FMLA leave only to provide care to a parent, spouse, or child—if you need time off to care for another close family member, such as a sibling, parent-in-law, or domestic partner, you can't use FMLA leave.

Some state laws give workers more rights, apply to businesses with fewer than 50 employees, or provide longer leave periods. Some large companies also have their own leave policies which are more generous than state or federal laws require.

If some unpaid time off work would help you organize long-term care for a spouse or parent, check your employer's policy and make sure it complies with the FMLA and the law of your state. If you return to work after unpaid leave and you find that your job has changed for the worse, you may have a legal claim under the FMLA or similar state laws.

For more information on the FMLA, contact the Department of Labor at 866-487-9243, or visit its website at www.dol.gov, where you will find helpful fact sheets on your rights under the law. For information on your state's laws, contact your state labor department. The National Partnership for Women and Families in Washington, DC, has free information available on your rights under the FMLA, including a question-and-answer guide to the law's provisions and information on state leave laws. This information is available on its website at www. nationalpartnership.org.

Finally, if the family member who needs care has long-term care insurance, check the policy to see if it provides for respite care. Respite care pays for home care aides who give short-term breaks to family members who care for an elder. (See Chapter 9 for a discussion of long-term care insurance.)

Long-Term Care: A Glossary of Terms

In this book, we use "long-term care" to mean regular assistance with medical care (nursing, medicating, and physical therapy) or personal needs (eating, dressing, bathing, and moving around) provided by someone outside an older person's family. There are many varieties of long-term care—ranging from part-time home care and adult day care, to independent living and assisted living residential communities, to personal care residences and nursing facilities. Some long-term care is temporary—for example, just long enough to help an older person recover from a broken hip or a stroke. Often, though, once begun, it lasts for the remainder of an older person's life.

Here, we provide brief definitions of various care options to help you keep the terms straight as you use this book. Bear in mind that most of these are not formal or technical terms—what people mean when they use these terms may differ slightly from place to place, or from facility to facility.

Long-Term Care: A Glossary of Terms (cont'd)

Adult day care. Services such as meals, social activities, and exercise programs, plus companionship, provided for free or low cost at senior centers or special adult day care centers. For seniors who live independently, either at home or with relatives. See "Supplements to Home Care" in Chapter 2.

Assisted living. A small private apartment, single room, or shared room in a residential facility (usually seniors only) that offers meals, assistance with the activities of daily living, some personal care and housekeeping, and close monitoring of residents' health and safety, but not nursing or other medical care, except by special arrangement. See "Assisted Living" in Chapter 3.

Board and care facility/home. A long-term care residence facility—often small, sometimes in a private home—in which a resident is provided a room (often shared), meals, assistance with personal care, activities, and health and safety monitoring, but not nursing or other medical care. Also called a residential care facility for the elderly, a personal care facility, or a sheltered care facility. See "Levels of Care" in Chapter 4.

Continuing care retirement community. A multilevel facility that permits a resident to remain in the facility while moving among independent living, assisted living, and nursing facility care, as the resident's needs require. See "Combination Residential Facilities" in Chapter 3.

Convalescent home. A general term that could describe either a nursing facility or a board and care or sheltered care home. Like "rest home," the term is being used less and less.

Custodial care facility. Any long-term care residential facility—including nursing facility, board and care home, residential care facility for the elderly, personal care facility, and sheltered care facility—in which residents get a private or shared room, meals, assistance with personal care, physical and social activities, and round-the-clock monitoring. Depending on the level of the facility, residents may also receive regular nursing or other medical care. See "Levels of Care" in Chapter 4.

Extended care facility. A long-term care residence offering more than one level of care within the same facility. It may combine independent living with assisted living, assisted living with a custodial care facility, a custodial care facility with skilled

Long-Term Care: A Glossary of Terms (cont'd)

nursing care, or some other combination of these. it does not necessarily offer all levels of care, as a continuing care retirement community does. See "Combination Residential Facilities" in Chapter 3.

Geriatric care manager. Someone who assists in locating and arranging short-term or long-term care for an elder, either at home or in a residential setting. See "Geriatric Care Managers" In Chapter 1.

Home care. Short-term or long-term care at a senior's residence, offering assistance with the activities of daily living, personal care, housekeeping, and meal preparation. If it also includes "home health care" (see below) provided by a certified home health care agency, it can provide nursing and some other medical and therapeutic services. Home care can be provided in private residences or in (most) assisted living facilities, either by a home care agency or by independent paid or family providers. See Chapter 2.

Home health care. Usually short-term care following a serious illness, injury, or surgery. Provides nursing and other medical and therapeutic care during recovery. Can be combined with nonmedical home care, including help with activities of daily living, personal care, and housekeeping. Must be provided by state-licensed home health care agency. See Chapter 2.

Home health care agency. Certified by each state and by Medicare, these agencies can provide everything from skilled nursing care and therapy to assistance with grocery shopping and personal paperwork. See Chapter 2.

Hospice care. Hospice is a special type of care, usually provided in the home, for people who are terminally ill and likely to live less than six months. Hospice does not treat the illness but instead focuses on the patient's comfort, particularly pain and other symptom relief. It also provides respite care for primary caregivers. Medicare pays almost the entire cost of hospice care. See Chapter 6.

Independent living residence/community. A building or community specially designed for and restricted to seniors, offering a rented or purchased apartment or house. It provides on-site common facilities and services, but not personal or health care. See "Independent Living" in Chapter 3.

Long-Term Care: A Glossary of Terms (cont'd)

Intermediate care nursing facility. A residential facility that provides some nursing and other medical care, but not as much as a skilled nursing facility provides. these facilities provide long-term care of the chronically ill or disabled, or short-term care until a patient/resident can be moved to a custodial care facility. See "Levels of Care" in Chapter 4.

Long-term care. An extended period—either permanent or during recovery from a serious illness or injury—of assistance with basic activities of daily living (sometimes called personal care), such as bathing, eating, dressing, and moving around. It includes monitoring of health and safety and may also include nursing care and physical or other therapy, meals, social activities, and housekeeping. Long-term care can be provided in a private home, an organized senior residence, or nursing facility.

Long-term care facility. Any of several types of residences designed and operated to provide on-site assistance with basic activities of daily living and to monitor health and safety. See Chapter 4.

Multilevel facility. Same as "extended care facility," above.

Nursing facility/home: A residential care facility that provides long-term custodial care. Depending on the type of facility, it may also provide more or less extensive nursing care and physical or other therapy. See Chapter 4.

Personal care facility. Same as "board and care home," above.

Rehabilitation facility. Similar to a skilled nursing facility (see below), rehabilitation facilities provide a variety of short-term inpatient therapies (physical, occupational, and speech) during recovery from a serious illness, injury, or surgery.

Residential care facility for the elderly (RCFE). Another name for a personal care facility or board and care home.

Respite care. Temporary, part-time company for a dependent elder intended to give the primary caregiver (usually a spouse or another family member) some time off. See Chapter 2.

Rest home. An old-fashioned term, not used much any longer, for a long-term care facility.

Long-Term Care: A Glossary of Terms (cont'd)

Senior residence. A residential building or community that is designed for and limited to seniors. This term is often used to refer to independent living or assisted living. See Chapter 3.

Sheltered care. Usually refers to a "board and care home" (see above) but sometimes refers to "assisted living" (see above).

Skilled nursing facility (SNF). An inpatient facility that provides round-the-clock medical monitoring and daily, intensive nursing and therapy, as well as all necessary personal care. Usually limited to short-term stays following serious injury, illness, or surgery. See "Levels of Care" in Chapter 4.

Make a Realistic Family Commitment

Whether older people have the option to receive long-term care while maintaining their independence often depends on the extent to which family members are able and willing to help. But family situations vary widely in terms of whether relatives are willing and able to provide care, transportation, companionship, or financial support to an elder. Before any long-term care program is organized—particularly when the elder is to remain at home without a spouse—family members must get together and discuss what each of them will do to help meet needs that cannot be met by outside care or would be prohibitively expensive if provided by paid caregivers.

Staying at Home

An older person's ability to stay at home while receiving long-term care may depend on several kinds of family help. The elder may need daily or weekly assistance with personal or medical care that is not provided by a home care or other outside agency. Help with housekeeping, shopping, and home maintenance may also be necessary. And there will certainly be a need for regular visits and transportation to allow the elder to maintain contact with the outside world. The elder may also need help to plan, coordinate, and oversee outside care programs and to plan and administer financial matters.

Moving in With Family

If older people are unable to maintain themselves in their own homes, they may still be able to avoid the cost and loss of independence a residential care facility requires by moving in with willing family members and receiving long-term home care there. This kind of arrangement may permit family members to supplement home care provided by outside agencies with direct care of their own, which can help keep down costs while allowing the elder more personal control.

But such an arrangement is obviously not for every family. It requires physical space and financial resources. And both the elder and the relatives with whom the elder lives must be willing to make it work. Everyone involved has to give up some room and some privacy and make adjustments in daily habits and expectations. Relatives with whom the elder does not live must also be willing to share the responsibilities by visiting, taking the elder on outings, and providing financial assistance. Obviously, all this takes a lot of talking, planning, and ongoing cooperation among all family members.

Entering a Residential Facility

Recent surveys of nursing facility residents have shown that contact with the world outside—leaving the facility for visits and outings and receiving visits, phone calls, and mail from family and friends—is their single greatest concern. So even when an elder moves into an organized residential setting that provides personal care and social activities, or into a long-term care facility that provides complete care, family participation remains of the utmost importance.

To prepare for any residential care setting, family members must be willing to discuss how much each is *realistically* able and willing to help. But most important, family members must discuss the future directly with the loved one who needs care.

What Can You Afford?

Most communities have a wide variety of home care programs and residential facilities, but almost all of them are quite costly. Paid home care can be much less expensive than residential care if only needed on a part-time basis. But as extensive paid home care is used, its costs can exceed residential care.

Residential facilities also vary greatly in cost—independent living facilities begin at around $25,000 per year, and the least expensive assisted living and personal care facilities cost about $30,000 per year. The average cost of a nursing facility is about $60,000 to $90,000 per year, depending on the state. And prices for each of these types of facilities may reach $150,000 per year in more expensive urban areas.

Unfortunately, government programs and private insurance pay a much smaller chunk of these costs than most people think. Medicare pays only about 10% of all nursing facility costs—and this all goes to short-term skilled nursing care, not long-term residential care. Similarly, Medicare pays only for short-term home care for people who need actual nursing—it pays nothing for long-term care at home. (See Chapter 7 for a discussion of Medicare, Medigap insurance, and veterans' benefits.) Medicaid (or Medi-Cal in California)—the federal program for low-income people—pays about half of all long-term nursing facility costs and a significant amount of home care charges. But Medicaid will pay for these only after you have used up almost all of your savings to pay for your own care. And Medicaid might not pay anything at all for assisted living or some residential care facilities. (See Chapter 8.) Private long-term care insurance may pay some portion of nursing facility and home

Medicare, Medicaid, Veterans Benefits, and Insurance: An Overview

	Home Care	Senior Residences	Assisted Living	Nursing Facilities	Hospice Care
Medicare A federal government program for which virtually everyone 65 and over is eligible	Short-term only; skilled nursing and therapy, but not custodial care	None	None	Skilled nursing facility only, following a hospital stay; full payment for only 20 days, partial payment for up to 100 days; only in facilities certified by Medicare	Covers almost all costs for six months' care (sometimes more) at home
Medigap Insurance Private insurance policies that can be purchased by individuals 65 or over	Some policies provide limited coverage for short-term care if Medicare also covers it; no coverage for long-term care	None	None	Many policies cover short-term stays in skilled nursing facilities if Medicare also covers them, paying the amount Medicare does not; no coverage for long-term custodial care	None
MediCare Part C; Medicare Advantage plans Managed care or other plans specifically for people on Medicare	Limited coverage for short-term care under Medicare rules; some plans offer extra home care coverage under easier rules than Medicare's; no coverage for long-term care	None	None	Short-term stays in skilled nursing facilities under rules similar to Medicare; no coverage for long-term custodial care	Same coverage as regular Medicare

Medicare, Medicaid, Veterans Benefits, and Insurance: An Overview (cont'd)

	Home Care	Senior Residences	Assisted Living	Nursing Facilities	Hospice Care
Medicaid (Medi-Cal in California) Varies in each state; to be eligible, you must have very low income and few assets, not counting your home, car, and household goods	Personal as well as medical care; usually limited in amount	Usually no coverage	Partial coverage in many states for Medicaid-certified assisted living facilities; limited eligibility and coverage	Extensive coverage in facilities certified by Medicaid: no time limit	Same coverage as Medicare
Veterans Benefits Some long-term residential and home care for certain veterans, and monthly benefits payments for some veterans and surviving spouses	Some home and community-based care programs for eligible veterans. Also, loans and grants available to modify a home	None	None	The VA operates its own nursing homes for qualifying veterans, and contracts with private nursing homes where no VA nursing home is available	Hospice available as part of VA medical benefits
Long-Term Care Insurance Private insurance policies; vary greatly in coverage and amount of benefits	Some policies cover only home care; more expensive comprehensive policies cover both home care and residential care; amount of coverage depends on amount of premium paid	None	Some policies cover long-term care in residential care (shelter care) or assisted living facilities if policyholder is unable to perform certain amount of activities of daily living	Coverage in licensed nursing and board and care facilities for custodial care if medically necessary or if elder is unable to perform activities of daily living; benefits depend on cost of policy and rarely cover full cost of care	Not usually any additional coverage

care costs, but it usually doesn't pay for everything—and it pays nothing at all for many types of residential care facilities.

Medicare, Medicaid, Veterans Benefits, and Insurance

Throughout this book, we discuss Medicare, Medicaid, veterans benefits, and private insurance coverage (or lack thereof) of long-term care costs. Chapter 7 is devoted entirely to Medicare, private Medigap insurance, and veterans benefits coverage of long-term care. Chapter 8 covers Medicaid eligibility and coverage and how to protect personal assets and still qualify for Medicaid coverage. Chapter 9 covers long-term care insurance.

The chart above gives a brief introduction to each of these types of coverage so that you will be familiar with them as you begin to read about long-term care alternatives.

Determine Income and Assets

The first step in figuring out what money is realistically available for someone's long-term care is to add up that person's income and available assets (and subtract their liabilities). Once you have a complete picture of someone's income and assets, you may be able to take certain steps to protect some of those assets from long-term care costs. (See Chapter 8.)

Family members can also begin to think about their own financial contributions. While there may be no immediate need for money from relatives, the decisions you make now about long-term care may determine if and when money from beyond the elder's own resources will be required. The earlier this is discussed, the easier it will be to plan and provide for it.

Here are the most common items (and some that you might overlook) to factor in as you try to get a complete picture of your income and assets. The last category—liabilities—is a set-off which you subtract from available financial resources. Because this list is only for your own reference, you don't have to use precise figures.

INCOME AND ASSETS

I. Estimated Income

Ongoing business income _____

Social Security retirement or disability benefits _____

Pension benefits _____

Income from rental property _____

Income from patents or royalties _____

Other income _____

II. Liquid Assets

Cash _____

Savings and money market accounts _____

Checking accounts _____

Certificates of deposit _____

U.S. savings and other bonds _____

Gold, silver, rare coins, and other precious metals _____

III. Personal Property Assets

Interest in ongoing business
(ownership, stock option, and profit-sharing) _____

Value of any patents or copyrights _____

Brokerage accounts and other stocks _____

Money owed to you _____

Automobiles, boats, and other vehicles _____

Antiques and works of art _____

Valuable jewelry _____

Face value of life insurance _____

Miscellaneous _____

IV. Real Estate (full or partial interest)

Property #1 (principal residence) _____

Property #2 _____

Property #3 _____

V. Liabilities (what you owe)

Mortgage debts
(all money you owe on real property listed above) _____

Personal property debts (loans) _____

Miscellaneous debts _____

> ## Organize Your Records
>
> As you fill out this list, you may discover that your financial and ownership documents are located in a number of different places. If so, this is a good time to gather them together and put them in one safe place, then give a list of the documents and their location to family members or others you trust. *Get It Together,* by Melanie Cullen and Shae Irving (Nolo), can help you gather and organize this information.

Geriatric Care Managers

Geriatric care managers (also known as private care managers for the aging) are professional counselors or guides who, on a one-time or ongoing basis, help assess long-term care needs and organize services to meet those needs. They can be particularly useful when family members don't live in the same city as the person who needs the care.

Geriatric care managers can assist with placing elders in different types of assisted living, residential care, and nursing facilities. They can be invaluable in guiding you through the maze of home health care and supporting services needed for long-term care in the home. Care managers are generally familiar with residential facilities and can help find a facility that meets the elder's care needs and ability to pay. They can also evaluate home care agencies. They may know of difficult-to-find services that may supplement care provided by an agency or of individual caregivers who can fill gaps in home care. And, they can help you set up a coordinated program of care among several providers. They also follow up, monitoring ongoing care and helping make changes as necessary.

Despite a care manager's expertise, decisions about long-term care are too important to leave solely in the hands of any one advisor. You and other family members should consider and evaluate a care manager's recommendations. You should also meet with all caregivers and visit any residence the care manager suggests. Keep in mind that you know best the abilities, needs, and personality of the elder who requires care. Also, the more you learn about long-term care choices and participate in the decision-making process, the better able you will be to choose among the alternatives a care manager may offer.

Where to Find Geriatric Care Managers

As with other long-term care resources, your personal physician, a local senior citizens center, or friends and neighbors might be able to refer you to a geriatric care manager.

You can also find geriatric care managers by searching online or in the white pages of the telephone directory under "Geriatric Care," "Geriatric Management," "Older Adults Care Managers," or something similar. Your local senior information or senior referral directory—usually listed separately in the white pages (sometimes under county or city offices or public health department)—can also make referrals. You can also find geriatric care managers near you by using the online directory of the National Association of Professional Geriatric Care Managers at www. caremanager.org, or by calling them at 520-881-8008.

Evaluating a Geriatric Care Manager

There is no easy way to know in advance whether a particular geriatric care manager is likely to be effective. Some care managers are connected to organizations dedicated to elder care; other excellent care managers work on their own. Unfortunately, there are no firm guidelines and no state certifications yet for this relatively new field. Here are some ideas on what to ask before hiring a geriatric care manager:

- **Where has the care manager worked before?** Experience with a local public agency that deals with the elderly is a good sign, as is work at a local nursing facility or home health care agency. Whatever the form, some public health experience is essential. The care manager should provide you with references from previous employment if you ask for them.

• **What is the care manager's professional training?** Normally, a care manager should have a license or degree in public health nursing, public health management, social work, or gerontology. If not, make sure the person has an extensive work history that you can check personally.

• **Does the care manager belong to any state or national professional organizations?** Membership in a professional organization, such as the National Association of Social Workers, Visiting Nurse Association, or National Association of Private Geriatric Care Managers, does not guarantee quality of work, but it may indicate a professional attitude and a willingness to have credentials verified.

• **How does the care manager structure fees?** Find out in advance exactly how much you will have to pay—and what you will get for your money. Some organizations with public or philanthropic support offer free or low-cost services to low-income individuals and families. Many private care managers charge a flat fee ($200 to $500) for the initial family visit and evaluation, then an hourly fee ($50 to $250) for making arrangements and follow-up visits. Whatever the terms, make sure to get them in writing.

• **How extensive is the follow-up?** After initial arrangements have been made, to what extent is the care manager available for personal or telephone consultations? For emergencies? What are the charges? Are there continuing services available, such as weekly or monthly reviews or visits, either by phone or in person? And, what happens if a service or provider the care manager has arranged for does not work out? On what terms will the care manager arrange for replacement services?

- **Does the care manager have a business contract of any kind with a particular home care agency or residential facility?** If so, be cautious about accepting the care manager's recommendation of that agency or facility because the care manager has a motive to steer business there. Make sure that the care manager presents you with some alternatives.

- **Does the care manager have any clients or former clients who can give a personal recommendation?** Speaking with someone who has used the care manager's services may give you confidence in the care manager and a better idea of what to expect.

Stay Involved in the Process

Even if you rely on a care manager, you should still do some research of your own. Check with friends, relatives, and any other potential sources of information about possible care options. There is information on finding home care in Chapter 2, choosing an organized senior residence or assisted living facility in Chapter 3, and locating long-term care facilities in Chapter 4.

Two good general resources about home care and residential care in your area are:

- Eldercare Locator: (800-677-1116, www.eldercare.gov), a nonprofit, government-sponsored free service run by the National Association of Area Agencies on Aging, and

- Total Living Choices: www.tlchoices.com.

Although these services cannot tell you which option or facility would be best for you, they can give you a list of choices to investigate, either on your own or with the help of a geriatric care manager.

Other Legal and Financial Matters

When you consider long-term care needs, you should also review other legal and financial matters. A person who needs long-term care may have increasing difficulty taking care of personal matters; this is usually a good time to review legal and financial documents and arrangements. These issues are discussed more fully in Chapters 8, 9, and 10.

Health Care Directives

When long-term care becomes necessary, you should start preparing to make decisions about future health care choices. In particular, you need to think about what kind of medical treatments you would like to receive if you become terminally ill or are no longer able to communicate your wishes about your medical care.

To make sure that your medical choices are respected, you can create two basic legal documents:

- a medical directive (sometimes referred to as a living will or advanced health care directive), which sets forth the type of care you wish to receive if you become incapacitated, and
- a durable power of attorney for health care, in which you name someone you trust to make sure that you get the kind of medical care you want—and, in some states, to make decisions about your medical care if you are unable to do so.

We discuss these documents in detail in Chapter 10.

Durable Powers of Attorney for Finances

As you grow older, you will want to make sure that someone will make financial decisions in accordance with your wishes if you are no longer able to handle your financial matters on your own. A durable power of attorney for finances can take effect right away or only if and when you become legally incompetent to handle your own financial decisions. It can help ensure that your finances are handled as you wish, by someone you trust, without the expensive, cumbersome, and time-consuming process of going to court. (See "Financial Decisions" in Chapter 10.)

Wills

Although an elder's need for long-term care certainly does not mean that death is imminent, it may be a signal of decreasing competence to make decisions about income, assets, and estate. It is a good idea to review any existing will—which may be old and out of date—and to make a new will that meets with the current wishes of the elder.

However, if there is any question about an older person's mental competence to make a new will, or about whether the elder's decisions about leaving property to others, might be unduly influenced by another person, consult with a lawyer who specializes in wills and probate matters before taking action.

See "Estate Planning Resources From Nolo" in Chapter 10 for information about will and estate planning self-help resources.

Living Trusts

A living trust is a legal document that allows you to retain control over your property during your lifetime and arrange for that property to be transferred, at your death, to beneficiaries you name—all without going through probate. You designate what property goes into the trust and who gets it when you die. During your lifetime, you act as the trustee—and you have the right to change the trust property, change the beneficiary, or revoke the trust altogether. On your death, the trust property is distributed directly to the named beneficiaries, without going through probate or any other legal proceeding. ●

At-Home Care

Until recently, older Americans and their families had few choices for elder care. The options were either family care at home or residence in a nursing facility or "rest home." Family care often placed an overwhelming burden on adult children and grandchildren and seriously strained family relations. Care in a nursing facility, on the other hand, often created guilty feelings, drained family finances, and restricted the elder's comfort and independence.

Fortunately, the number and kinds of home care services have increased substantially in recent years. New technologies have made many medical treatments—such as oxygen and intravenous therapy—mobile enough for home administration. As a result, more elders who need care can remain at home or live with relatives without putting undue stress on the family.

Another reason to use home care is its cost: It can be a cheaper alternative to residential nursing facilities, which have become increasingly more expensive. And, agencies and programs have increased the kinds of therapeutic, nutrition, homemaking, and other personal care services they offer for home care in response to the larger number of people receiving medical care at home.

This trend toward home care is particularly welcome in light of public health surveys indicating that up to half of all nursing facility residents could live independently if they had adequate and affordable home care services. Other studies have shown that the longer people remain independent from institutional care, the better their overall physical and emotional health.

Unfortunately, though, long-term home care is not always a practical solution. Home care may be adequate and affordable if the elder needs help with:

- some physical movements around the home (for example, bathing or getting meals)
- exercise or physical therapy, or
- monitoring a chronic health condition.

But, if the elder needs extensive medical treatment or close monitoring for many hours each day, the difficulty of arranging different types of care may make home care impractical—and the cost may become prohibitive. In most cases, long-term home care also requires family members to fill in gaps that the outside care services do not cover. For many people without such family assistance, long-term home care is simply not an option.

Home Care May Not Last Forever

Even if home care is a workable alternative, it may not remain so. An elder's physical needs will change over time; home care that now works well may later become impractical. For this reason, you may want to begin planning for the possibility of residential care at some later date. This is particularly true if you or your family member is facing Alzheimer's disease (a progressive condition) or some other form of dementia. (See Chapter 5.)

Your planning should take two forms. First, get to know the kinds of residential facilities in your area. (Elder residences are discussed in Chapter 3, long-term care facilities in Chapter 4.)

Also, begin to consider how you might pay for residential care. If it appears that Medicaid may be an option, explore ways to protect some of your assets while still qualifying for Medicaid coverage. (Medicaid is explained in Chapter 8.)

What Is Home Care?

The term "home care" encompasses a multitude of medical and personal services provided at home to a partially or fully dependent elder. (Although home care is available for people of any age who require long-term care, we focus on the needs of older people.) These services often make it possible for an older person to remain at home or with a relative, rather than enter a residential facility for extended recovery or long-term care. In this book, the terms "home" and "home care" refer to the private house or apartment where the elder lives alone, with a spouse, or with other family members or friends, or an assisted living, board and care, or other residential facility where the home care would supplement the care the facility provides.

Depending on what is available in your community, home care and related supplemental services can include:

• health care—nursing, physical, and other rehabilitative therapy, medicating, monitoring, and medical equipment that is usually only short-term and may only be provided by a state-licensed home health care agency, under a physician's orders.

• personal care—assistance with personal hygiene, dressing, getting in and out of a bed or chair, bathing, and exercise

• nutrition—meal planning, cooking, meal delivery, or meals at outside meal sites

• homemaking—housekeeping, shopping, home repair services, and household paperwork, and

• social and safety needs—escort and transportation services, companions, telephone check, overall planning, and program coordination service.

(See "Services Provided" and "Kinds of Providers," below, for a complete discussion of the home care services.)

Not everyone using home care will need all of the services available. Not every community will offer every possible service, and a single program or agency might not provide everything that the elder requires. An elder's additional needs may have to be filled by community agencies or organizations, adult day care or senior centers, individuals hired through informal networks, family, and friends. Geriatric care managers can help establish a home care program for elders who require a mix of care—different services from different providers. (See "Geriatric Care Managers" in Chapter 1.)

Independence

One of the great advantages of home care is that it permits an older person to maintain a feeling of independence and comfort in familiar surroundings. Also, you and your family may be better able to control the care received—and to avoid care that isn't necessary or desired.

On the other hand, for home care to work well, you and your family must take the initiative to find services, coordinate different programs and personnel, monitor home care needs and performance, figure costs and budgets, and make changes when required. And, the family will be making all of these decisions without a professional institution to help. This decision-making responsibility can add an extra burden to the daily task of meeting the elder's needs for physical care.

Remaining at home also isolates some people from social activity and limits mental stimulation. Although friends and family often intend to provide lots of companionship, too many elders wind up spending their days in bed asleep or watching television. An organized elder residence, on the other hand, offers both a community of people and a constant stream of activities.

Financial Savings

In addition to the physical and emotional advantages of remaining at home, there can also be significant financial savings if the care you need is not too complicated or frequent, and family and friends help out. While residential care facilities average $30,000 to $150,000 a year, home care can average from 25% to 90% less, depending on what care is required. You save by not paying for unnecessary services or institutional overhead. The things you provide yourself at home—food, drugs, and supplies—come without any nursing facility mark-up.

For a good sense of the cost of both home health aides and home care assistants in your geographic area, search online for:

• Met Life's *Market Survey of Long-Term Care Costs*, or

• Genworth Financial's *Cost of Care Survey*.

However, home care often becomes more expensive over time. Home care needs may become more extensive or complicated and family members may not be able to pick up the slack, which could require additional paid care and services.

Hospice May Provide up to Six Months' Home Care

Hospice is a program of comprehensive pain and symptom relief and comfort care, usually delivered in a patient's home, for someone who is not expected to live more than another six months. Hospice is a very intensive kind of at-home care, with substantial attention from nurses, aides, and attendants. It can provide a substantial boost in home care for people who depend almost entirely on nonpaid caregivers. It can allow a person to leave a hospital or nursing facility when he or she otherwise would not have sufficient resources to be cared for at home. And, it offers respite care, which can give nonpaid caregivers a regular break from their care responsibilities.

Outside of hospice, this kind of home care would be quite expensive. And, ordinarily, Medicare does not pay for any home care unless the patient is in the process of recovering from an injury or illness. (See Chapter 7, "Medicare and Veterans' Benefits.") But one of the great benefits of hospice is that Medicare pays for almost the entire cost of care, including all drugs needed for pain and symptom control. Hospice coverage can last for up to six months and, occasionally, even longer. For a complete discussion of hospice, see Chapter 6.

Sometimes, hidden expenses make the true cost of home care too high. Families often fail to calculate peripheral expenses: the continued or expanded cost of running a home (such as taxes, utilities, insurance, and maintenance), the cost to family members of transportation and missed work (to help care for the elder), and the cost of temporary care workers to fill in when family members can't make it or regular care falls through.

Quality of Care

While the comfort and financial advantages of home care sound attractive, you may have some doubts about how the quality of care at home compares to the care provided in a nursing facility or other elder residence.

Nursing, Therapy, and Other Medical Care

Nursing, therapy—physical, occupational, and speech—and other medical care at home may only be provided by a state-licensed and Medicare-certified home health care agency. (See "Kinds of Providers," below.) Home health care is supposed to be provided according to a care plan based on orders from the treating physician and developed under the supervision of the home health agency's physicians and nurses. If the patient or patient's family has any question about whether the home health care is being provided safely, properly, and adequately, the patient or family should get in touch with the clinical or nursing supervisor at the agency or the patient's personal physician.

Nonmedical Care

The care people need at home is not primarily medical or nursing care, but help with what are called the activities of daily living (ADLs). These include bathing, using the toilet, dressing, eating, getting in and out of bed or a chair, and walking around. For people with Alzheimer's or other cognitive impairments, home care may consist primarily of making sure that the person does not become lost, disoriented, or injured. For these kinds of nonmedical assistance, home care is often better than residential care. Home care is provided one-on-one, whereas residential facilities have staff-to-resident ratios of one-to-ten or more. By choosing and monitoring a home care agency or individual home care providers, you may be better able to control the quality of care you receive. On the other hand, tracking the effectiveness of home care is primarily up to the family, whereas residential facilities have professional staff members who are supposed to check regularly on the quality of nonmedical care provided.

How to Find Home Care Services

As you've probably gathered by now, arranging a program of home care involves some searching and organizing and often requires you to use services from more than one source. To do this, you need to learn where to find these services and how to locate recommended agencies and individuals.

Much of home care—particularly nursing and other medical services—can be provided by a home care or home health care agency. (The services such agencies provide are discussed later in this chapter.)

Friends and Relatives

While the opinions of professionals are often helpful, you should start your search by talking to friends and relatives who have had home care experiences. Friends may know of a program or person unfamiliar to an agency or professional or warn you about providers to avoid—despite their apparently sound credentials. Call a few friends or relatives and tell them the kind of help you think you need. They may be able to tell you about other people they know who have arranged for similar help. This kind of networking can snowball, with each phone call leading you to others to contact for information or services. Don't be shy. Call around and start the snowball rolling.

Hospital Personnel

If you are looking for home care following a stay in a medical facility, most facilities have a "discharge planner" or "social services" administrator who can refer you to a home care agency capable of meeting your needs. Many hospitals and skilled nursing facilities operate their own home health care units. Although you should not automatically sign up with the hospital or nursing facility's home care unit, it is a good place to start comparison shopping.

Geriatric Care Managers

A geriatric care manager has knowledge about the types and sources of home care available in a local area. The care manager is likely to have experience with local home care agencies and may also know of good sources of independent caregivers. To find a geriatric care manager near you, you can use the online directory of the National Association of Professional Geriatric Care Managers at www.caremanager.org, or call them at 520-881-8008.

Physicians

Your own physician may have worked with a good home care agency. Your doctor may also be willing to put you in contact with other patients who've used home care, so you can ask them about their experiences.

Nursing Registries

If you need at-home nursing, contact your local hospital—many have a registry of visiting nurses. The local chapter of the Visiting Nurses Association provides visiting nurses and may also be a good source of referrals for other care.

National, State, and Local Agencies and Organizations

If you need home care because of a particular illness or disability, ask for referrals from the local chapter of a volunteer organization that focuses on that illness or disability, such as the American Heart Association, American Cancer Society, American Diabetes Association, or Alzheimer's Foundation.

Public agencies that specialize in the needs of older people can refer you to home care agencies in your area. Area Agencies on Aging operate federally funded programs that might help. The area agencies can also refer you to Medicare-approved home care agencies.

Most states have their own Agencies on Aging—and there may be local offices of the state agency in your own community. Check the state government listings in the white pages of the telephone book.

City and county Agencies on Aging may offer low-cost programs of their own. They can also refer you to reputable home care agencies. You can find referral services online and in your phone book under listings for Senior Referral, Department of Social Services, Family Service Agency, or Information and Referral. Often these services have a social worker or public health worker who specializes in referrals for older people.

Check the Resource Directory

You can find contact information for many of these organizations and agencies in the Resource Directory in the appendix of this book.

Senior Centers

Because it is part of the job of local senior centers to provide information for seniors, they are usually happy to help with referrals to agencies and individual services. Home care providers know that senior centers supply this information, so they often make their services known at the centers. You can also get personal recommendations and opinions from other older people at the centers.

Volunteer Organizations

A number of community volunteer organizations not only provide referrals, but also administer their own home care programs. Your local United Way, for example, is a good clearinghouse for different services. Churches or synagogues and local religious, ethnic, or fraternal agencies and organizations are often very helpful in coordinating home care services and making informal care arrangements.

Older People Helping Older People

The Retired Senior Volunteer Program (RSVP) is a federally funded program through which retired older people volunteer to help other less mobile elders. RSVP, together with the Senior Companion Program, provides all sorts of general assistance with nonmedical daily needs, free of charge. And, if RSVP is not equipped to help you directly, it may be able to refer you to a program or agency that can. To find your local RSVP, look in the white pages of the phone book under Retired Senior Volunteer Program or contact the national office of Senior Corps at 800-942-2677 or at its website, www.seniorcorps.gov. The national office will help connect you with the branch nearest you.

Services Provided

Home care services range from highly skilled medical care, nursing, and therapy to simple household tasks, such as cleaning and cooking. Home care agencies can also provide respite care from a stand-in home care provider who visits with an elder while a regular caregiver—usually a family member—takes a break.

Medical Services

Most home care agencies and Visiting Nurses Associations can provide or arrange for a number of medical services, including skilled and basic nursing, rehabilitation therapies, and dietary services.

Nursing

With a physician overseeing the course of treatment, a home care agency or nursing registry can provide geriatric nurse practitioners, registered nurses, and licensed vocational or practical nurses. These highly skilled nurses plan and monitor health care, give injections and intravenous medication, and instruct you on self-administered medications, injections, and treatments.

More routine nursing care is provided by vocational and practical nurses and by aides who work under the nurses' supervision. They monitor pulse, blood pressure, and temperature; administer simple diagnostic procedures, such as drawing blood and other samples for the laboratory; and instruct home patients on how to use portable testing equipment.

Therapies

Most home care agencies provide a physical therapist, respiratory therapist, speech therapist, or occupational therapist. These specialists give short-term assistance to people recovering from an illness or injury and ongoing therapy to those with permanent disabilities.

Nutrition

Most agencies either have someone on staff or can arrange for someone to help plan a diet and show how to prepare foods that provide proper nutrition and meet special dietary needs. You may also be able to get help in shopping for and preparing meals or have prepared meals brought to your home.

Medical and Safety Equipment and Supplies

Home care agencies can provide medical equipment and supplies, such as a hospital bed, wheelchair, walker, oxygen equipment, and various home testing and monitoring equipment and supplies for incontinence and other conditions. You can buy or rent the equipment from the agency or from a medical equipment company with which the agency does business.

Some home care agencies will also inspect your home for safety needs and arrange to install any necessary equipment, such as support railings, access ramps, or an emergency response system.

Comparison Shop

Find out whether you are required to buy or rent all medical equipment and supplies from any home care agency you are considering. If so, and if you need substantial medical equipment or supplies, make sure their prices are competitive with what you would pay if you purchased the equipment or supplies on your own. Always comparison shop before buying equipment or having any work done through an agency.

Nonmedical Personal Care

Home Health Aides

Most people who consider home care do not need skilled medical care as much as they need assistance with personal tasks that have become difficult because of frailty or other physical debility. This type of care is provided not by skilled medical personnel, but by "home health aides" or "home care aides."

Aides are the people who spend the most time with the elder. Their tasks vary, depending on your needs, the rules of the agency, and the willingness of the individual aide, but in general they include:

- assistance with personal care, such as bathing, grooming, toilet needs, and eating
- help with movement or exercise, such as getting in and out of a bed or chair, getting around the house, stretching, or taking a walk
- simple health tasks, such as taking blood pressure and temperature and helping with self-administered medications, salves, and breathing equipment, and
- minimal homemaking, such as helping to plan and cook simple meals.

More general homemaking services (grocery shopping, meal preparation, and clean-up, light housecleaning, and laundry) are often available through home care agencies. Not every home care agency provides homemaking services, however, and you may need to make separate arrangements through informal networks of friends, relatives, and neighbors or with an independent home care provider.

Ask About Other Services

Just because something is not on a home care agency's or individual aide's list of offered services does not mean it is not available. Depending on how flexible your home care aide is, any light task around the house might be included. If the aide will not help or is not allowed by an agency to assist with certain needed tasks, the agency may be able to provide someone who can.

Respite Care

With home care, the primary responsibility for care and companionship often still rests with family members. Particularly if an elder requires extensive monitoring, it can become a substantial burden on family members to always stay around the house. Some agencies provide temporary respite care—a companion for the elder, whose presence allows a family member to leave the house and go to work, attend to other business, or simply have a break. Obviously, you can also make private arrangements for someone to fill this need.

Respite companions are often volunteers, organized through a community group. If your agency does not have respite care, it should be able to refer you to a community group or organization that does. (See "Supplements to Home Care," below.)

Kinds of Providers

Home care providers range from hospitals or other high-tech organizations with highly trained medical staffs to full-service home care agencies to the ten-year-old kid down the block who takes out your trash. Getting the most sophisticated and well-equipped home care provider is not the point. The goal is to find providers who can give you the specific care you need, for the best price.

Full-Service Agencies

Most home care agencies provide a wide variety of services, though only a state-licensed home health care agency may provide medical care such as nursing and therapy. Of the services discussed below, some agencies will provide all of them while others will only provide services that are nonmedical. Even if you use a home care agency, you may still find it convenient and less expensive to fill in some of the gaps in nonmedical care by using independent caregivers as well.

Home Care Agency Choices

Many home care agencies will create a written care plan and include a written estimate of costs as part of any contract you sign for their services. Review the care plan and contract carefully to make sure you are not obligated to buy, rent, or pay for any services or equipment in the future.

Home care agencies are often affiliated with hospitals, nursing facilities, and nursing organizations. But since most home care is *not* direct medical care, the fact that an agency is connected with a medical institution does not necessarily mean it will provide better overall personal care.

On the whole, full-service agencies tend to be more expensive than independent providers or support care agencies that do not provide nursing or medical therapies. Despite their higher cost, full-service agencies can be extremely useful in coordinating different levels of care and when no family members are available to organize and oversee separate independent providers.

Home Care Personnel

Home care agency workers go by different titles—and offer different types of services and skills. Knowing what these titles mean can help you make the best use of the services an agency has to offer. Because fees are higher for more skilled workers, understanding the different options available can also help you avoid paying for an *overqualified*, and therefore overly expensive, home care provider when a less skilled but equally effective provider would do.

Supervisors and Planning Coordinators. The planner (probably the first person you will have contact with) assesses your needs and capabilities and develops an overall plan for care. The planner may also oversee personnel assignments and assist you in making changes in services or personnel after your care has begun.

Clinical or Nursing Supervisors. A clinical supervisor, usually a public health or geriatric nurse, monitors your direct home medical care, including diet and nutrition. This is the person with whom you, your family, or your doctor should speak if you have a question or problem with the skilled medical care you receive.

Social Workers. The agency's social worker, resource manager, or caseworker can help coordinate your care with other programs and services not provided by the agency and can help with financial and insurance planning and paperwork.

Nurses. Every home health care agency should have at least one nurse practitioner or registered nurse (RN) on call at all times to monitor patient nursing needs. Nurse practitioners generally supervise other nurses and can prescribe some medicines, give injections, and diagnose routine medical problems. Registered nurses handle complex nursing functions, including administering intravenous medication, drawing blood, making an overall assessment of patient needs, and creating a nursing care plan to meet those needs.

A licensed vocational nurse (LVN) or licensed practical nurse (LPN) handles the more routine nursing tasks, such as monitoring blood pressure and pulse, checking fluids, administering oxygen and some medications, and doing some basic physical rehabilitation.

If you require a special physical rehabilitation program—after a hip injury or a stroke, for example—a certified rehabilitative nurse (CRN) may plan the program, begin you on it, and monitor your progress, sometimes in conjunction with a rehabilitation therapist.

Rehabilitation Therapists. Physical, occupational, speech, and respiratory therapists plan and carry out a program of rehabilitative therapy. Once you are on a regular program, routine therapy assistance is often handled by trained assistants or technicians.

Home Care Aides. The home care aide is the foot soldier of home care. The aide handles simple, everyday health and personal care tasks:

bathing; grooming; moving around; exercising; helping with self-administered medications, creams, and therapies; and monitoring blood pressure and temperature. The aide may also help you with minimal homemaking—planning and preparing simple meals, for example. But the home care aide is not a housekeeper or house cleaner; these services may or may not be available through your home care agency. An independent home care aide, on the other hand, may be more flexible about doing a certain amount of household work.

Companions. An elder's greatest need, particularly if housebound, may simply be company. Some home care agencies provide, often through a community group, people known as "companions." These people will spend time with the elder at home or go for a small outing—shopping, to the library, to the park, or just for a walk—to offer some company and conversation. Companions may also help with personal paperwork, make phone calls, and organize slightly more complicated outings.

Support Care Agencies

Support care agencies provide personal, household, and respite care, but not skilled nursing or medical therapies. They are often sponsored by community or charitable organizations. Because they do not maintain highly skilled medical staffs, some can provide home aides at lower rates than full-service agencies. (In choosing a support care agency, refer to the criteria discussed in "What to Look For," below.)

Independent and Informal Arrangements

As emphasized throughout this chapter, not all care has to come through a formal agency. More important, not all *good* care comes from an agency. Independent home care workers are often more flexible in the tasks they will perform—and less expensive—than agency personnel.

Some communities have what are called in-home support services that refer home attendants and aides for nonmedical home care. And many public agencies, community or charitable organizations, and churches, while not sponsoring home care agencies, offer referral lists of independent home care aides that the organizations or agencies have referred successfully in the past.

You can also find professional nurses and nonprofessional aides through informal networks. Friends and relatives may know of an individual who suits your needs but does not work through an agency and may not have any formal certification or training. Many people have found that "unofficial" aides provide very personal, flexible, and competent assistance and charge considerably less than certified nurses or aides.

Keep in mind, though, that the range and quality of care you get depends entirely on the knowledge, skill, and attitude of one caregiver. There is no outside supervision, no one to make sure you are getting high quality care. Also, no agency has done a background check on the person who will be spending a considerable amount of time in your home. And while agencies routinely post a "bond" for their aides to protect the consumer from theft or damage by the home care aide, most independent aides are not bonded.

Finally, independent aides sometimes get sick or are otherwise unavailable—which can pose significant problems if you depend on their care. If you will need an independent aide regularly, it is a good idea to have a back-up to call on short notice.

What to Look For

You may find good quality and less expensive care without using a home care agency. If you do choose to use one, however, here are some things to look for.

Certification

Although it's not necessarily a guarantee of quality care, a full-service agency should be approved by both Medicare and your state's Medicaid program. The government checks to make sure certain staff, supervision, and basic training requirements are met. If your state licenses home care agencies, make sure your agency has a state license as well. To find out, call your area or local Agency on Aging. (See the Resource Directory in the appendix.)

Some agencies are also accredited by national health care organizations. For example, the Joint Commission for Accreditation of Health Care Organizations (www.jointcommission.org) is an umbrella organization that accredits home health care agencies.

Reputation

Here are some questions you can ask to find out about an agency's reputation:

- How long has the agency been in business? Look for an agency that has stood the test of time.
- Does the agency belong to the National Association for Home Care or to a state home care association? Membership may indicate adherence to certain standards of care.
- Can the agency give references to doctors, public health workers, and clients who have worked with or used the agency? Talk directly with the references. If you will need medical care, ask your doctor to do so, too.

Alzheimer's Care Requires Special Skills

If you are looking for a home care agency to provide care for someone with Alzheimer's disease, make sure that both the agency and the specific personnel it plans to send to your home have experience with the disease. Chapter 5 discusses the particular problems faced by those who must find or provide home care for an Alzheimer's patient.

Services and Flexibility

No matter how many services an agency claims to offer in its brochure, the important thing is to match its services with your needs. If you have any special scheduling needs, make sure the agency will accommodate you. Also, find out if there is any extra cost for night or weekend services.

Flexibility in care is also very important. An agency may be able to meet your needs now, but what if your needs change? Can the agency also provide different, more specialized medical services, a more unusual schedule, or help with household work? It is not necessary that the agency *directly* provide every service you might need in the future, as long as it has the capacity to arrange the service through coordination with other providers.

Before choosing an agency, ask the planning coordinator about the availability of services through other providers. What are their regular arrangements with other programs or agencies? What is the extra charge for such services? Can they arrange for services that they do not already have on call?

Personnel Standards

Find out about an agency's personnel before you begin to receive care. What are the skill levels of both in-home and planning personnel on staff? What training and experience are required for different positions? Even nonmedical home care aides should have completed some formal training.

Because home care workers will be spending a significant amount of time in your home, often with no one else present, you should find out how the agency screens an employee's background.

Matters of Less Significance

Although these might seem like important factors to consider when choosing an agency, they don't mean that much in practice.

Nonprofit, Church-Related, or Charitable Organization

If an agency is nonprofit, will it be less expensive? If the agency is sponsored or owned by a church or a charitable organization, will it have the client rather than money or reputation foremost in mind?

The answer to both questions is: not necessarily. Some organizations that operate home care agencies acquire nonprofit tax status by associating with a larger nonprofit group. This means they pay less in taxes, but it does not mean that the rates they charge will be cheaper; only comparing their rates with those charged by other agencies can answer that question.

Nor does nonprofit status mean the quality of care is any better. Just because a church or charitable organization sponsors an agency does not mean it is involved in the agency's daily operations. These are usually handled by independent administrators—and it is their work that determines the quality of care.

National Chain

An agency that is part of a large nationwide organization may seem like a safer bet than a small, independent agency. In certain respects, that may be true—for example, standardized personnel duties or computerized billing may make some aspects of home care easier to manage. But gains in paper efficiency may be lost in personalized care. The quality of care you receive from any agency, national chain, or small independent depends on the skill and attention of the people who will be in your home every day.

Hospital Connected

An agency affiliated with a hospital may seem better able to provide medical care than other agencies. But, keep in mind that most home care does not involve complicated medical treatment. An agency that focuses on high technology health care may be giving too little attention to what most home care recipients need most—thoughtful human attention.

Getting Started

Whether or not you use the services of an agency, settling on a home care plan is an important first step. You may also have to supervise the care and update the care plan as needed.

Developing a Care Plan

If you are using an agency, personnel there should consult with you and your family in developing a care plan, rather than imposing a standard package on you. Some agencies automatically deliver more care than is needed, partly because the more services they provide, the more money they make. This raises costs unnecessarily and, for many people, stops them from doing things for themselves, which can be an important part of continued psychological well-being. Agency or not, family members should be involved in the planning since they will probably be involved in providing additional care.

If you have special needs—rehabilitative therapy, a restricted diet, or Alzheimer's disease (see Chapter 5), for example—specialists in those areas should also participate in planning. Consultations with your doctor should also play a role. A home care plan must take into account your overall comfort and need for human contact as well as specific medical care—for example, it may be important to you for your aides to speak a language you are comfortable speaking or to not smoke. In search of such a match, an agency planner should make at least one extensive visit to the home where you will be receiving care *before* finalizing a plan. And, although you will certainly be keeping an eye on your own financial limits, an agency planner should also take your finances into account.

If you are making up your own care plan, using a checklist like the one below can help you keep track of your care. Be sure to include family members and friends who will help with care as well as paid or volunteer outside aides.

Getting Regular Providers

A home care plan is only as good as the people who carry it out. In addition to the training and experience of home care personnel, how well you get along is also important—and harder to evaluate. It helps to meet and interview home care aides before they begin to provide care. Be warned, however, that some agencies discourage advance selection to prevent clients from overshopping for the "perfect" aide.

Continuity of caregivers is also important. Once you have developed a relationship with caregivers who understand your needs, you want to be able to count on them regularly. On occasion, there are legitimate reasons, such as illness or vacation, for a temporary substitute. But even in these instances, substitute care should be provided only by an aide regularly employed by the agency and not by an independent or "freelance" caregiver—unless that person's qualifications and background have been subjected to the same scrutiny as regular employees.

Checklist for Home Care Plan

1. Medical and Rehabilitation Care

Service: _____

   Provider: _____

   When provided: _____

   Additional nonprofessional: _____

   Follow-up care (who and when): _____

Service: _____

   Provider: _____

   When provided: _____

   Additional nonprofessional: _____

   Follow-up care (who and when): _____

Service: _____

   Provider: _____

   When provided: _____

   Additional nonprofessional: _____

   Follow-up care (who and when): _____

2. Nonmedical Care (including personal assistance, meals, homemaking, escort, companion, transportation, and phone check)

Service: _____

   Provider: _____

   When provided: _____

Service: _____

   Provider: _____

   When provided: _____

Supervising and Reviewing Your Care

If you use the services of a home care agency, that agency should regularly review the care plan to make sure your needs are being met. The original plan may not have addressed your needs adequately, your needs may have changed over time, or the people actually giving you care may not be doing their jobs properly.

A staff member skilled in the specific care you require should regularly supervise and review your care. A certified therapist should be checking on your therapy aide, and a registered nurse should be checking on health care aides. The frequency of reviews should depend on how much care you receive. Medicare, for example, requires that a supervisor visit the home *at least every two weeks* to check on care for a chronic or acute illness. If no skilled medical care is involved, home visits by supervisors can be less frequent—every four to eight weeks, perhaps—but a supervisor should talk with a caregiver at least once a week.

The agency should provide an easy way for you to complain to a supervisor about the care you are receiving. You should have frequent telephone contact with a supervisor and regular visits from a supervisor to review your care—with your family members present, if you wish.

Costs of Home Care

As discussed in Chapter 7, you cannot count on Medicare, Medigap health insurance, or managed care to pay for much of the cost of long-term home care. Medicaid (Medi-Cal in California) will pay for long-term home care, but only if you have little income and few assets. (See Chapter 8.) Even if you have long-term care insurance coverage for home care, it will probably pay only a portion of your total home care costs. (See Chapter 9).

Because you will probably have to pay most long-term home care costs out of your own pocket, you should take a close look at the way a provider—particularly a home care agency—calculates its charges. Many agencies will give you a written estimate of charges based on the care plan they develop with you. Before signing up, read the estimate carefully, making sure it does not include charges for services you do not need or want. After you have been receiving home care for a while, check the agency's bills against the estimate to make sure you are actually receiving everything you have paid for.

Use Certified Providers

For financial or convenience reasons, you might use independent home care workers rather than going through a home care agency. But, if you do use an agency, make sure it is state licensed and Medicare and Medicaid certified.

Medicare and Medicaid Approved. Even if the care you receive initially is not covered by Medicare or Medicaid or you are not eligible for Medicaid, make sure the agency you use is certified by both. Your physical situation may change, making your care eligible for Medicare coverage. (See Chapter 7.) Or your financial situation may change, making you eligible for Medicaid. (See Chapter 8.) If the agency is certified, you will have continuity in your home care.

State Licensed. Some states have minimum quality standards and issue home care licenses or certificates only to those agencies or individual providers that qualify. If you have private Medigap insurance, Medicare managed care, or long-term care insurance that covers home health care, you will probably have to use a state-licensed provider. (Medigap and managed care coverage of home care is discussed in Chapter 7, long-term care insurance in Chapter 9.)

Sliding-Scale (Income-Based) Fee Policy

Many public agency, community, church, and philanthropic organization home care providers base eligibility and fees on the care recipient's income. In other words, you only qualify if your income is below a certain level—and the lower your income, the lower the charge. These are not always full-service home care agencies, but they may offer significant savings if they can meet your needs.

Cost Depends on Skill Level

Most agencies and individual providers charge by the hour or by the visit. Agencies sometimes also impose a minimum daily or weekly charge. Generally, the amount charged reflects the skill level of the provider. Therefore, you shouldn't receive simple care from a highly skilled provider when someone less skilled can provide it just as well. You can expect to pay rates in these ranges:

- nurse practitioners and registered nurses, $50 to $100 per hour
- practical and vocational nurses, licensed rehabilitative therapists, and geriatric social workers, $35 to $75 per hour
- trained home health aides, $10 to $30 per hour
- homemakers, home workers, and companions, $8 to $20 per hour.

The rates charged by independent care givers are usually lower than those charged by agencies. Rates also vary in different parts of the country.

Beware the Hidden Charges

When you discuss rates with a prospective home care agency or other provider, make sure to find out about possible hidden charges. For example, there is sometimes a minimum charge per visit, per week, or per month. There may also be higher rates for night and weekend visits, which could mean a significant cost increase if you require this kind of care. Some agencies also charge extra for in-home assessments, evaluations, and visits by supervisors. These are necessary elements of overall home care planning and service, however, and should *not* be charged as "extras."

Coverage for Home Care Costs

Medicare, Medicaid, Medigap insurance, managed care coverage, and long-term care insurance all may pay some of the costs of home care. Unfortunately, only Medicaid pays the full cost of long-term care. Here is what you can expect:

- **Medicare.** Pays for short-term home health care—one week up to a couple of months—but not for long-term care. Pays for home care only if you need skilled nursing or rehabilitation. (See Chapter 7.)

- **Medigap insurance and Medicare managed care plans.** Medigap policies pay nothing for long-term home care. The same is generally true for Medicare managed care plans, although a few managed care plans offer some home care coverage for an extra premium. (See Chapter 7.)

- **Medicaid.** Pays for long-term home care by certified providers. You will qualify only if you have very low income and few assets. (See Chapter 8.)

- **Long-term care insurance.** Some long-term care insurance policies cover home care. Payments begin only when you meet their benefit standards—meaning that, according to their rules, you need the care. (See Chapter 9.)

- **Veterans benefits.** If you qualify for VA medical benefits coverage, it can include home care. (See Chapter 7.)

Financing Home Care Through Reverse Mortgages

An older person who has very low income and few assets may qualify for Medicaid, which may pay for the entire cost of home care. (See Chapter 8.) Or an elder may have a long-term care insurance policy that will pay a portion of home care costs. (See Chapter 9.) However, many older people are caught in the middle. They have no long-term home care insurance coverage and they do not have enough income or liquid assets to pay for the long-term home care they need, but they do not qualify for Medicaid coverage.

Many of these same people own their own homes or condominiums outright, or have considerable equity in them. By using a reverse mortgage, elders can convert home equity into cash while continuing to live at home as long as they are physically able to do so. A reverse mortgage is a loan against the value of a home paid as a lump sum, monthly amount, line of credit, or some combination, which does not have to be repaid until the borrower sells or otherwise permanently leaves the home.

Reverse mortgages also have a side benefit. Because the money they provide is a loan, it is not taxable as income, nor does it count as income against Social Security benefits if you haven't yet reached full retirement age. The interest you accumulate on the loan, however, is not tax-deductible until the loan is paid off.

When the borrower sells the home, he or she must pay back the loan out of the proceeds. If the borrower permanently leaves the home—moves in with relatives or to a nursing facility or other location—or dies, the lender must be repaid within a certain time, usually one year to 18 months. This often means that the borrower or the estate will have to sell the house to repay the reverse mortgage. The final repayment amount is determined by the size of the loan, the interest rate, the cost of insurance, and the length of time the loan is outstanding.

If the property is sold for more than the amount of the mortgage, then the owner or owner's survivors keep the difference. On the other hand, if the property receives more under the reverse mortgage than the home is eventually sold for, neither the owner nor the survivors owe the mortgage company anything more; the mortgage company has to take the loss.

There are several types of reverse loans and mortgages, each with somewhat different terms and purposes:

- **Property tax deferral programs.** On a small scale, there are publicly funded and operated property tax deferral programs available in many states. These programs, available to low-income elders, defer the cost of the owner's property tax and take a lien for that amount against the property, payable when the home is sold. Although these deferrals are for relatively small yearly amounts, they free up some cash for home care or other needs. For information about whether such a program is in place where you live, contact your county property tax collector or your Area Agency on Aging, or call your local senior information and referral number (look in the white pages of the telephone directory).

- **Deferred home improvement loans.** Some state and local government agencies also make loans to low-income elders to repair or improve their homes, deferring repayment as long as the elder continues to live in the home. Although these loans are for limited amounts and specific purposes, they can help finance necessary improvements on a home, either to fit it specially for assisted living or merely to repair it so it remains livable. And the money an elder borrows to make home improvements can free up other money for use on home care services.

- **Reverse mortgages insured by the federal government.** The Federal Housing Administration (FHA) insures some reverse mortgage loans through its Home Equity Conversion Mortgage (HECM) program; the loans are processed through private lenders and are available to any homeowner age 62 or older, regardless of his or her income.

The loans are available to any owner or occupant of a single-family primary residence including condominiums (but not co-ops and motor homes). A homeowner can usually borrow 40% to 60% of a home's value.

- **Privately insured reverse mortgages.** In addition to government-insured loans, certain private mortgage holding companies also insure reverse mortgages administered by local lending institutions. These loans have less stringent qualifying standards and higher equity limits than government-insured loans, but they also charge higher fees and interest rates.

Drawbacks of Reverse Mortgages

Although reverse mortgages have some attractive features, they also have some serious drawbacks. They often have high initial fees, such as those for appraisal, credit checks, and insurance, as well as closing costs, origination costs, and service charges. So, if you die or move out of the home before you have drawn much on the mortgage, you wind up paying a very high cost for what will have turned out to be a short-term loan.

There are also continuing fees and interest payments each year, which may take a serious bite out of the money you actually receive. When considering any reverse mortgage, have the lender show you in writing exactly what these total annual loan costs (TALCs) will be—not just for the initial year, but for the entire life of the loan.

Even more significantly, interest under a reverse mortgage loan compounds; in other words, you wind up paying interest on interest as the loan period goes on. In addition, as you borrow more monthly or under a line of credit, the principal also goes up. The combination of these two spiraling debt factors means that over a period of years, a modest initial reverse mortgage can cost considerably more than conventional forms of borrowing and can eat up all the equity in the property. An elder who wants to preserve some equity to pass on to heirs or to use in some other way after selling the house may instead wind up with a piece of property that has no residual value.

A reverse mortgage also ties the borrower to the house. Most reverse mortgages require that the loan be repaid when the borrower no longer lives in the house. If the borrower moves in with relatives, moves to another area, or enters a nursing home to receive better care, monthly payments and any line of credit stop—and the borrower must repay the loan within a certain time. Elders who borrow under reverse mortgages may one day find themselves faced with the unhappy choice of paying off the loan in order to move to a more comfortable, healthy, or secure setting, or staying put to continue receiving the mortgage benefits.

Protecting Your Interests

There are several things that people who shop for a reverse mortgage should insist upon to protect themselves and their home equity.

First, the mortgage must have a "nonrecourse" clause. This means that the lender cannot go after any source of debt repayment other than the house. This limits the debt—no matter how long the borrower lives, how high the interest payments pile up, or how many other assets the borrower has—to the value of the house.

Second, do not consider any reverse mortgage that requires you to transfer title to your property or transfer title out of your name. A reputable reverse mortgage is a loan with an interest in your equity, not a transfer of title.

Third, never pay any application or processing fees until you have actually decided to apply for a specific loan. If a company tries to get you to pay before you even try to enter a contract with them, you can be sure it will try to squeeze money from you all the way down the line.

All government-insured loans require potential borrowers to receive counseling from a financial advisor unconnected to the lending institution. This advisor can explain all aspects of the loan and highlight its advantages and disadvantages. If you are considering a nongovernment loan, follow the same procedures. Consult with an independent financial advisor unconnected with the institution offering you the reverse mortgage, to find out all of the mortgage's benefits and risks.

Get More Information on Reverse Mortgages

For information on where to locate reverse mortgages and how to evaluate the ones being offered, see the Resource Directory in the appendix at the end of the book.

Cashing in a Life Insurance Policy

Life insurance policies offer another source of funds for seniors who are terminally ill. By cashing in a life insurance policy, an elder can get a substantial amount of money relatively quickly—without having to worry about how the money will get paid back.

However, there are potential drawbacks to cashing in a life insurance policy that may make the option somewhat less attractive than it first appears. First and most obviously, the policy benefits will no longer go to the original beneficiaries. And the amount you receive will be considerably lower than the policy's face value (the amount that would be paid after your death). Also, the payments may be subject to state capital gains tax; although the federal government exempts these amounts from taxes, some states consider them taxable income. Because of this potential tax consequence, plus the complicated terms of the settlements themselves, you should consult with a financial advisor before entering an accelerated benefit or life settlement agreement. (See "Life Settlements," below.)

Perhaps most significantly, the amount you receive may disqualify you from receiving Medicaid coverage for home or nursing facility care. (See Chapter 8.) Medicaid does not consider the face value of a life insurance policy as an asset, or require a Medicaid applicant to cash in a policy. But if a policy is cashed in, Medicaid will count the money received as an asset. And if the benefits push the elder over the Medicaid eligibility limits, cashing in the policy will have created a double loss: The elder won't qualify for Medicaid coverage and will receive much less than the policy's face value.

For many terminally ill people, however, the benefits of getting the cash clearly outweigh these negatives. If getting the money before death seems worth it to you, there are two avenues for selling or exchanging a life insurance policy: accelerated or living benefits and life settlements.

Accelerated or Living Benefits

Some life insurance policies may be cashed in directly with the insurance company itself—a procedure known as collecting accelerated or living benefits. The amount of these benefits runs between 60% and 80% of the face value of the policy, depending on its terms. If the policy provides for accelerated benefits, it usually requires the treating physician to declare the policyholder terminally ill—meaning that he or she has less than two years to live.

The procedures you have to follow to claim accelerated benefits depend on the terms of the individual policy. To learn whether a policy may be cashed in for accelerated benefits and how that process works, check the terms of the policy and speak with a representative of the insurance company that issued it. Do not rely on an insurance agent to explain the details; ask to be referred to staff that specializes in accelerated benefits.

Life Settlements

Even if you do not qualify for accelerated benefits—either because your policy does not permit it or because you are not terminally ill—you can achieve similar results by making a "life settlement" (also called a "senior settlement" or "investor-owned insurance settlement") of your policy. Life settlement companies pay a lump sum to a life insurance policyholder who is 65 and over. The amount they pay depends on the amount of the policy benefits, the amount of the monthly premiums, and the age and health of the policyholder. Settlement amounts run between 50% and 80% of the policy's face value. The younger and healthier the person selling the life settlement, the lower the settlement amount.

The company that buys the policy pays the premiums until the policyholder dies. The benefits are then paid to the settlement company rather than to the original beneficiaries of the policy. This can be an effective way to raise cash to pay for long-term care. The obvious drawback is that whoever you originally intended to be the beneficiary of the life insurance will no longer get the benefits.

To shop for the best life settlement, compare at least two or three companies. Begin with your own insurance agent or one of the organizations that monitors life settlement companies. (See the appendix at the end of this book for resources.) Regardless of how you find a life settlement company, check with your state's Department of Insurance to make sure the company is licensed to do business in your state. A state license means that the company's business practices are subject to some official oversight.

Hurry Up and Wait

Most people cash in a life insurance policy because they need the money immediately. But, make sure you take the time to consider several companies, compare all the options offered, and carefully review all the paperwork before deciding on a settlement. It might also be a good idea to consult with an accountant, lawyer, or other financial advisor. Because the insurance and settlement companies also take their time considering your application and plowing through their bureaucratic steps before any money actually changes hands, you shouldn't expect to see your money for two to four months.

Supplements to Home Care

A number of free or low-cost programs now provide older people with certain services not offered by most home care agencies. These programs supplement home care services, keep costs down, and often make the difference between being able to stay at home and having to enter a nursing facility. Most of all, many of these services give the person receiving care a break in the routine—and give family members some relief from their responsibilities.

Meals on Wheels

Meals on Wheels is perhaps the best known supplement to home care. Although good nutrition is essential to health, many older people begin to neglect their diets when shopping, cooking, and cleaning become difficult, or when dietary problems restrict their food choices. Meals on Wheels brings easily affordable food that is hot, tasty, nutritious, and ready to eat. It also provides daily, friendly human contact that is a welcome diversion in a long day at home.

Almost all communities now have some kind of low-cost meal delivery system for housebound elders, although in some areas there is a waiting list for this service. Funding for Meals on Wheels varies, and the service often depends heavily on volunteers, but all of the programs work essentially the same way. For a very small fee, Meals on Wheels delivers a hot, nutritious meal once a day, usually around lunchtime. Often, for a slight extra charge, you can also get a snack or another meal, either cold or easily heated, for later in the day.

To find a Meals on Wheels local program near you, you can use the directory on the website of the Meals on Wheels Association of America at www.mowaa.org. Or, you can find information about a Meals on Wheels program near you using the Eldercare Locator at 800-677-1116 or www.eldercare.gov.

Adult Day Care and Respite Care

Adult day care can be an excellent supplement to home care. Adult day care centers offer daytime monitoring, meals, companionship, and activities for people who need assistance with the activities of daily life. They do not usually provide much in the way of medical services. Respite care provides a few hours a week of low-cost companionship without any active care services. Both are less expensive than paid home care services.

Adult Day Care Centers

Adult day care centers provide meals, companionship, social and physical activities, and social services. Some centers also offer limited medical care and monitoring. And they give family caregivers an alternative to full-time home care. These centers can often make it possible for an elder to continue living at home rather than entering a long-term care residential facility.

A few centers affiliated with hospitals or skilled nursing facilities offer medical care—including administering medications and treatments, physical and other rehabilitative therapies, health testing, monitoring, and screening—as part of a personalized, written health care plan. At centers run by community or public service organizations, more modest levels of medical care may be available.

All day care centers offer meals, personal care assistance, exercise, recreation, and social and educational programs. Social services, including referrals to other agencies and programs, are also usually available. But above all, adult day care centers offer companionship for elders who might otherwise be housebound—and a little time off for their family members.

Adult day care centers may offer half-day or full-day programs, one to five days a week. Some require scheduled attendance, while others permit drop-in visits. Some centers also provide or arrange for transportation. Prices depend on the range of services offered and the nature of the sponsoring organization. Many centers charge according to the elder's ability to pay.

Finding Adult Day Care

To get a referral and references for a center nearby, contact:

National Adult Day Services Association, Inc.
Toll-free phone: 877-745-1440
www.nadsa.org

Or, go to the U.S. Department of Health and Human Services' Eldercare Locator at www.eldercare.gov. Although the federal government provides links to adult day care, there is no federal licensing or oversight of adult day care providers.

Respite Care

Like adult day care, respite care serves as a break in routine for both those who give and those who receive care. Unlike adult day care centers, however, respite care does not involve organized activities or services. It provides companionship and monitoring, often by volunteers, for short periods of time on a regular or occasional basis—a few times a week, one weekend a month, or for a full weekend or week when primary caregivers are unavailable. Respite care can be provided at home (yours or the caregiver's), at a church or community center, or in a nursing facility. It is often sponsored by a community organization. Unless it is provided at a medical facility, it is usually low-cost or even free.

If your home care agency or geriatric care manager cannot direct you to organizations that provide respite care, you can find referrals through your state Area Agency on Aging or the government-sponsored Eldercare Locator at 800-677-1116 or www.eldercare.gov.

Senior Centers

Most senior centers provide free social and recreational activities, education, information, and exercise programs and a hot meal on a drop-in basis to physically self-sufficient elders. Generally, there is no fixed schedule required for participation, although elders may have to sign up for meals and some programs in advance.

While senior centers do not offer personal assistance care, they do provide some respite care, nutrition, organized activities, and informal companionship for an elder who does not need monitoring. Senior centers often arrange for transportation to and from the center and sometimes organize outings to places of interest. They are excellent sources of information about services available to seniors, particularly about the individual, independent caregivers who can be reliable and less expensive alternatives to agency care.

County Health Screening

One of the functions of skilled home health care is to monitor the health of the elder receiving care. If you require less extensive care, however, you may be missing regular health monitoring and screening. As a supplement to doctor visits, many city or county health clinics regularly offer free or low-cost health screening and testing. These clinics can provide adequate general health monitoring if used as part of an ongoing care plan. The public health nurses at these clinics can help schedule a regular program of screening and testing.

Family Education Programs

A number of public agencies and community organizations—United Way, Red Cross, Visiting Nurses Association, and many hospitals—offer instruction for elders and their families on various aspects of home health care: personal care assistance (such as bathing and movement techniques), exercise, nutrition for special dietary needs, and monitoring health conditions and vital signs. Learning these techniques helps ensure the safety and well-being of the elder and permits family members to assist with a wider range of home care—and avoid some of the dependence on professional providers. A family education program can also be a good source of information about other available programs, as well as a chance to share information and experiences with other elders and their families.

Additional Services

In addition to the programs discussed above, there are other specific services available free or at very low cost which can help lighten the burdens of home care.

You can find services to supplement home care in much the same way that you find home care itself. With supplemental care, however, the referrals are more likely to come from local rather than state or regional agencies, and from volunteer and community organizations rather than from institutions or medical sources. The local senior center is usually an excellent source of information, as is the senior referral telephone service listed in the white pages of your phone directory. Geriatric case managers can be particularly helpful in finding the small, independent, or little-known extra services not provided by home care agencies.

Some of the supplemental services available in many communities are described below.

Senior Escort Service

Some people can get around on their own or with minimum assistance, for short trips to the store or the bank or the park, for example. However, they may be concerned about their safety on the streets. Escort services provide someone to accompany you on short trips; they're often available on fairly short notice.

Transportation Service

Many people would love to go to a senior center, the library, a park, or organized activities if only they could get there. There are a number of public agencies and community groups that provide free transportation, often with wheelchair access.

Companion Service

Similar to respite care, a companion service can send someone for a few hours a week on a regular schedule, to provide company but not care. The occasional company and conversation of someone who brings good cheer can be a wonderful diversion. These services are mostly volunteer staffed and community funded, so there is usually no charge for using them.

Housekeeping and Grocery Services

Many state and local government departments of social services or volunteer programs offer grocery shoppers and part-time housekeepers to do occasional work for low-income physically disabled or impaired elders. When available, these housekeeping and grocery services are offered free or at a very low cost.

Telephone Safety Service

Particularly valuable for people who live alone and do not have family in the vicinity, telephone reassurance programs make a daily call, at the same time each day, to check in with an elder living at home. Besides being a safety check, these calls allow the elder to have a brief conversation with someone during the day.

A related service, called Lifeline, is available in many places. It provides a telephone emergency response service usually connected directly to a hospital or other emergency health facility. The line can be connected to your phone and maintained for a nominal cost.

Organized Senior Residences

Many seniors are no longer able, or no longer willing, to live completely independently at home. For some, home care may offer help, but it may not deliver the sense of security and companionship that the elder needs. For seniors at the other extreme, the amount of home care they need may be prohibitively expensive, but they may neither want nor need the institutional care of a nursing facility.

Elder residences have evolved to fill this gap. They combine some of the comforts and independence of living at home with some of the care and security of a nursing facility. Elder residences come in various shapes and sizes, provide different services and levels of care, and carry different price tags. But they share at least one thing: They provide shelter and services for the elderly without the institutional feel and high cost of nursing facilities.

These organized residences range from seniors-only apartment complexes and retirement communities for relatively independent elders, to assisted living facilities for people who need help with activities of daily living (ADLs). Some residential communities offer both independent living and assisted living in the same location. Still others provide continuing care, including a nursing facility, which guarantees that a resident can move from one level of care to another as needed.

While organized senior residences may provide excellent living situations, they are not for everyone. Some facilities deny entry to seniors who are over a certain age, while others mandate a certain level of physical capability. And most carry substantial price tags or monthly payments that are beyond the means of many elders. The exception is federally subsidized housing for low-income seniors, which may charge rent and provide some services on a sliding scale based on income.

And financial assistance is hard to come by. Medicare, Medicaid, and private insurance do not cover any of the cost of independent living residences. Nor do they pay for most assisted living facilities, although this is slowly changing. (See "Assisted Living," below.) Nonetheless, most of the residential alternatives discussed in this chapter are less expensive than nursing facilities and are worth considering if some care short of a nursing facility is needed.

How to Find Residential Facilities

A growing number of sources offer help in finding suitable residential facilities:

- Eldercare Locator, run by the U.S. Administration on Aging, can provide referrals. Phone: 800-677-1116; Internet: www.eldercare.gov.
- Leading Age can provide you with information about its member residential facilities in your area. Phone: 202-783-2242; Internet: www.leadingage.org.
- Assisted Living Federation of America provides a list of assisted living facilities that belong to the federation. Phone: 703-894-1805; Internet: www.alfa.org.
- Your local Area Agency on Aging provides information about subsidized housing and residential facilities. (See the appendix for contact information.)
- A senior referral and information service listed in the white pages of the telephone directory can refer you to local facilities.
- A geriatric care manager may be able to direct you to residential facilities (especially assisted living facilities), might know the reputation of particular local residences, and can help you evaluate whether a particular place is likely to meet your needs. (See "Geriatric Care Managers" in Chapter 1.)
- Religious, ethnic, or fraternal organizations are often good sources of information about senior housing.

Independent Living

Independent living complexes are housing built or renovated for older people who are, for the most part, able to care for themselves. The main purpose of these residences is to provide senior-friendly housing and social services.

If More Care Is Needed

Independent living residences do not provide personal care or monitor a resident's physical condition. But, some include separate floors or wings with assisted living units where such care is provided. In these facilities, a resident may move to a higher level of care when needed, but only if such a housing unit is vacant.

Other independent living residences are combined with both assisted living units and a nursing facility. In these continuing care communities, residents are guaranteed whatever level of care they need. A resident whose health or physical condition changes may move to a different level of care without having to wait for available space. This guarantee makes continuing care communities more expensive than multilevel facilities that permit seniors to move only when there is a vacancy.

The Basics

Independent living residences come in many forms. For people with a good deal of money and independence, there are luxury, gated housing developments, often with a golf course or other extensive indoor and outdoor recreation amenities. In these developments, people purchase their own homes or townhouses.

There are also more moderately priced rental apartment or condominium complexes with a selection of differently sized units, common dining and socializing areas, and services for residents, but without the extensive private grounds and recreation facilities of gated communities.

Independent living residences may also be simple urban apartment buildings with small rental units, limited common areas, and few services. Some of these senior apartment buildings are subsidized by the federal government, which means that rent is considerably cheaper than market rates for units of the same size.

Many independent living residences refer to themselves as communities. This may seem like a big claim for what may be no more than a small apartment building, but a sense of community is just what these residences seek to create. The amount and type of services offered by an independent living facility vary, depending in large part on cost. But all independent living residences provide a specially tailored and protected living space—a community—by:

- limiting residence to seniors, which means the people who live there tend to have similar experiences, physical capabilities, and limitations

- designing and outfitting common areas and individual living units specially for elders, with elevators, ramps, wide hallways, good lighting, handrails, and extra safety and security devices

- having common dining areas and providing meals—some included in the general fees paid, others for an extra charge—specially prepared for older tastes, digestion, and nutritional needs

- providing some laundry and housekeeping services, although there may be extra charges for these

- offering some commercial services on the premises, such as banking, a beauty salon, shops, a library, or local transportation

- organizing social, educational, and recreational events both on and off the premises, and

- having a nurse or paramedic on duty, or some other medical emergency system.

Independent Living Plus Home Care

You may be one of many people considering a move to an independent living community, but wonder whether you are independent enough. You may need more personal care than an independent living community offers, but not need all the services an assisted living facility provides. The difference may be something as simple as needing help to shower. If you need only a little personal care, you may not want the close monitoring and regulations of assisted living—or the higher cost of help that you don't need. But without a small amount of extra care, you cannot quite manage on your own.

One solution may be for you to arrange for outside home care in your independent living residence. (See Chapter 2.) You may be able to hire just as much home care as you need, without the unwanted and costly care provided by assisted living. Some independent living facilities even maintain a roster of reliable outside home care providers and will help arrange the care.

Other independent living communities, however, have rules about the type or frequency of outside care permitted. And some independent living facilities require that all residents maintain a certain level of physical capability—being ambulatory and able to get in and out of bed unassisted, for example. Such rules may make home care in those communities less useful than it could be. (See "Rules and Restrictions," below.)

Costs

Independent living residences range from federally subsidized studio apartments rented for a few hundred dollars a month to luxury homes sold for over a million dollars. And there are other important questions about cost to consider: Are there fees in addition to rent or purchase price? How much are rent and fees likely to be raised over time? What services are included in the price you pay, and what services cost extra?

Renting

Many independent living complexes offer studio, one-bedroom, or two-bedroom rental apartments. Because of the services, facilities, staff, and common areas that are also provided, rent for these units generally runs 50% to 100% higher than for a comparable apartment in the same locale. On the other hand, they are usually significantly less expensive than comparable assisted living units. Some are federally subsidized, which means that the rents are lower for those who meet the eligibility requirements: a low fixed income and very few assets.

Although the initial rent for an independent living apartment may be affordable, you also need to consider rent increases. Because they provide more than just housing, independent living complexes are almost always exempt from city or county rent control laws. However, you may be able to control your own rent for a short time through a lease. Most independent living facilities will offer a one-year lease; some will offer two or three years. Longer leases are rarely offered and are probably not a good idea, either. If it turns out that you do not like living in the apartment, or your needs change and you can no longer manage in independent living, a long lease might tie you down.

Before moving into a rental apartment, ask to see the facility's record of rent increases over the previous five years. If it has consistently raised rents by large amounts, the practice will probably continue. On the other hand, if it has kept rent increases low over the years, it might also do so for the foreseeable future.

Buying

Many independent living complexes are enclosed subdivisions with single family homes or townhouses for sale. Also, many senior apartments are sold as condominiums or cooperatives rather than rented. The prices of these houses and apartments vary widely, depending on size, quality, location, and services. A senior housing unit tends to have less square footage than regular housing with the same number of rooms, but their special design, security, and included services make the properties more expensive.

Unlike open market housing, many senior independent living complexes restrict an owner's rights to resell or mortgage the property. In all senior housing, a new buyer must qualify under the community's general rules, which generally require residents to be over a certain age and have a defined physical independence. (See "Rules and Restrictions," below.) But some complexes place additional restrictions on resale or refinance. For example, a housing complex may reserve the right to buy back the unit for some percentage more than the seller paid—or some percentage less than any offer the seller receives. Rules may also restrict an owner's right to refinance the house or to obtain cash by taking out a reverse mortgage. There may also be strict rules against renting out the property.

If, at some point, you need to move to a higher level of care than you can receive in independent living, or for any other reason you want to move out, these restrictions may make it difficult to sell your home. They will also reduce its market value. Your survivors would experience the same difficulties if you died while living in the property. So, before entering into any agreement to purchase an independent living house or apartment, thoroughly examine any rules relating to resale or refinance. If you are not certain how those rules might affect you, get a full explanation from an attorney, accountant, or other financial advisor who is not connected to the facility.

Additional Fees

At many senior residences, the price to buy or rent a house or apartment is only one of several costs. There is often an entrance fee that is partially or entirely nonrefundable. Many residential complexes also charge monthly maintenance fees. And some places include certain services (such as one daily meal and occasional cleaning services) in the basic rent or purchase price, but charge extra fees for other services, such as additional meals, laundry, and access to recreational facilities.

Entrance Fees. If you buy an independent living house or condominium (and, in some cases, if you rent one), you may be required to pay a lump sum entrance fee, also called an endowment fee or a founders fee. These fees may range from $10,000 to $100,000—depending on how luxurious—or popular—the place is.

Sometimes, these entrance fees are fully refundable for a limited time—for example, if you sell the unit within the first three to six months after you buy it. Other times, you get back only a portion of the fee when you sell your unit—commonly, the entrance fee refund is reduced by 1% to 5% for each month you live in the residence.

Maintenance Fees. Most independent living complexes in which residents own their house or condominium charge a monthly maintenance fee. For rental units, the fees are usually part of the rent. Most complexes charge a maintenance fee even if they also charge an entrance fee. Before you buy a residence, find out if there are any rules that control how much the maintenance fee may be raised per year. If there are no rules about fee increases, check the facility's records for the previous five years to see how often and how much the fees have been raised.

Fees for Services. All independent living residences include some services in addition to a roof over your head. It is important to find out which services are included in the rent or purchase price and which cost extra.

Most independent living residences have a kitchen and common dining room in which at least one hot meal per day is served; some serve three meals, although breakfast and lunch may be informal buffets. But meals may not be included in your regular rent or maintenance fees; if you want meals, you may have to pay extra for them. Food is usually a senior's greatest expense after rent and health care. Shopping for, preparing, and cleaning up after meals can be a significant burden for many elders. And, good nutrition is a key to continued good health. For all these reasons, find out how many meals are included in your basic rent or maintenance fee and how much extra meals cost. This should be an important part of your investigation of any independent living residence. Quality is important, too. If you plan to eat the residence's food, make sure to sample it by having at least two meals before you agree to move in.

Choosing Between Inclusive and Noninclusive Contracts

Some independent living complexes offer what is called an inclusive contract or extensive agreement, which means that the rent or purchase price, plus maintenance fees, covers all the services the facility provides. If you can choose between an inclusive and a noninclusive contract, you must determine if the extra cost of the inclusive contract is worth the extra services. If the extra services are not things you particularly care about, you may not want to pay for them.

Choosing between the two types of contracts will be less difficult if you are permitted to pay for individual services without having to buy the whole inclusive package. You may be able to pick and choose the few extra services you want—lunch and sessions with an exercise instructor, for example—without having to pay for all the other things in the inclusive contract that don't interest you.

Among the services commonly offered is recreation—exercise and dance, for example, and golf, tennis, and swimming at the more expensive communities. You may be charged a separate fee for some of these services, or charged extra for unlimited or preferential access to them. Similarly, transportation, housekeeping, laundry, and shopping services may be offered, but some or all of them only for extra fees.

Some independent living facilities also offer temporary personal assistance. If you need long-term help with dressing, bathing, eating, or moving around, you will not be permitted to remain in independent living. But if your need for care is only short-term, some facilities provide it. Find out whether the facility offers this kind of personal care and whether it is included in your regular fees or requires paying extra.

Rules and Restrictions

Because they are organized facilities rather than merely a collection of residences, independent living communities tend to have numerous rules and regulations by which residents must abide. The rules range from simple things like the time meals are served or the decorations or modifications permitted in an individual living unit, to the extremely important matter of the physical condition a resident must maintain to live there.

Age and Physical Condition

Independent living facilities require residents to maintain a certain level of physical independence. There are usually two different standards: one to enter as a resident and another standard (somewhat less stringent) to remain.

Requirements to Enter. To qualify to buy or rent a housing unit, you must have reached a minimum age—usually 55 or 60. But, many residence complexes also have a maximum age; some have entry age limits of 75, 80, or 85.

In most residences, you must also be fully ambulatory—meaning that you are able to move around without a wheelchair or personal assistance. Most independent living complexes permit a new resident to use a walker, but some do not permit walkers or oxygen units in the common dining areas. Many independent living facilities also require that new residents be fully continent. Others insist that a resident must be able to eat without assistance, at least in the common dining area.

Rules for Couples

It often happens that one person in a couple—either a married couple, siblings, or some other combination of people who live together—loses some physical capabilities before the other does. If one member of the couple falls below the facility's physical requirements while the other remains physically qualified, what happens next depends on the rules of the facility and the availability of another housing unit within the same complex.

In some residences, the couple must move—or one of them must move while the other remains. If the same facility offers assisted living units, this rule would not create quite as much of a hardship. Other facilities permit the couple to stay if the less able one can reach the minimum physical standards with the help of the healthier one, but without outside assistance.

Any couple considering an independent living residence must understand these rules and make sure they are clearly spelled out in the written residence contract.

Requirements to Remain. Residents in independent living units might not be permitted to remain if their physical conditions deteriorate, for more than a short time, past a certain point. Any of the following problems might disqualify a resident:

- inability to get in and out of bed without assistance
- full incontinence, or
- inability to eat without assistance.

Because of such rules, if you are already frail and are likely, within the foreseeable future, to fall below a residence's physical condition requirements, you should consider:

- an independent living residence with less stringent requirements or no requirements for continuing residents

- an assisted living residence instead of independent living, or

- a facility with more than one level of care, so that if you must move, you will be able to remain in the same residential community.

Number of Residents, Guests, and Assistants

Many independent living facilities limit the number of people who may live in any given unit. The maximum is usually two; only one resident might be permitted in a small unit. All residents must be over a certain age—generally 55 to 65. That means that children or grandchildren may not move in, even if they could provide needed personal care for the resident. Some communities also require that couples who share a residence be related. This restriction prevents residents from reaping the great cost savings of sharing with a housemate—as well as older couples who are not (or cannot get) married.

Most residences also have rules about overnight guests. Some prohibit guests in the units but offer guest rooms or apartments for short stays, usually with an extra charge to the resident. Some permit guests for short stays, but prohibit children under a certain age. Most places allow guests to stay for meals, for an extra charge to the resident; some even provide a separate, private dining room for groups or special occasions.

When you consider an independent living residence, find out whether and under what circumstances it permits home care for individual residents. Having a personal care aide come to your home on a regular basis to help you with activities of daily living—dressing, bathing, cooking, and eating, getting in and out of bed, or taking a walk—may mean the difference between remaining in independent living and having to move to assisted living or a nursing facility. But some residences limit the number of regular visits by outside personal care aides or do not permit them at all except on a temporary basis while a resident recovers from an illness or injury. Such a restriction may not seem that meaningful to you if you are now hale and hearty, but it could become important if and when your physical condition takes a turn for the worse.

Watch Out for Changes in Ownership

Like many other businesses these days, senior residences are frequently targets for takeovers by larger companies. National corporations that run senior residences around the country are gobbling up good, low-cost, locally owned facilities. And when the ownership changes, the quality and the cost often change, too.

New owners often change things to make their acquisition more profitable, which may mean less comfort and higher costs for the residents. If you are considering moving into an independent or assisted living residence complex, find out how long the current owners have operated it.

If it has been sold within the previous two years, talk with the staff and residents about recent changes. Cuts in services and staff may make residents less comfortable than they have been, and future cuts may make things worse. Also, you can no longer rely on what the previous owners did regarding rent or fee increases. Ask management for information on increases the new ownership has imposed not only at this residence but also at other facilities they operate, particularly ones they have recently purchased.

Assisted Living

Assisted living combines much of the homelike atmosphere of independent living with some of the personal care of a nursing facility. It provides extensive personal assistance and services, plus round-the-clock monitoring—services not offered by independent living residences and very costly if arranged through home care. Assisted living also permits residents to maintain some of the privacy and independence that are lost in more institutional, and more expensive, nursing facilities. Assisted living is the fastest growing type of senior residence—with more than 50,000 facilities and close to a million residents—meeting the needs of people who cannot make it entirely on their own but who do not need nursing home care.

The residences referred to in this section as assisted living are sometimes also called sheltered care or catered living. Although each facility or residence differs somewhat in the type of housing and level of services and staffing provided, all of them have certain things in common. They provide:

- domestic services, including meals and housekeeping
- assistance with personal care and the activities of daily living, but not nursing care, and
- close monitoring to help ensure residents' health and safety.

The Basics

Assisted living provides a room or small apartment—usually rented—to help maintain a homelike setting. It also includes a range of services to assist residents with those tasks of daily life made difficult for them by the loss of some physical or mental capabilities.

Types of Living Spaces

There are several kinds and sizes of assisted living housing: full-size one-bedroom apartments; studio apartments with small kitchenettes; studios without a kitchen or with a partial kitchen that has no cooking facilities; single rooms; and shared rooms. An assisted living apartment or room may be furnished or unfurnished. Even if a space is furnished, some places permit residents to bring in some furnishings of their own, which can make a new place feel more like home.

Assisted living apartments and rooms tend to be smaller than living spaces intended for the general public. They are often fitted with safety devices such as handrails and special bathroom fixtures, and may include a hospital bed if needed. In addition to the small rooms and space-eating fixtures, people tend to bring more of their own furnishings than would otherwise fit easily into the space. As a result, many assisted living apartments feel crowded and even smaller than they are. It is often difficult for a new resident to adjust to the smaller, more cramped quarters.

Special Care for Alzheimer's or Disorientation

Assisted living is often an excellent solution for many people who suffer mild symptoms from the early stages of Alzheimer's or other age-related disorientation. Their need for monitoring and assistance make independent living too difficult or dangerous, but they do not need the high level of care provided by a nursing facility.

However, the kind of assistance these people need is different from that required by those who have only physical limitations. The same assisted living residence that provides good care for someone with only physical frailties does not necessarily work well for a person with mild dementia. If you are considering an assisted living facility for someone with early Alzheimer's or other mild dementia, read Chapter 5.

Services Provided

The main difference between assisted living and independent living residences is that assisted living gives residents more help in meeting their daily needs. While assisted living does not offer the medical care or the level of attention of a nursing facility, it does provide personal care in a resident's living space and common areas, meals, household tasks, and extensive monitoring of each resident's physical condition.

Personal Assistance. Most people move to assisted living because they need help with one or more of what are known as the activities of daily living (ADLs). ADLs include eating, bathing, dressing, continence and using the toilet, walking, and getting in and out of a bed or chair.

An assisted living facility will help a resident with any ADL—but not all the time, and not whenever a resident wants help. Instead, a schedule will be developed that takes into account the resident's needs and the staff's availability. For example, an aide might help a resident get in and out of bed in the morning, once or twice during the day, at bedtime, and once again during the night. Or a resident might be given a full bath three or four times a week, but not every day.

When you consider a particular assisted living residence, ask precisely what help it offers for the specific ADLs with which you need assistance. If the facility offers you the kind and frequency of assistance you need, make certain that care is spelled out in the written residence agreement you sign.

Health Monitoring. In addition to help with daily activities, an assisted living facility monitors a resident's health. That does not mean nursing or other active treatment of a medical condition, however. Rather, it means keeping track of and helping the resident take the correct dose of medications, helping the resident with self-administered health aids, such as prostheses and oxygen, providing emergency call systems, and checking on a resident's well-being during the night.

Most assisted living residences have a nurse on duty to check on any resident who has health difficulties or whose physical condition seems to be changing and to refer the resident for medical care if it seems necessary. Health monitoring may also include coordinating care with the resident's primary care physician and keeping track of a resident's medical appointments. And, most facilities provide or arrange transportation to and from those appointments.

Strict Rules Aren't for Everyone

Assisted living offers close monitoring of residents' physical conditions. This includes keeping track of medications, checking on residents at night, and making sure residents eat properly. Assisted living facilities accomplish this by setting up schedules that staff and residents must follow.

Sometimes, these schedules and rules are too restrictive for a competent, independent-minded person.

Depending on your needs, including your need to be left alone, independent living plus home care might fit your personality better than assisted living—even though you and your family will have to take charge of organizing your care.

Meals. For many people, one of the most attractive things about assisted living is that meals are provided. These facilities have a kitchen and a common dining room where at least two and usually three meals a day are served. The cost of meals is included in the resident's rent or fees. Residents are freed from shopping, cooking, and cleaning up; they are assured of nutritious food; and they are brought together for the informal social exchange of a meal with other residents.

There are several things to check about an assisted living residence's food service. First, find out how many meals a day are included, and whether they are all full, hot meals. Then check on the quality of the food; it won't do you any good if you won't eat it. Try several meals in their dining room, and see if the residents seem interested in their food and in each other.

It is also important to find out what happens if a resident is not able to appear for a meal or simply does not want a meal in the dining room. Are meals served at different times, or only at one set time? Under what circumstances are meals delivered to individual rooms or apartments? May a resident take food from the dining room back to a private room? If three meals a day are served, may a resident regularly choose to skip one or more of them? If so, does the resident need to prove to the staff that he or she is getting enough nutrition without the prepared meal?

Housekeeping. Assisted living facilities provide laundry service and also clean individual rooms or apartments. What that housekeeping includes, however, can vary considerably. Find out how often a resident's bedding and bath linen are laundered. Does the facility do a resident's personal laundry as well? Is there an extra charge for personal laundry? How often (and how well) is an individual room or apartment cleaned?

Social Activities and Exercise. It is one thing to assist residents with the basics of daily life, such as dressing and bathing; that help is guaranteed in a contract with an assisted living residence. It is another thing entirely to help residents lead mentally, physically, and socially active lives. This is not a matter of contract, but of the quality and style of service at a good residence. Most facilities plan group activities such as guest lectures and exercise classes, as well as regular gatherings for the residents to visit among themselves. The best facilities also help individual residents participate in these activities to the extent possible and provide alternatives—an assisted walk around the hallways, for example, or a one-on-one chat in a resident's private room—when it's not feasible to participate in a group.

There are several ways to get a sense of the quality of group and individual activities at a particular facility. You can always check what is scheduled for any given week, but it is also important to visit during one of these planned activities to see if residents participate and seem to enjoy doing so. As for more individual attention, find out whether there are any rules against staff spending nonscheduled time with residents. And on all your visits, watch how staff members interact with residents: Look for a friendly, relaxed manner on everyone's part. (See "Choosing the Right Facility" in Chapter 4—much of the information there also applies to assisted living.)

Costs

Most assisted living spaces are rented, not purchased.

Basic Rent

Obviously, rent depends on the size of living space. A small room with no cooking facilities will cost much less than a spacious one-bedroom apartment with full kitchen. The rent also varies with the amount of services and staff provided, the location, and the overall condition of the facility. Some facilities offer more than one type of rental agreement. A limited contract may include fewer meals and personal assistance than an inclusive or extensive agreement that includes all the services the facility has to offer. Given all of these variables, rent for an assisted living unit generally runs 50% to 100% higher than for a comparable independent living unit in the same facility. But it will still be one third to one half the cost of a nursing facility of the same quality, in the same area. However, most assisted living facilities have additional charges above and beyond basic rent (see "Additional Fees," below).

For a good sense of the cost of assisted living facilities in your geographic area, search online for:

- Met Life's *Market Survey of Long-Term Care Costs,* or
- Genworth Financial's *Cost of Care Survey.*

Rent Increases

As with any other rental housing, you must consider how much your rent may go up over time. A lease can guarantee the rent for a year or two. After that, rent increases are completely within the discretion of the facility's ownership, unless a yearly limit is included in your rental agreement. If there is no limit, check the facility's record of rent increases over the previous five years. If they have raised rents in large chunks, you have to consider whether they will price you out of your apartment in years to come.

Additional Fees

Almost all assisted living facilities charge fees in addition to rent. There may be a one-time nonrefundable entrance fee. And there may be a fee for certain services not included in the basic assisted living contract, such as extra or delivered meals, extra housekeeping service, local transportation fees, or personal care beyond the standard level of care offered in the facility.

Medicaid Coverage

Medicaid (called Medi-Cal in California) is a federal program, administered somewhat differently by each state, that pays medical expenses for people with very low incomes and few assets. (See Chapter 8.)

Until recently, Medicaid paid for home care and for nursing facility care, but not for any type of long-term care residence in between. Slowly, however, Medicaid administrators have begun to recognize that many people who live in nursing facilities paid for by Medicaid could be living more comfortably in much less expensive assisted living facilities if Medicaid would pay for it. So, many state Medicaid programs are now providing some limited coverage for assisted living for people who would otherwise require nursing home care.

There are no national standards for Medicaid coverage of assisted living, and each state makes its own rules regarding eligibility and extent of coverage. Most states that do provide some Medicaid coverage for assisted living offer it only to a limited number of Medicaid beneficiaries. And most importantly, they pay only a portion—sometimes only a small part—of the cost of residence in the facility. Also, many assisted living facilities do not participate in the Medicaid program, so the number of facilities available to a Medicaid recipient is likely to be limited.

Nonetheless, if you believe you might qualify for Medicaid now, or in the foreseeable future (after spending most of your assets), it would be wise to take these steps:

- Read Chapter 8 of this book regarding Medicaid eligibility.
- Contact the Medicaid office in the county where you plan to live to find out if the local program covers assisted living and if so, what the rules are.
- If Medicaid does cover some assisted living, get a list from the Medicaid office of all the assisted living facilities in the area that are certified to receive Medicaid payments.

It may be better to find out whether a particular facility is covered by asking the Medicaid office directly rather than asking facility administrators. If the facility does not accept Medicaid, your question may scare off the facility operators even if you are currently able to pay your own way. They might worry that you are asking about Medicaid because you anticipate running out of money at some point, which could make them reluctant to take you on as a resident.

Long-Term Care Insurance Coverage

Virtually none of the private long-term care insurance policies issued during the 1970s and 1980s covers assisted living—they are all essentially nursing home policies, some of which also cover home care. By the mid-1990s, however, some policies began to offer coverage for assisted living. This was due, in part, to increased competition among insurance companies and, in part, to the insurance companies' realization that if they have to pay on a policy, they would rather pay for assisted living than for a more expensive nursing facility.

If you have long-term care insurance and believe assisted living might be a better choice for you than either home care or a nursing facility, check the extent of coverage in your policy. If assisted living is covered, carefully examine the requirements to qualify under your particular policy.

Such policies usually require you to have physical or mental limitations to trigger the coverage—many policies will pay for assisted living only if you need assistance with at least two or three activities of daily living, or ADLs. Some policies make this requirement a bit easier to meet by also looking at what are called instrumental ADLs, such as the ability to keep house, manage money and bills, and manage medications.

There is also the question of who decides whether your condition meets these standards. The policy may require that your primary care physician certify that you meet the conditions, but the policy may also permit the insurance company to have its own doctor examine you before agreeing that the coverage trigger has been met. (Chapter 9 covers long-term care insurance in detail.)

Rules and Restrictions

Assisted living facilities take on the difficult task of providing different types and amounts of care and services to people who, like everyone else, have individual quirks and personality traits. One way these facilities manage is by setting standards about who is an appropriate resident and creating fairly strict rules by which all residents must abide.

Becoming and Remaining a Resident

Just as assisted living fits between independent living and nursing care, its residents' physical and mental capabilities are supposed to fit between complete independence and total dependence. To ensure this fit, assisted living facilities establish standards residents must meet to enter and remain.

The entrance requirements for potential residents may begin with a minimum age—55 or 60—and sometimes a maximum—80 or 85. Then there is the matter of the care needed by a potential resident. Facilities will usually accommodate someone who doesn't need much assistance but wants the personal attention offered by an assisted living facility (and is willing to pay for it). Some facilities (especially those with few vacancies) might suggest that a relatively healthy potential resident try independent living instead. But assisted living facilities are usually careful not to accept a resident who needs more care than they can deliver. Most of them scrupulously assess each potential resident's physical and cognitive capabilities before agreeing to let the individual into the facility.

Rules for entering and staying in such facilities commonly mandate that residents:

- require regular staff assistance with no more than two to four of the activities of daily living (ADLs)—eating, bathing, dressing, transferring in and out of a bed or chair, using the toilet, and walking

- not be completely incontinent

- not require daily nursing care, and

- not present a danger to themselves, staff, or other residents and not require extremely close monitoring or physical control—unless the facility has a special care unit for Alzheimer's or other dementia sufferers.

Unless it is part of a continuing care community which guarantees each resident the right to remain in whatever level of care is required, an assisted living facility may force a resident to move out—usually to a nursing facility—if he or she falls below the facility's standards.

However, assisted living facilities are often more flexible with existing residents than with potential ones. For example, a facility may permit a resident to remain if he or she hires outside assistance for the extra care the facility is unable to provide, depending on the facility's rules regarding how much outside assistance is permitted.

Who Decides Whether You Must Move?

A resident must meet physical standards to remain in an assisted living facility. But who decides exactly what a resident's condition is? The answer to this question is very important, because it could determine whether you are required to move to a nursing facility

Some changes in condition will obviously require a change. If a resident becomes completely bedridden, there will be no argument that he or she no longer meets the facility's standards. But often, the issue is murky. The degree of a resident's incontinence may be unclear, for example. Or a resident might suffer a fall that results in permanent disability—or long-term recovery.

An assisted living contract should clearly describe how this decision is made. A facility always reserves the right to make the final decision. But this decision should take into account the resident's primary care physician's opinion and be reviewed by an independent physician or geriatric social worker.

Outside Assistance

Some assisted living residences place strict limits on visits by outside nurses and personal care aides. Some permit them only on a temporary basis while a resident recovers from an illness or injury. Others permit regular visits by outside help, but limit the type or frequency. If the personal care assistance offered by an assisted living facility does not seem to match your needs, but you believe you can fill the gaps with outside help, find out whether the facility's rules would permit it. If so, make sure the rules are clearly spelled out in your written residence agreement.

Staff Control Over Residents

One of the important services provided by assisted living staff is round-the-clock monitoring of the residents' well-being. This is often achieved through strict schedules by which staff and residents must abide. For example, some facilities serve meals at precise hours and require residents to appear in the dining room for all of them. Or a staff aide might enter each resident's room one or more times every night to check on the resident's condition. Or the staff might control all of a resident's medications, even nonprescription ones, to ensure that the resident uses them properly and to protect against adverse drug interactions.

This constant caretaking is more than some residents need or want. It is therefore important to find out not only about the facility's rules and schedules but also about its flexibility. For example, if a resident does not want three meals a day in the dining room, do the rules allow checking in without having to appear? Can some meals be delivered to a resident's quarters, or must the resident provide his or her own food if a meal is skipped? Can nightly check-ups be eliminated if the resident finds them more disturbing than beneficial? May medications be left with the resident if the resident has sufficient awareness and orientation to monitor them without help?

Right to Return

Many assisted living residents have serious medical crises that force them into the hospital or a nursing or rehabilitation center for extended stays. Often, no one knows for months whether the resident will recover sufficiently to again live in assisted living, or instead will need to move to a long-term care nursing facility. During this time, the resident may not want or be able to pay for an unused assisted living room or apartment to which the resident might never return.

Most facilities have rules regarding a resident's right to return after an extended absence. Many facilities will hold a room or apartment for a short time, then offer a longer period—often six months or a year— during which the former resident has priority over new applicants for the next available equivalent room or apartment. Without such protection in an assisted living contract, one serious medical crisis— even one from which you eventually recover—could force you to search for a new home.

Combination Residential Facilities

The first two sections of this chapter discuss independent living communities and assisted living residences, while Chapter 4 covers nursing facilities. But many senior communities combine two or three of these care levels in one place. This section explains the different combinations available—and the benefits and risks of each.

Extended Care Residences

Many senior residence communities offer both independent living and assisted living in the same complex of buildings and grounds. Because many design features and services are common to both, it can be economical for the same ownership to build and operate the two levels together. This makes it possible for a senior to move into an independent living residence and conveniently transfer to assisted living, if necessary.

That both independent living and assisted living are offered within the same seniors community, however, does not necessarily mean that you may move from one to the other whenever you choose. In an extended care community, you may be given an opportunity to move from one level to another, but not a guarantee. This differentiates it from continuing care and life care communities in which, for considerably more money than a simple extended care facility, you lock in the right to move to a different level as needed.

In an extended care community, an independent living resident may move to assisted living only if there is a vacant unit that fits the resident's needs and budget. Some people move into assisted living first, then to independent living if they regain strength or mobility. But, most move first into independent living and later to assisted living.

If there is no vacancy, the resident must wait. This is not always a major problem—often a resident's need for increased care develops slowly, as physical strength diminishes. And the wait may be shorter if the facility gives priority for vacancies to existing residents. That should be spelled out in the written residency agreement.

If you do eventually need assisted living, an extended care community offers advantages that may make it worth the potential delay:

- You can remain within a familiar physical setting and routine. In most places, many of the community's common areas are used by both independent living and assisted living residents. And although your private living space would change if you moved from one level to another, it would still have a familiar look and feel—in design, bath, and kitchen fixtures, for example.

- Many of the people on staff will be the same, so you don't need to get to know a whole new crew, and they don't need to become newly acquainted with you.

- The other residents whom you have come to know will still be your neighbors.

- You avoid the strenuous and disorienting process of packing up, moving to a new location, settling in, and getting to know a new area, a new living space, new rules and regulations, and new people.

Continuing Care Retirement Communities (CCRCs)

A continuing care retirement community (CCRC) provides any level of care and services you need—independent living, assisted living, or custodial nursing care—for as long as you are a resident. (See Chapter 4 for information on custodial-level nursing care.) The basic agreement of a CCRC is that the resident pays a hefty entry fee and monthly charges to live in the community, and the facility guarantees that the resident may move from one level of care to another as the resident's physical and mental condition require. The phrase often used to describe this guarantee is "aging in place"—that is, to live in the same place through all the stages of growing old. And while some CCRCs truly offer an age-in-place guarantee, others fudge a bit on the "place."

Some CCRCs offer a year-to-year arrangement to residents, after an initial entrance fee. These facilities may also have monthly maintenance fees; these fees are sometimes tiered—meaning that they are higher for assisted living than for independent living, and highest for nursing care. Other CCRCs offer an extended lease, which locks in maintenance fees and other charges for the period of the lease. And, a special, more expensive kind of CCRC arrangement, called a life care contract, promises care for as long as the resident lives. (See "Life Care Contracts," below.)

Basic Arrangements

All CCRCs provide continuing care, but not all of them do so in the same location. Almost all CCRCs offer independent living and assisted living in the same place. And some CCRCs also have an on-site nursing facility. But many CCRCs have no separate nursing wing; instead, a resident who needs nursing care must receive it in an assisted living apartment. When that is not practical, the resident must move into a separate off-site nursing facility with which the CCRC has a contractual arrangement.

On-Site or Off-Site Nursing Facilities

A CCRC with its own nursing facility is not necessarily better than one that has contracted with an outside facility. In fact, some on-site nursing facilities are no more than rooms in a separate section of assisted living where nursing care is delivered. Of course, there are advantages to remaining in the same location with some of the same staff and your neighbors nearby. But if an on-site nursing wing does not get much of the community's attention, expertise, and money, it may be better to move to an off-site nursing facility that provides only one level of care and does it well.

Find out whether a CCRC's on-site nursing facility is certified by the state. If not, find out whether it contracts with a separate local nursing facility to take residents for whom they can no longer care. If it does, visit that facility and assess it as thoroughly as possible. (See Chapter 4.)

Be aware that some CCRCs only admit residents who are initially able to qualify for independent living. It costs less for the CCRC to provide care and services for an independent living resident, and facility administrators want to make sure that they get several years of providing this less expensive level of service before they have to provide more costly assisted living or nursing care. Some CCRCs also have a maximum entry age of around 80.

Costs

Because of its guarantee of care and services at any level needed at any time, a house or an apartment in a CCRC is usually substantially more expensive than a comparable living space in a multiunit facility that offers no nursing care and provides no transfer guarantee.

Consider the Future

People who consider moving into a CCRC do so because they want to provide not only for their immediate needs, but also for the care they may later require. Unfortunately, when investigating specific communities, too many people focus on the independent living quarters and services where they will live first, and only casually look into the assisted living and nursing facility care. This nearsightedness is often encouraged by the community's sales staff, who know that independent living is always a more cheerful and inviting part of the community to show a prospective resident.

Investigate the assisted living and nursing facility living quarters, services, and costs as closely as you do independent living. You may never need those levels of care, but if you do, you will want them to measure up. You will have already paid a lot of money for them, and if, someday, you need the care they offer, you will have to depend on them. This advice is important for all CCRCs, but doubly so if you are considering a life care contract.

Rentals. If an independent living house or apartment in a CCRC is offered as a rental, you can expect to pay anywhere from 25% to 100% more than for a comparable rental in a non-CCRC independent living community. The amount of rent may depend on how steep the entry and maintenance fees are; sometimes high fees mean lower rent. The rent may also depend on the level of care and services you receive. That is, while you have guaranteed access to assisted living or nursing care if you need it, there may be higher rent for those services than for independent living.

You should also look into the possibility of rent increases. Some facilities agree in the rental contract to a percentage limit on rent increases. Others have no such limit, however. If there is no contractual limit on rent increases, it is important to investigate the facility's recent record on that score.

Purchases. Some CCRCs offer equity purchases rather than rentals. This usually means that you are buying an interest in a specific condominium. But in other CCRCs, you buy an interest in the whole community—a membership, so to speak—which does not give you ownership or the right to sell any particular living unit.

How resale works—what's yours to sell and under what terms—is a crucial aspect of a CCRC agreement. If you buy into a CCRC, you must fully understand the limits placed on your ability to resell your interest if you choose to move out someday, as well as the equity that may remain for your survivors if you die while still living in the community.

Entrance and Maintenance Fees. There is usually a large entrance fee that is only partially refundable, and only for a short time, should you decide to move out of the CCRC. Fees range from $50,000 to $300,000 and up. The entrance fee may vary with the overall quality of care and demand for space in the particular CCRC, the size of the independent living unit, and the type of nursing care contract.

There may also be monthly maintenance fees. Those fees may increase if you move from one level to another. And the amounts will go up over time. In the best residence contracts, the percentage that maintenance fees may be raised per year is strictly limited. If it is not limited at all, fee increases over the years could eat up your savings and, if you can't afford them, force you to move out.

Nursing Care Fees. Although all CCRCs guarantee nursing care should it become necessary, the terms of that care vary greatly from one community to another. We've already covered the issue of where care is provided—on-site or in a separate facility. But there is also the question of extra charges for nursing care, depending on where and for how long you receive it. Different types of residence contracts cover these variables in nursing care fees. Some communities offer only one type of contract; others offer a choice, at different prices:

Medicare Covers Only Very Limited Nursing Care

When considering the cost of nursing care in a CCRC, don't count on Medicare to provide any long-term financial support. Medicare coverage of nursing care is extremely limited, either under Medicare Part A (nursing facility coverage) or Medicare Part A or Part B (home health care coverage). Medicare Part A will pay for nursing care in a CCRC only if you require daily, skilled nursing care immediately following a hospital stay, and the section of the CCRC you are living in qualifies and participates in Medicare as a "skilled nursing facility" under Medicare rules. If Medicare does provide coverage, it does so only for a part of the cost of care, and only for up to 100 days within any one recovery period.

It may also be possible to receive Medicare coverage for nursing care in a CCRC under Medicare's coverage for home health care. But in that case, the nursing care must be provided by a Medicare-certified home health care agency—not usually the CCRC itself—and is approved only for a very limited amount of nursing and only for a short time while recovering from an acute illness, injury, or surgery.

For a complete explanation of Medicare coverage for nursing facility care and nursing care under home health care, see *Social Security, Medicare & Government Pensions*, by Joseph Matthews and Dorothy Matthews Berman (Nolo).

- An extensive or all-inclusive CCRC contract provides unlimited nursing facility care of all levels, either on-site or in a separate facility, without any extra charge. (See Chapter 4.) Because there is no limit to how much expensive nursing care you might receive under such terms, the entrance and monthly fees for these contracts are the highest. A life care contract includes unlimited nursing care.

- A modified CCRC contract guarantees a certain number of days (usually 30 to 90) per year of free nursing care. The number of days may vary depending on whether the care is delivered on-site or requires moving to a separate nursing facility. After you have used your free days, you are charged additional fees, ranging from $50 to $300 per day, depending on the level of care provided. These contracts are less expensive than all-inclusive arrangements.

• A fee-for-service CCRC contract guarantees you nursing care as needed, provided in your living unit, in the community's own nursing wing, or in a specific separate facility, but charges you a daily fee for the care. The amount of the fee often varies, depending on the level of nursing care you receive and where you receive it. Because these charges partially offset the community's cost of providing nursing care, the entrance and monthly fees for such a contract are the lowest.

Decisions About Levels of Care

It is one thing to know that many levels of services and care are available to you in a CCRC. It is another thing to know who decides which level of care you need. No CCRC permits a resident to have the sole authority to decide what level of care is appropriate. On the other hand, you should not enter any CCRC that reserves for itself the exclusive right to decide when to move you in or out of independent living, assisted living, or nursing care.

A CCRC should have specific written standards in its residence contract that spell out what physical or mental conditions require or permit residence in one community level or another. Whether you need nursing care should be determined by your primary care physician. The CCRC, however, may reserve the right to decide whether you are to receive that nursing care in your residence, in a nursing care wing of the community, or in a separate, off-site nursing facility. That decision should be made only after the community's management obtains an assessment of your condition and needs from a physician, nursing supervisor, or geriatric social worker, in consultation with your primary care physician.

Life Care Contracts

One form of arrangement with a CCRC provides care for the life of the resident. A life care contract makes a very large promise: If you enter a residence in your seventies, as many people do, the facility might have to provide you with 20 or 30 years of care. In exchange, the entrance fee is extremely high—$100,000 to $500,000 or more. And that may not include the cost of your individual residence and other fees. In other words, that may be merely the cost of your lifetime membership in the community.

Because your investment is so large, you must judge a life care contract and the community that offers it with extraordinary care. What you buy with a life care contract is no different from what you get in any other CCRC; it is just guaranteed to last longer. And the length of the contract is the source of its two major potential problems. The first is uncertainty concerning the quality of care the community will provide in the future. The other is the amount of monthly maintenance charges the facility will levy years down the road.

A resident is not handcuffed to the community. If the quality of care and services becomes poor, or the maintenance fees too high, you are free to leave. But you will have lost the lifetime benefit your huge entrance fee was intended to cover. And losing that money may make a move somewhere else unaffordable. Also, if you have purchased an equity interest in specific living quarters, the contract terms may prevent you from recouping much of your equity when you sell.

Diminished Quality. There are many scenarios in which a dazzlingly luxurious and well-staffed life care community might become unable to provide high-quality services after ten, 20, or more years. The operators of the community may not have calculated fees and costs properly or may be poor administrators who squander the funds needed to maintain high-quality premises, services, and care over the long haul. Or the buildings and equipment may not be constructed to last and may require unaffordable refurbishing. And, there is the problem of profit taking: Owners may take too much money out of the business for themselves, leaving too little to maintain high-quality operations. Similarly, the business may be sold to new operators who have a stronger commitment to their profits than to the quality of care.

Increased Fees. To make up for poor planning and management (or simply to increase profits), the owners might begin to raise monthly maintenance and nursing care surcharges at a steeper rate as both you and the facility age. Unless your contract limits how much the fees and surcharges may be raised, they may get to levels that are difficult for you to pay, or that eat up the money you had intended to pass on to your survivors or use for other purposes. ●

Nursing Facilities

n recent years, increases in the availability of home care and assisted living have meant that the percentage of people over 65 who live in nursing facilities has actually dropped, even though there are many more people living longer and needing care. Still, more than 1.6 million people live in nursing facilities. Nearly one out of three women and one out of five men over age 65 will spend at least some time in a nursing facility. Most of these stays are relatively short-term:

- about 60% of all nursing facility stays are for less than three months, including people coming directly from the hospital while recovering from surgery or severe illness

- about 75% of all nursing home stays are for a year or less, and

- about 8% of stays are for three years or more.

Planning and Finances

If at all possible, searching for a nursing facility should not be a hurried, emergency procedure. As soon as you begin to see that your current living arrangements may become insufficient and neither home care nor assisted living will provide the care or monitoring you need, begin planning.

Finding out what long-term care facility might be the best in a particular area can take time. Many good ones operate at full capacity, so they may not be able to accept a new resident on short notice.

You must also consider how you will pay the facility. You'll have to calculate family assets and income along with reverse mortgages (see Chapter 2) and the amounts that might be contributed by Medicare and veterans' benefits (see Chapter 7) and any long-term care insurance (see Chapter 9). Medicaid coverage may be available for people with low incomes and few assets other than a home. (See Chapter 8.) It helps to understand Medicaid rules, both perhaps to save some assets by advance planning and to make sure that Medicaid will cover care in a particular facility if and when the resident qualifies.

There is a great range in the levels of care available in nursing facilities. Skilled nursing facilities provide short-term, intensive medical care and monitoring for people recovering from acute illness or injury. Other facilities—called nursing homes, board and care homes, sheltered care homes, or something similar—provide custodial care: long-term room and board, 24-hour assistance with personal care and health care monitoring, but not intensive medical treatment or daily nursing.

Many people would prefer to remain outside a care facility. However, some seniors, because of their conditions, circumstances, or the unavailability of in-home services or affordable assisted living residences, can only receive adequate care in residential care facilities. Unfortunately, as we've all heard on the news, some facilities provide substandard living conditions and even a dangerous lack of care. Still others give basic care that meets technical health standards but offer little else and have an atmosphere that is debilitating or demoralizing to the residents.

However, there are also excellent nursing facilities that provide high-quality care while assisting residents to maintain active lives with a full measure of dignity. But, because there are many levels and types of nursing and personal care, your task is to find a good, affordable facility that is right for you.

How to Find Out About Local Nursing Facilities

The federal government and the states have teamed up to create an online service that lists and compares the qualities of every certified nursing facility in the country. This service is called "Nursing Home Compare" and can be found at Medicare's official website, www.medicare.gov.

This service provides contact information about every nursing facility in any geographic area you choose. And, for any particular facility, the service lists information from the facility's official record regarding staffing, resident care, and inspections.

However, while this website is a good starting point and reference, you should not depend primarily on its information when choosing a facility. The site statistics—which are often well over a year old—may provide you with an important warning about a facility with a bad record. But "good" statistics cannot tell you much about the quality of life for residents in a facility. Only several in-person visits, looking at and talking about the various factors discussed in this chapter, can give you a good sense of the facility.

You should also speak with people who have personal experience of nursing facilities in your area. Your doctor may have a good or bad impression of certain local facilities. And your relatives, friends, and neighbors may have had experience with a nursing facility or know someone who has.

Levels of Care

Care in long-term residential facilities ranges from intensive 24-hour care for the seriously ill, which is called skilled nursing care, to long-term personal assistance and health monitoring with very little active nursing, often called custodial care. Some facilities provide only one level of care, while others provide several levels at the same location.

Most people who are in nursing facilities cannot function without 24-hour monitoring and extensive personal assistance and nursing care because of illness or physical or mental limitations. Some residents are in relatively good physical and mental health, but too frail to live alone at home. If they had more family or resources, many of these people might be able to make do with extensive home care (see Chapter 2) or residence in an assisted living facility (see Chapter 3). For lack of an alternative, they become nursing facility residents.

Your task is to find a good and affordable nursing facility that provides not just care, but the right type of care. For someone with severe physical or mental limitations, it is crucial to find a facility that provides the kind of attention and care that meets the individual's specific needs. For people who need little or no actual nursing care, the task is to find a facility that provides physical, mental, and social stimulation rather than just bed and board.

Your toughest challenge may be footing the bill. Long-term care facilities of all levels are very expensive, but depending on the type of care needed and the type of insurance you have, you may get some help covering the cost. Skilled nursing facilities run more than $500 per day, although stays there are relatively short and Medicare or private health insurance often picks up much of the tab. (See Chapter 7.) Long-term custodial care—the kind that may last for years—averages between $5,000 and $10,000 per month and can go even higher. Neither Medicare nor Medigap private insurance supplements pay any of the cost of custodial care. Long-term care insurance, for those who have it, may cover some of the cost of custodial care. (See Chapter 9.) And Medicaid pays the full cost of custodial nursing facility care for people with very low incomes and few assets. (See Chapter 8.) Some veterans may also find coverage for custodial care through the Veterans Administration. (See Chapter 7.)

If a facility is certified by the federal government, it may also be more affordable. The Health Care Financing Administration has certified about 85% of all nursing facilities; HCFA certification means that the facility is eligible to receive Medicare and Medicaid payments. Some facilities do not meet HCFA standards. Other facilities charge high prices and simply do not want to accept residents who depend on Medicaid payments. Unless you have an unlimited supply of money to pay for long-term care, make sure that any facility you consider is certified. Certification means that the facility meets certain minimum health, safety, and care standards. And, certification also means that if someday you should need and qualify for Medicaid coverage for your stay, you will be able to receive it without having to move to a different facility.

Hospital-Based Skilled Nursing Facilities

Hospital-based skilled nursing facilities, also known as extended care facilities, are departments within hospitals. They provide the highest levels of medical and nursing care, including 24-hour monitoring and intensive rehabilitative therapies. They are intended to follow acute hospital care due to serious illness, injury, or surgery.

Unlike other nursing facilities, a hospital-based facility is not for permanent residence, but for a short-term stay until a patient can be sent home or maintained elsewhere. Hospital-based facilities are very expensive, but the average stay is generally short (usually a matter of days or weeks) and, for those who qualify, is usually covered by Medicare or private insurance. (See Chapters 7 and 9.)

Skilled Nursing Facilities

Nonhospital-based skilled nursing facilities (SNFs) provide a relatively high level of nursing and other medical care, as well as personal care and assistance, for people whose illnesses or impairments require close monitoring.

Around-the-clock nursing is available from licensed vocational or practical nurses, with at least one supervising registered nurse on duty at all times. In addition to nursing, most other prescribed medical services can be provided, including various rehabilitative therapies. An SNF is almost always for short-term recovery from a serious illness, injury, or surgery that requires hospitalization. A few people may spend months in an SNF, but most stays last only days or weeks.

The cost of SNF care is usually more than $500 per day. Medicare, Medicaid, and private insurance usually pay for SNF care, but only up to specific coverage limits.

Inpatient Rehabilitation Facilities

Similar to skilled nursing facilities, inpatient rehabilitation facilities (IRFs) provide short-term rehabilitation while a patient recovers from a serious illness, injury, or surgery, usually immediately following a period of hospitalization. IRFs provide around-the-clock care and all necessary medical services. They specialize in intensive physical, occupational, and speech therapies. Some people may spend months in an IRF, but most stays are for days or weeks.

The cost of an IRF is usually over $500 per day. Medicare, Medicaid, and private health insurance cover IRF care, but only up to specific coverage limits.

Intermediate Care Facilities

Intermediate care facilities (ICFs) provide less nursing and other medical care than SNFs. ICFs are for long-term residents with chronic illnesses or impairments whose conditions are not as acute as those of SNF residents. Residents in an ICF are usually ambulatory, for example.

Staff is geared as much toward personal care and assistance as to medical care, although there is always a licensed vocational or practical nurse on duty. ICFs generally care for people who need a long recovery period from serious illness, injury, or surgery, but who no longer need the level of nursing care and high-tech monitoring that an SNF provides.

Costs range from $250 per day and up. Medicare does not cover ICFs and private insurance coverage is rare, usually requiring prior approval. Medicaid, however, may cover much of the cost of ICF care. (See Chapter 8.)

Very few facilities are set up solely as ICFs; most are part of an SNF or a custodial care facility.

Medicaid Certification

One of the first things you should check about any facility is whether it is certified by Medicaid (called Medi-Cal in California). If it is certified, Medicaid will pay for the resident's care in the facility if the resident qualifies for Medicaid benefits. If you plan to pay for the facility out of your own pocket and are not currently eligible for Medicaid (see Chapter 8), this may not seem important. But if you stay in the facility for an extended period, you may spend enough of your assets to qualify for Medicaid coverage. If this happens, you will want Medicaid to pay for your care in the facility where you have been living—and this can happen only if the facility is Medicaid certified.

Custodial Care Facilities

Custodial care facilities come in a variety of shapes and sizes—and offer a variety of services. They also go by a number of different names: nursing facility, board and care home, rest home, congregate living facility, sheltered care facility, group home, and RCFE (residential care facility for the elderly), among others. Some are small facilities, with five to ten beds in a converted private home. Others are 100-bed facilities with large common areas and extensive social, physical, and educational activities—and that unmistakable institutional feel. Costs range from $50,000 to $150,000 per year. Costs depend on geographic location— they are 20% to 40% higher in urban rather than rural, small town, or suburban areas. Costs can be up to 50% higher for a private rather than a semiprivate room.

Despite these differences, all facilities that provide custodial care share these basic elements:

- They provide room, board, assistance with the activities of daily life (ADLs), health monitoring, and social, recreational, and exercise activities.

- They do not provide nursing, physical therapy, or other skilled medical care.

- They are intended for people who need help throughout the day and night with personal care and mobility but do not need constant medical attention or intervention.

- Residents are there for the long term—for months or years—and not merely while recovering from an acute physical condition.

- Because residents live in rooms—often shared—rather than a private apartment, and because no expensive medical care is provided, these facilities cost much less than skilled or intermediate care nursing facilities.

- Because residents receive all meals and round-the-clock monitoring and assistance, these facilities are more expensive than assisted living facilities.

The Significance of the Type of Facility You Choose

The title a facility uses—for example, nursing facility, board and care home, or residential care facility for the elderly (RCFE)—may tell you something about the state rules and regulations that the facility must abide by. It won't, however, tell you much about the quality of life it provides residents. Instead, you have to judge a facility by whether it will offer the services you need at a price you can afford.

Different types of facilities are subject to different sets of rules and are certified and inspected by different state agencies. In some states, a nursing facility may have to follow stricter rules (about number and training of staff members, for example) than a board and care home does, even though the facilities are very similar in most respects. In some states, nonnursing facilities have very few rules to follow—and are subject to almost no inspection or other oversight by state agencies. If you are seriously considering a particular facility, ask what state agency oversees it. Then, contact that agency to find out whether it has information for consumers on the rules and regulations the facility has to follow. And be sure to review the facility's recent inspection reports.

Choosing the Right Facility

Once you have determined which facilities in your area are affordable and provide the appropriate general level of care, you must decide which one best suits your needs and preferences.

The experts to turn to for guidance are the residents themselves. Studies have shown that most nursing facility residents care very little about high-tech medical gear, or even about medical care. Rather, their most important concerns involve their ability to maintain some independence, to participate in decisions about daily life, and to retain contact with the outside world.

Veterans Nursing Facilities

If you are a military veteran, you may be eligible for free long-term care in a nursing home run by, or contracting with, the Department of Veterans Affairs (VA). (See Chapter 7.)

Because these and other concerns discussed below cannot be guaranteed in writing or demonstrated in a quick tour, it is important to spend as much time as possible at a facility before making a decision to receive care there. Make separate visits during the day, evening, and night, and during one or more meals. And to the extent possible, talk with current residents and their families.

Special Considerations for Those With Alzheimer's

All of the factors discussed in this section apply to people with Alzheimer's disease or other forms of age-related dementia. However, choosing the right nursing facility for these elders will require you to consider other issues as well. These matters are treated separately in Chapter 5. Before you move on to that chapter, read through the information in this section. Then use it—along with the material in Chapter 5—to choose a facility that will fit the bill.

Ownership and Management

The quality of daily life in a nursing facility is determined primarily by on-site management and hands-on care personnel. And the owners of a facility determine how well management can do its job through the funding provided for equipment, food, and staffing. However, the form of ownership (for example, whether a facility is a nonprofit or is run by a particular religious group) may not tell you much about the quality of care it provides.

For-Profit Facilities

About three fourths of all nursing facilities are operated for profit, often by big corporations. There is a popular, but not necessarily accurate, belief that in profit-making facilities, the dominating desire to make money means skimping on patient care. Research has shown that this is not always the case. Profit-making facilities may be better managed than nonprofits, and therefore deliver better care for the dollar. Similarly, studies have found that patient satisfaction is important to for-profit facilities because their economic health depends on keeping their beds filled. As a result, a for-profit facility may be just as likely as a nonprofit facility to provide good quality care for the price.

Nonprofit Facilities

The flip side of negative beliefs about profit-making facilities is the notion that those run by nonprofit philanthropic, charitable, or religious organizations will provide quality care because their only interest is to "do good" for residents. But nonprofit organizations often give no more than their name and tax advantages to a long-term care facility, while everyday management is contracted out to others. Even when the nonprofit organization takes an active role in running the facility (usually several facilities), there is no guarantee it will be any better at the job than profit-making managers. The test of care quality comes on the floor of the facility itself, not in the boardrooms of its owners.

Group Affiliation

Some nursing facilities are operated by or affiliated with religious, ethnic, or fraternal organizations. Depending on your interest and on how the affiliation affects daily life in the facility, this can be either good or bad. A particular affiliation may mean that you and the other residents will have similar backgrounds and interests, which can make for a real feeling of community. Also, there may be specially targeted activities at the facility in which you will enjoy participating.

On the other hand, if a group or organization to which you do not belong dominates the social activity of a facility, it may make you feel like an outsider and may limit the availability of other, nonsectarian activities.

Cost

Although it may generally be true that higher costs lead to better quality, that is not necessarily the case with nursing facilities.

With nursing facilities, high price often means sophisticated and expensive medical equipment and staff. Although most residents will never need them, every resident ends up paying for them. Similarly, some facilities are expensive because they have to foot the bill for a shiny new building.

Many smaller, less expensive facilities with less high-tech equipment can provide a more comfortable setting with more individual attention and participation for residents. Of course, you must make certain that lower cost does not reflect a lack of essential services or qualified personnel. But these are things you will have to investigate—the cost of the care alone won't tell you much about the quality of the facility.

For a good sense of the cost of custodial care nursing homes in your geographic area, search online for:

• Met Life's *Market Survey of Long-Term Care Costs*, or

• Genworth Financial's *Cost of Care Survey*.

Larger Doesn't Mean Less Expensive

While one might guess that larger facilities cost less because they operate on an economy of scale, in general, it is just the opposite. On the average, larger facilities cost more to operate than smaller ones, due in part to their higher-level medical services and larger administrative staffs.

The Facility

Location

For a number of reasons, the location of a facility can be extremely significant. Continuing contact with people and life outside the facility is one of the residents' greatest concerns, and location can affect that contact in a number of ways.

Visiting. Can friends and relatives get there easily? Is it near public transportation? The ease with which people can visit has a direct bearing on how often they come.

Outings. Are there places nearby—a park, library, or senior center— where elders can be taken for outings, either by visitors or by staff?

Immediate Surroundings. Is the surrounding area noisy, peaceful, ugly, safe? What can be seen and heard through the windows during the day and night? Are short walks or a bit of lounging outside possible?

Number of Beds and Residents

As with most questions about nursing facilities, there is no simple guide-line about whether a large or small one is best. It is mostly a matter of your own needs and tastes, and the quality of care delivered. When assessing large facilities (those with over 100 beds), consider whether their size means they're too institutional or too cold. Do they still provide personal attention and permit residents to participate in their own care?

A small facility, on the other hand, may not have all the services and skilled personnel (such as dieticians, rehabilitative therapists, and social workers) that a larger one has. But smaller facilities tend to be more personal and homey and allow residents greater control over their daily lives.

The Facility's "Feel"

What is your first impression when you walk through the door? It is probably the same general impression, conscious or unconscious, that a resident has all the time.

Homeyness. A facility should be as unlike a hospital as is consistent with good health care. It should be colorful, with personal, individual touches on walls and tables. Some facilities encourage residents to decorate their rooms and common areas; others have regulations against it. There should also be plenty of light, both from windows and lighting.

Check the Inspection Report

Most licensed nursing facilities are inspected regularly by state health care officials—usually about once a year. The inspectors check for violations of state and federal health, safety, and care standards. The state agency then describes those violations, along with residents' complaints, in a written report called a State Inspection Report or Compliance Survey. All facilities are supposed to make these reports readily available to the public. Most good facilities will post the most recent report on a bulletin board and have other copies available.

Read a facility's latest report carefully. Even the best among them will have some minor violations or complaints from residents. But a report that mentions many serious health violations or repeated neglect of residents should raise a red flag. The administrators at a facility should be willing to discuss the report with you and to explain what they are doing to address violations and complaints.

While a bad report means the facility has some explaining to do, a good report does not necessarily mean everything is hunky dory. Most facilities know roughly when an inspection is due—and some load up with extra staff to bring the facility up to par for the inspection, then sink back to fewer staff and poorer conditions as soon as the inspectors leave. When evaluating a facility, depend first and foremost on your own inspection.

Healthfulness. The facility should be clean and free from strong odors. Infections and viruses pass easily in group living situations, and they can be very serious for elders. The space should not feel cramped; crowding is both physically and psychologically unhealthy. And the air should not be too hot, too cold, or too stuffy.

Odors may mean that food, linen, residents' clothing, or personal hygiene are not receiving proper attention.

Public Areas

Prospective residents often pay much less attention to common rooms than to residents' private rooms. But the comfort and attractiveness of the public areas affect the amount of time a resident spends out of his or her room or out of bed—and so may have a bearing on how active the resident remains. Consider each of the following areas.

A Quiet Room. Although one advantage of a nursing facility is that residents do not spend too much time alone, this can also be a problem. Most residents share rooms, and privacy can sometimes be difficult to find. It's important that some room or area is available where residents can enjoy some solitude or at least quiet—where there is no radio, television, or group activities and where it is understood that people are to be left to themselves.

Eating Areas. Food and rules about eating are discussed more fully below, but you should spend time where the food is served and eaten—dining room, private rooms, or other areas of the facility—while residents are actually eating. If possible, you should also eat a few meals there with the residents.

Social, TV, and Activity Rooms. While television can be good company for facility residents, it can also become a real annoyance. If televisions are always on in all common areas, that can interfere with other activities such as having a simple conversation. It may also signal that the staff is using television as a distraction rather than interacting with the residents.

Whether or not there is a "quiet" room, it should be possible to socialize somewhere without a TV blaring.

The social and activity rooms should be clean and comfortable and should have some personal touches. A simple way to tell whether the residents find these common rooms inviting is to see how many people are using them.

Outside Areas. Is there a garden, courtyard, or other outside area where residents can spend time? Both the fresh air and change of scene can be very inviting to residents.

Visiting Areas. Is there a place other than the resident's room for private visits? Must visiting take place in a room used for other purposes as well? Does the facility encourage visiting or make it seem like a bother?

Residents' Private Rooms

Many people who enter a nursing facility have not shared a room with anyone else for a long time, yet most nursing facilities provide only double or triple rooms. Adjusting to the loss of privacy and need for compromise that go with sharing a bedroom can be difficult. The set-up and rules of the facility can make this transition easier or harder. Here are some things to look for:

Size. Are there single rooms, doubles, or triples? Are there adjoining bathrooms? Are the bathrooms set up to ensure privacy?

Light. Is there a window that lets in natural light? Is there an individual reading light near each bed? Can the light be used without disturbing a roommate's sleep?

Structure. Does the set-up of the room, furniture, and perhaps a curtain between beds allow some privacy for each roommate? Is there someplace to sit other than on the bed? Are there places for visitors to sit and visit privately? Can furnishings be moved around?

Security. Theft is a common problem in nursing facilities. Is there a place where personal possessions can be kept safely and easily retrieved? Is there a call button within reach of each bed that connects to the central aide station and can only be turned off at the bed?

Comfort. Is private furniture allowed in the room? Can residents in the room control its temperature? Are telephones, radios, or televisions permitted in the rooms? If so, what rules protect roommates from too much noise?

Get Advice From an Ombudsman

Every licensed nursing facility has one or two volunteers or employees of the state or county, called ombudsmen, who act as advocates for residents and their families when conflicts arise about facility rules or with facility staff.

The operators of the nursing facility can give you the name and phone number of the local ombudsman for that facility or let you know when he or she is slated to visit. The local ombudsman should be able to provide you with good, unbiased opinions about the facility and its staff, compare it with other area facilities, and discuss whether the facility is particularly good or bad with residents who have similar physical or mental capabilities.

There is also a state ombudsman who oversees the local programs and tracks formal complaints and health and safety violations against nursing facilities. If you call the state office, you may be able to get an overall assessment of several facilities you are considering. The state office can also give you the phone number of the local ombudsman near you. To find the office of the state ombudsman for your state, search online using the term "long-term care ombudsman" and the name of your state.

Services and Activities

Nursing facilities do not all offer the same services and activities beyond basic personal and medical care. Some facilities focus on exercise and therapy for physical impairments, others on social or educational programs, still others on developing residents' independence and memory. It is important to match services and activities with your needs. For example, if a resident does not have the physical or mental capacity to be very active, recreational and social programs may be much less important than how much attention personal staff pays to cleanliness, comfort, and conversation. For more active residents, though, activities that encourage independent thought and movement may be crucial to maintaining the highest possible levels of health.

You cannot match services and activities with needs entirely in advance, because you may have trouble anticipating what needs will be most important. Also, needs change over time. Try to choose a facility that encourages resident input into services and activities and is attentive to a resident's individual needs. Discuss the flexibility of services and activities with the staff and listen for indications that residents' dignity, independence, and individual differences are valued.

Rehabilitation Therapy

Is the particular physical, respiratory, speech, or other therapy you need regularly available in the facility, or must you make special arrangements? Will you have to go outside the facility to receive the therapy? Will it cost extra?

Social Activities and Other Services

The greatest concern of many nursing facility residents is to maintain contact with the outside world—by seeing family and other visitors, physically leaving the facility, and receiving news, phone calls, and mail.

Outings. Does the facility regularly organize outings to places and activities such as trips to the library, park, local senior center, or shopping areas? Is transportation provided? Are escorts available for a simple walk?

Incoming Activity. Are visiting speakers and activities scheduled regularly? Is there a program of outside volunteers who participate with residents in some program or activity?

Organized Events. Look at the facility's weekly or monthly calendar of events. Is there stimulation for mind and body—education, information, and exercise—as well as entertainment? Do organized activities take place in the evening as well as the day? Do people from outside the facility participate?

Personal Care. Are there services for personal grooming and cleanliness, such as a visiting barber or hairdresser, and a way to have clothes washed and cleaned? Does a dentist or dental hygienist visit the facility?

Social Service Assistance. Is there a counselor or social worker who can assist with family problems, paperwork, financial organization, and referrals for outside services?

Facility-Wide Rules

Every facility has rules by which all residents and visitors must abide. Ask to see the written rules and try to find out about important rules of daily life which are not listed. Do they seem reasonable? Do the administrators seem willing to be flexible with those rules to meet individual needs?

Visiting. When and where is visiting allowed? Are there any particular rules about children? What about phone calls in and out? Can visitors eat facility meals with residents?

What You Can Learn From Consulting Care Plans

By law, a licensed nursing facility must develop a written care plan for each resident. When considering a facility, ask to see some of the resident care plans that have recently been developed. This plan includes an assessment of the resident's physical and cognitive abilities, needs, personality, and social skills. Based on that assessment, the facility develops the plan for care, which should include nursing, therapy, and physical and memory exercise requirements; prescribed medications (and medicine combinations to be avoided); social activities the resident favors and is able to join; and nutrition needs, including dietary restrictions and required eating assistance.

Privacy need not be an issue when you request to see plans—names can easily be blackened out. The plans should not all look the same; they should be tailored to meet each resident's individual limitations and needs. Also, ask about the facility's procedures for regularly updating the plans and ask to see plans that have been changed to meet a resident's changing condition and needs.

Meals. Are mealtimes flexible? If you miss a meal, is there other food available to eat? Must meals be eaten in the dining area? Can you bring in food from outside the facility?

Hours. Is there a set time when all residents are awakened? Is there a rule about having to get dressed? About going to bed? Watching television? Lights out? Is there a curfew for residents who have gone on an outing?

Bathing. If a resident needs assistance bathing, does he or she retain a reasonable choice about when and how often?

Privacy. Can a resident keep the private room door closed at will, or only during night hours? Must staff knock before entering? Is there privacy in the bathroom?

Privately Hired Aides. Some facilities allow residents to supplement the personal care staff with privately hired aides. This flexibility may be a good thing, but be wary if the practice is common. It may mean the staff relies on the outside aides and gives less care and personal attention to residents.

Medication Control

Overmedication is a serious problem for many older people. Some elders have trouble keeping track of dosage amounts, when and how often they are supposed to take their various medications, or. And, sometimes, a doctor may prescribe medicine without carefully considering how it might interact with other drugs the patient is taking. Long-term care facilities can add to these problems by encouraging a resident too strongly to take "as needed" medications—such as sedatives, relaxants, and sleeping medications—instead of dealing with the resident's specific problem or need.

For all these reasons, it is important to find out how carefully a facility monitors residents' medication. The facility should:

- keep a written record for the personal physician and family to review

- have a policy of periodic review of all medications a resident is taking

- have a policy that any new medication shall be cleared in writing with a responsible family member, and

- have a clearly stated rule about the resident's right to refuse unwanted medication, including "as needed" medication.

Medical Records

Although technically required to keep records only of certain medical and nursing procedures provided, a thorough facility will also keep a written record of a resident's medical condition and outside treatment by doctors, clinics, and hospitals. It can also be very helpful to a resident and to his or her physician if the facility keeps a written record of health problems that have not warranted medical treatment but have affected the resident's comfort and well-being—such as problems with elimination, digestion, sleeping, depression, too much time in bed, bedsores, eating problems, or weight changes.

Special Warning on Drug Use and Restraints

A few nursing facilities prescribe and administer psychotropic drugs, also known as "chemical straightjackets." Not only do these drugs rob residents of their humanity while they're directly under the influence, but they can do lasting physical and emotional damage as well.

Any good nursing facility should be willing to show you its written policy on psychotropic drugs. The policy should specify that no such drugs can be administered to a resident without the written consent of either the resident or certain designated family members, that any such written consent will be valid only for a limited period of time, and that the designated family members and the resident's physician will be notified of the administration of any such drugs.

There are legal limits on the use of physical restraints to hold a resident in a bed or chair. Both health care experts and nursing facility advocates seriously frown on the practice. Although in some limited circumstances restraints may be necessary (for people who are in danger of falling if left unattended, for example), some facilities use restraints like psychoactive drugs merely to "manage" residents who require more attention than the facility wants to give. Find out what the facility's policy is on the use of restraints. It should permit restraints only when a resident presents an immediate danger of physical injury to himself or herself or others and should require a designated family member to be notified when restraints will be used.

Other Residents

When considering a nursing facility, try to make several visits there and speak to some of the residents as you consider the matters discussed below.

Similar Levels of Care

Small facilities should only admit residents with relatively similar care needs; large facilities should provide only one level of care in each separate area or wing. There are several reasons for this. First, when care is kept to one level, personnel can be specialized—they may be better at what they do if they have fewer things to do. Costs may also be lower because residents aren't paying for services they don't need.

There are other reasons for putting people with similar care needs together. Residents can share their concerns and methods for coping with similar problems. Also, they need not be confronted on a daily basis with problems that are different or more severe than their own. This is particularly important where mental orientation or capacity is concerned. Good facilities may separate the rooms of severe Alzheimer's or other dementia sufferers from the rooms of other residents. When all the residents are together, the staff should pay special attention to residents who are disoriented.

Room Assignment

Some small nursing facilities offer residents private rooms. Larger facilities that offer private rooms usually charge considerably more for them. However, most facilities have two beds per room; some large nursing facilities have three beds in each room.

In facilities where people share a room, resident surveys show that roommate selection is very important to the residents' happiness and well-being, ranking only behind contact with family and friends. Some people prefer to have a roommate in similar physical condition so that they can better understand each other's needs and concerns. Other people do not mind having a roommate with greater needs; it allows them to be of help. Still others would prefer a roommate in better physical condition so that they can receive extra help. Whatever your preference, find out whether the facility will take it into account in assigning a roommate.

There is also the matter of finding someone with common interests, religious or ethnic background, language, and habits—smoking or late nights, for example. Will the facility consider these things when assigning a roommate? If so, make sure to let them know the things that are most important to you.

Residents' Condition and Activity

You can tell a lot about a nursing facility simply by walking around and looking carefully at the residents. Are most extremely ill or disabled? Do people appear comfortable? Are they reasonably neat and clean? Do you see smiles, hear friendly conversation among residents and between residents and staff? Are residents moving about the facility and being active in some way, or are they mostly in their rooms? Are people sitting alone and unattended in chairs or in wheelchairs in the hallway?

By checking the common areas, you can tell whether the residents are doing things together or only on their own. It may take several visits, at different times of the day, to get a feel for this. Are there any ongoing communal activities, such as a newsletter, a garden, regular outings, or some volunteer project? Be sure to ask.

Staff

Getting a sense of the staff also requires spending some time at the facility during a normal day's activities.

Personal Care Aides

In virtually every nursing facility, 90% of direct resident care is provided by personal care aides—also called assistants, attendants, or orderlies. These are the foot soldiers of long-term facility care, and their competence and attitude are most important to the health and well-being of residents. There are several things to find out about them.

Numbers. Although there are no hard and fast rules about how many attendants there should be for each resident, there must be enough so that the residents receive attention most of the time when they want it—and any time they need it. Generally, a good facility will have one aide on duty in a given wing or section of a facility for every five or six residents there. At night, the figure may drop to one aide for every 15 or so residents. On the other hand, during meals, when resident needs are high, aides should be supplemented by volunteers or other assistants so that there is one person to help every three or four people. In addition to these numbers, use your eyes to judge whether there are enough aides: Are there residents who seem to want or need attention from an aide but are not getting it?

Turnover. How long have people worked at the facility? Long-term employment generally means that both management and residents are satisfied with the aides' work. A rapid turnover of aides may be a bad sign, although even the best facilities sometimes have a hard time keeping staff (particularly in the aide jobs, which are usually high in stress and low in pay).

Language. If English is not the first language of the resident, how many people on the staff speak the resident's first language? The reverse may also be important. If English is the resident's first language, what percentage of the staff can communicate in English?

Intangibles. The courtesy, friendliness, and efficiency of the personal care aides to both residents and visitors are very important considerations. But the only way to judge this is to see the aides and residents in their daily interchanges. Is there easy conversation? Do the aides seem to pay attention to what the residents want? Do the aides have a neat and professional appearance?

Remember, as with any group of people, not every aide and every resident are going to get along. The crucial thing is not that every interaction is smiling and efficient, but that most contacts are cordial and responsive to a resident's needs.

Available Professional Staff

It doesn't really matter how many people with impressive certificates and licenses are listed on a facility's letterhead. What counts is how much time any of them actually spends with residents. How often does the facility's physician check on medical care standards? How often do licensed nurses make rounds? How easy is it to schedule a rehabilitation therapist? How much hands-on care do professional personnel provide, and how much do they just supervise? To what extent can a resident request direct care from one of the professional staff?

Except in emergencies, direct physician care will come from your own physicians, not from the facility's doctors. Find out whether the facility restricts visits from outside physicians and whether it provides transportation to outside medical appointments. Also, many physicians will not make visits to a nursing facility. Ask whether your primary care physician will make such visits, and if so, whether he or she will come to the particular facility you have in mind.

Outside Help

Find out whether the facility permits or arranges for extra outside help.

Volunteers. Many facilities make good use of volunteers from public service agencies and programs. Some simply provide extra personal attention or companionship, while others bring special educational skills or social programs. These volunteers are a good link to the outside world and give residents a change of pace and face from the regular staff.

Private Aid. Does the facility allow part-time private assistance of any sort from outside the facility, such as a private duty care assistant, chiropractor, massage therapist, or private duty nurse?

Food

In a nursing facility, the importance of meals goes beyond merely getting the right nutrients. Meals are central activities in a resident's day—a social event and a source of pleasure when many other events and pleasures may be limited. In inquiring about a facility's food service, don't restrict yourself to looking at a menu or seeing that a dietician is an official member of the staff. Instead, visit the facility's dining areas during one or more meals and eat the food with residents. There are several things to ask, look, and taste for:

Tastiness. Don't overlook the simple fact that the nutritional value of food doesn't matter if you don't eat it. If food tastes lousy, people eat less of it. Freshness and variety also help keep people interested. Check menus from a week or two and see how often fresh foods are served and how often dishes are repeated.

Preferences and Restrictions. No group living facility can cater to the different food whims and desires of all its residents. But residents should be offered some choice in meals, and the facility should respond to strong likes and dislikes. Dietary restrictions, whether for health, digestive, or religious reasons, must be strictly followed. The facility should keep a written record of any such restriction for each resident, and the kitchen staff should consult it when planning and preparing meals.

Extra Food. Not everyone's appetite runs by the standard meal clock. Some people prefer, or need, to eat a little bit several times a day. Other people who are up at "odd" hours get hungry. And many people get pleasure from special foods made by friends or relatives or a favorite neighborhood bakery. A facility that is too rigid about food is not taking care of important needs.

Does the facility serve snacks, tea, or coffee between meals or at least make such things available to residents? Do the snacks include fresh fruit and other healthful foods? May residents eat the snacks where and when they want—particularly in their own rooms—or only at designated times and places? May residents be given food from outside the facility? And if so, is there an easily accessible place where it can be kept?

Dining Area. The first thing to pay attention to when you visit the dining area during a meal is whether the residents are eating the food. That will tell you a lot. Observe whether the staff is helpful with residents who need assistance eating. Are residents comfortable? Is the area clean? Ask if dining times are flexible. Do residents have enough time with their meal, or is food rushed in and out?

Family Involvement

One benefit of a nursing facility is its ready-made community of companions and helpers. However, active family involvement in the resident's life also provides important benefits. Residents rate personal contact—by visits, phone, mail, and outings—at the top of their list of concerns. And no matter how good a facility's own outreach programs are, a resident's ability to stay in touch with the larger community requires help from friends and relatives.

Whether family and friends are actively involved in a resident's life depends to no small degree on whether the facility encourages their participation. Families should be regularly invited to participate in activities with residents. Visiting should be encouraged rather than merely tolerated. There should be adequate space, comfort, and privacy in visiting areas and wide and flexible visiting hours. Visiting should be permitted during meals, and there should be wide latitude in taking residents for outings.

Together, the staff and resident's family should regularly review the resident's condition and care. Find out what the procedures are for family consultation about problems or changes in the resident's care plan or room or roommate assignment. Ask whether there is an organized family support group or network for residents' families to keep in touch.

Decision Making

Residents' long-term health and comfort depend directly on a facility's procedures for making decisions about their care. A good facility should have standardized procedures for making daily care decisions. Review them before deciding on a particular facility. If a licensed facility refuses to respond to a resident's complaints, there are state and local government agencies that can step in. (See "Nursing Facility Ombudsman," below.)

Residents' Problems and Complaints

It is a sad but widely recognized truth that patients are abused and neglected in some nursing facilities. There are also many smaller problems that, if unattended, can make a resident's life miserable. Therefore, a facility must have specific procedures for residents and family members to lodge a complaint or discuss a problem about a particular staff person, a method or type of care, or a facility rule or condition.

The danger of not having an explicit complaint procedure is that a resident will not know with whom to speak or will get a runaround from staff members who claim they have no authority to do anything to right the wrong. Find out how complaints are handled and make certain that the process guarantees a response from an identifiable person in authority.

Similarly, there should be a regular procedure for registering complaints or discussing problems about a roommate or other resident. Find out what these procedures are and what a resident must do to request a room change.

Facility-Imposed Changes

For financial and other reasons, a facility may want to move residents around when there are vacancies in double rooms. Or, because of a change in a resident's condition that requires a different level of care, the facility may believe a room change is necessary. However, the resident may not want to move. It is, therefore, important that a resident have a right to be notified in advance of a room change and that the facility have rules that limit the circumstances under which such changes can be made.

As with a room change, the facility may decide that the particular nonmedical care a resident has been receiving is no longer necessary or that new types of costlier or more restrictive care are required. Find out how these decisions are made and what rights the resident has. Also, make sure there is a provision for consultation with, and notification of, the family.

For all decisions about medical care or changes in condition, specific written rules should be set out, including:

- what decisions can be made by aides and what must be decided by the nurse on duty

- when the facility's attending physician must be consulted about a change in medical care or condition

- when the resident's personal physician must be consulted about a change in condition or a possible change in care, and

- when the resident's family must be notified of a change in care or condition.

Nursing Facility Ombudsman

The federal government funds a program, administered by each state's Agency on Aging, which makes available to nursing facility residents an ombudsman—a kind of troubleshooter to mediate unresolved problems between residents or their families and a nursing facility. The ombudsman has regular visiting hours and days at the facility and should also be available by phone. There is no charge for using the services of the ombudsman.

Your Written Contract

All facilities have a formal written document that both the resident and a facility representative sign. It does not matter whether this document is called a "contract" or an "agreement" or something else. What does matter is that all important terms and conditions of residence and care are included, so that both you and the facility are clear about them. If you are unsure of any terms and conditions, have an attorney or someone else familiar with nursing facility care review it with you before signing. Even if you do not consult with anyone else, take the agreement home and review it carefully before signing.

If something important to you is not included in the facility's preprinted agreement, discuss it with the proper facility official. When you've reached an agreement, write it on a separate piece of paper, signed and dated by both of you, and attach it to the rest of the agreement.

What Your Agreement Should Cover

The agreement should spell out the specific health care, personal care, equipment, and supplies you will get for your regular daily, weekly, or monthly fee. This should include frequency of nursing care, physical or other therapies, number of meals, and special dietary needs.

Room. The agreement should specify the number of beds in the resident's room, as well as any other distinguishing features of the room, including anything that is important to you—such as the room size, bathroom facilities, windows, or location in the building.

Extra Charges and Adjustments. The agreement should specify what services, equipment, and supplies are charged as extra (above the regular rate). The agreement should also specify whether you will get any discounts for such things as meals eaten outside of the facility and time spent off the premises, such as vacations or time in the hospital.

Some contracts require residents to purchase their medications at the facility's own pharmacy. Because the rates there may be considerably higher than at outside pharmacies, this is, in effect, a forced extra charge. Find out in advance whether this is the policy at any facility you are considering.

Rate Changes. The agreement should spell out whether, and how much, the regular rate will go up or down if the level of care is changed, whether the regular rate is guaranteed to remain the same for any length of time, and how much notice must be given before rates are raised.

Illegal to Ask for a Family Guarantee

In the past, a nursing home commonly asked family members to become financially "responsible parties," personally guaranteeing payment of its fees, before it would allow a family member to become a resident. This practice is now illegal under federal law (42 Code of Federal Regulations sec. 483.12(d)(2)). Still, some nursing home admission contracts contain fine print making the "cosigner" personally responsible for the resident's bills. Check the admission papers carefully to make sure it does not contain such a clause. And do not sign any side agreements or attachments that would make you financially responsible for your family member's nursing home costs.

However, if you have a power of attorney over your family member's finances, it is lawful for the nursing home to ask you to agree to act in that capacity to use your family member's funds to pay the nursing home bills. Signing that agreement, though, does not make you personally responsible for the bills.

Other Matters to Understand

Make sure you know what your coverage is upon entering a facility. Medicare and private insurance coverage for nursing facility care is very limited. (See Chapter 7.) Medicaid coverage, while extensive, is not available to everyone at all times. (See Chapter 8.)

Change in Funding. It's also important to know how a facility will respond to a change in circumstance (and what your personal responsibility would be upon such a change). Some facilities provide certain rooms for Medicaid residents and other, better rooms for private paying patients. In that situation, once Medicaid begins to cover your stay, you could be forced to move to a different, less desirable room.

Financial changes to consider include:

• using up your allotted Medicare skilled nursing facility coverage

• moving from skilled to intermediate or personal care, neither of which is covered by Medicare or private insurance

• becoming eligible for Medicaid, and

• declaring personal bankruptcy; many facilities require proof of your ability to pay for two years as a condition of admission.

Discharge Policy. There are situations in which you might want to either move out of the facility or the facility might want to discharge you even though you want to stay. Find out the facility's policies and procedures, including how much written notice must be given, in discharge situations such as:

• if the resident's need for care changes and the resident wants to leave the facility to receive different care

• if the resident's need for care changes and the facility wants the resident to move out and receive care elsewhere, or

• if the resident's source of funds changes.

Check the Policy on Temporary Hospitalization

It is not uncommon for a nursing facility resident to need hospitalization for some period of time. Find out what the policy is on holding a resident's bed during hospitalization. If you may be going back and forth to the hospital and you can easily lose your place in the facility while hospitalized, you may want to choose a different facility.

Care for Elders With Alzheimer's Disease

Long-term care for those with Alzheimer's disease presents special problems, both for the elder and for the caregivers. This chapter explains the special needs of Alzheimer's patients—and the ways those needs can be met at home, in assisted living residences, and in long-term care facilities. General information about home care and assisted living and long-term care facilities is covered in Chapters 2, 3, and 4 of this book.

As discussed below, Alzheimer's disease is a progressive condition. It begins with mild symptoms and slowly, but inevitably, becomes worse. What type of care is appropriate depends in large measure on how far an elder's disease has progressed. An elder with mild Alzheimer's symptoms can often manage very well at home, or in a family member's home, with a combination of home care and strong family support. Or the elder could receive home care in an organized senior residence. When the elder's symptoms become more severe, however, providing care at home can become extremely difficult. For many people in the middle stages of the disease, some sort of assisted living or long-term care residential facility works best. And as the disease progresses to its most severe stages, patients almost always require the round-the-clock care provided in a custodial care nursing facility.

Other Types of Cognitive Impairment

This chapter focuses on the particulars of Alzheimer's disease. But older people may suffer diminished mental capabilities—called "cognitive impairment" or "dementia"—from other causes, such as a stroke, Parkinson's disease, or the loss of brain cell function that has traditionally been called "senility." Whatever its cause—and no matter what name it goes by—diminished mental capacity often presents the same symptoms as Alzheimer's, such as disorientation, memory loss, anxiety, sleeplessness, loss of balance and coordination, and eventual difficulty with body functions. This chapter provides information about dealing with these and related symptoms, whether they result from Alzheimer's disease or from another type of cognitive impairment.

The Symptoms and Stages of Alzheimer's

If you are organizing care for yourself or for a loved one with Alzheimer's, you should learn the symptoms of the disease in its various stages *before* those symptoms fully appear. Alzheimer's is a progressive disease in which a person's condition slowly deteriorates. The course of the disease—from mild, early symptoms to severe late stages—may last from five to 20 years. But, within that slow decline, symptoms may appear abruptly, without warning. Knowing what to expect can help you cope with these changes as they develop.

This section looks at the three stages of Alzheimer's disease as the medical and care communities now understand and describe them. But the symptoms of Alzheimer's and other forms of dementia vary widely from person to person. Some people will show only some of the symptoms on the "standard" list or suffer a milder version of some symptoms and a more severe version of others. Other people will develop the classic symptoms but not in the order or severity of the disease's normal progression. No clear dividing line separates one stage of the disease from another. Although learning about the disease's usual progression can help you prepare for the future, no brief summary can cover the many ways in which this complex disease appears. And long-term care is for a person, not a disease. It is that person's individual needs that must dictate care, not those of a theoretical person with supposedly "average" Alzheimer's symptoms.

Early-Stage Alzheimer's

In the earliest stage, Alzheimer's symptoms may be subtle and hard to recognize. How do you distinguish between the "normal" signs of aging—lower energy, slower movements, and thinking that isn't quite as sharp—and the more serious loss of cognitive functions that may indicate the onset of Alzheimer's? Even physicians find it very difficult to make the distinction. And, these same symptoms can result from an undetected physical problem, such as a small stroke, Parkinson's disease, overmedication, or a potent interaction of several medicines. If you begin to notice some of the symptoms listed here, see a physician who is experienced with Alzheimer's. If your personal physician does not have that experience, ask to be referred to a doctor who does. This doesn't mean you cannot continue to be treated by your regular physician, even if you do have Alzheimer's. But an accurate early diagnosis of Alzheimer's, if that is what you have, will help you, your family, and your physician plan for what is to come.

As the early stage of Alzheimer's progresses, even its relatively minor symptoms can make life difficult and dangerous for the person who has the disease and for those with whom that person lives. Once several of these symptoms are occurring regularly, you will need to arrange for close monitoring and care. (See "Home Care for Alzheimer's," below.)

These are the most common early symptoms of Alzheimer's disease:

• **Confusion about time and place.** One of the tell-tale signs of early Alzheimer's is increasingly frequent mistakes about the day, time, or location. Some loss of date and time awareness is common in older people, especially if they have no fixed daily schedule. But, elders who are confused on a regular basis or seem not to know where they are should be checked for Alzheimer's.

• **Short-term memory loss.** Some memory loss is a normal aspect of the aging process. Over time, most elders will suffer from fading long-term memories—an inability to reconstruct events long in the past. But elders with Alzheimer's begin to lose short-term memory. In the afternoon, a person may not be able to remember what happened that morning. Or, for example, a person might repeat a task he just completed, because he has no memory of having done it already.

• **Difficulty with routine tasks.** A person with early stage Alzheimer's may be unable to figure out how to write a check, count out the right amount of bills to pay at the grocery store, or change channels on the radio or television.

• **Making senseless decisions.** An Alzheimer's sufferer may make choices or decisions that are illogical, like putting on a heavy coat to go out on a hot summer day, putting the cordless phone away in the fridge, getting undressed for bed right after breakfast, or putting ten loaves of bread in the grocery basket.

• **Mood swings.** Those who have Alzheimer's sometimes "lose" their normal personality. A person with early stages of the disease may become moody, restless, and irritable for no apparent reason, may be unable to concentrate on anything, or indifferent to surroundings. These mood swings tend to occur most often and acutely at dusk, as the light is changing—which is why doctors refer to this phenomenon as "sundowning."

Information and Referrals About Alzheimer's

There are two excellent national nonprofit organizations that can provide a wealth of information to people coping with Alzheimer's disease. These organizations offer materials that can help you understand the disease, its symptoms, and its treatments. They also provide descriptions of and referrals to local health care organizations and facilities that specialize in Alzheimer's care. They connect families caring for someone with Alzheimer's to support groups of other families in the same situation. And, they provide a continuing stream of valuable information via newsletters, brochures, and websites. Anyone dealing with Alzheimer's should make use of the resources of one or both of these organizations:

Alzheimer's Association
800-272-3900
www.alz.org

Alzheimer's Disease Education and Referral Center
800-438-4380
www.nia.nih.gov/alzheimers

Middle-Stage Alzheimer's

An elder in the middle stages of Alzheimer's disease may suffer a more severe version of the early stage symptoms—and will begin to exhibit new symptoms. Some medications—antidepressants, sleep aids, and antianxiety drugs—can help alleviate some of these symptoms, at least for a while. But the disease's progression can only be slowed, not stopped. It becomes increasingly difficult for elders with Alzheimer's to communicate and care for themselves. This makes it much harder for family members to be the sole caregivers. You can get outside help from a home health agency or independent personal attendants, either in a family home or in an organized senior residence. As the symptoms worsen, however, the patient will require extensive monitoring, supervision, and assistance. At this point, many families will have to make the difficult choice to move the elder to an assisted living or long-term care facility.

These are the symptoms most commonly associated with middle-stage Alzheimer's:

- **Confusion as to time, place, and persons.** An elder's confusion about times, dates, and places worsens. This is compounded by one of the most heartbreaking aspects of Alzheimer's: the elder's inability to recognize other people. An Alzheimer's patient will mix up names and identities; as the disease progresses, the patient will no longer recognize even the most familiar faces.

- **Memory loss and transposure.** The short-term memory loss that begins in the early stages of the disease becomes acute. People with middle-stage Alzheimer's may remember very little that they have recently done. Long-term memory is also affected. Those suffering from Alzheimer's often transpose events and people, creating a hodgepodge of recent recollections and childhood memories that they can no longer sort out.

- **Wandering.** People with middle-stage Alzheimer's have a tendency to wander away from home—or from a companion on an outing—and become lost. This can cause great anxiety and difficulty for both patient and caregiver—and a variety of dangers (from exposure, traffic, or crime, for example) if the person winds up in unfamiliar territory.

- **Loss of simple logic.** Patients are no longer able to go from one simple thought to the next, or to figure out the basic steps they will have to follow to complete a task. For example, an Alzheimer's patient might not realize that a door must be unlocked before it can be opened.

- **Language problems.** As Alzheimer's progresses, people lose their facility with language. Someone with middle-stage Alzheimer's may have trouble finding even simple words, may use words incorrectly, and will likely have difficulty reading.

- **Motor function difficulties.** The early symptoms of Alzheimer's are mostly cognitive—that is, they affect the patient's ability to think and understand. In the middle stages, the patient's body begins to suffer, too. Elders may lose hand-eye coordination, making simple tasks difficult. They may have trouble with balance, meaning that dangerous falls may occur. And they may become incontinent.

- **Extreme mood swings.** People with middle-stage Alzheimer's often ride an unpredictable roller coaster of emotions, from deep depression to high good humor, from intense anger to weepy sentimentality.

- **Impulsive behavior.** People with Alzheimer's are known to "act out" in impulsive and unexpected ways, such as loud talking or shouting, arguing, disrobing, making inappropriate personal commentary, or touching others and engaging in other antisocial or embarrassing behaviors.

- **Paranoia and hallucinations.** As the disease progresses, a person may begin to exhibit paranoid behavior, showing fear or mistrust of strangers, caregivers, and even close family. Those with Alzheimer's in the middle stages may also begin to have visual or auditory hallucinations—that is, they might start to see or hear things that aren't there—which can be very disturbing to patients and caregivers alike.

Late-Stage Alzheimer's

Because Alzheimer's disease may take up to 20 years to run its full course, many people die of some other disease or condition before their Alzheimer's progresses to its final stages. Those who do reach the late stages of the disease almost always require care in a nursing facility. At that point, the disease weakens the body as much as the mind.

In its late stages, Alzheimer's can cause:

• **Complete loss of cognitive functions.** People with late-stage Alzheimer's are unable to recognize anyone, to communicate, or to help with their own care.

• **Physical deterioration.** Someone with late-stage Alzheimer's has difficulty chewing and swallowing, suffers severe weight loss, is completely incontinent, and often develops troubled breathing.

Home Care for Alzheimer's

In its very earliest stages, the symptoms of Alzheimer's may be no more than a nuisance. With the help of a spouse or other family members, someone with Alzheimer's may be able to manage without any outside care. As the early-stage symptoms become persistent, however, elders will require some assistance from outside personal care aides. Caregivers can come to the elder's home, a family member's home, or an organized senior residence. However, once patients reach middle-stage Alzheimer's, with its deepening confusions and disorientation, they will require round-the-clock monitoring, often in a residential care facility.

Before considering the issues peculiar to home care for someone with Alzheimer's, read Chapter 2 to familiarize yourself with more general matters of home care.

Family Participation Is Crucial

To care for someone with Alzheimer's at home, you will need substantial family participation. Patients in the early stages won't need much assistance. But as their condition worsens, they will need monitoring and assistance round the clock. Most people cannot afford 24-hour outside help—which means that they will have to rely on their spouse, grown children, and grandchildren. Unless family members are ready and willing to make this commitment, home care won't be a workable solution over the long term.

Care in a Family Home

Staying in the comfortable surroundings of home can be very important to someone with Alzheimer's—even more so than to an elder with frailty or other physical problems. As elders lose their memories and grow increasingly confused, the familiar faces and layout of a family home can provide a sense of stability and well-being.

With the help of a healthy and physically capable spouse, someone with Alzheimer's may be able to get along well at home for quite a while. The spouse can serve as the main caregiver and organize other sources of care. This will be easier, and less expensive, if adult children or grandchildren live nearby and can help out. If no adult children or grandchildren can provide substantial help, a spouse may have to consider moving with the patient to an organized senior residence or moving the ill spouse to an assisted living or residential long-term care facility.

Patients who don't have a healthy and physically capable spouse to help with care might consider moving into the home of an adult child, grandchild, or sibling. If there are a number of people living in the home, they can share the caregiving responsibilities. A person with Alzheimer's will probably find a family home is more comforting than a residential facility. And it will be less expensive, at least initially.

The larger the number of family members helping to provide care—either in the elder's own home or in a family home—the less outside care will be needed. As the elder's need for care increases, however, it will become more difficult for family members to handle alone. And the more outside assistance is required, the more expensive home care becomes, until at some point the elder will probably have to move to an assisted living or residential long-term care facility.

In addition to the factors listed in Chapter 2, here are some additional things to consider when setting up home care for an elder with Alzheimer's.

Caregiver Experience

As explained in Chapter 2, you can get home care assistance from a home care agency or independent home care aides. Someone in the early stages of Alzheimer's will require safety monitoring, minor assistance with daily tasks, and companionship—but not necessarily medical or therapeutic care. Therefore, you probably won't need the more medically skilled personnel offered by a home care agency, at least at the beginning. Instead, you should look for an individual caregiver who has the right skills and temperament for Alzheimer's care.

Caring for an elder with Alzheimer's requires a special kind of patience, a soothing personality, and an ability to sort through the workings of a confused mind. Someone who has these personality traits but doesn't have experience working with Alzheimer's patients may turn out to be a wonderful caregiver. Generally, however, you should try to find outside caregivers with Alzheimer's experience. A home care agency that can guarantee that it will send Alzheimer's-experienced aides will save your family the time and effort of finding experienced help. If the agency cannot guarantee experienced aides, however, you should consider spending the time to find aides on your own. Your efforts will pay off in higher quality care—and in lower expenses, as independent aides generally charge less than a home care agency.

Continuity of Caregivers

Someone with Alzheimer's should see the same aides, at the same time of day, to the extent possible. The aides will get to know the patient's individual needs and preferences—and will learn what works (and what doesn't) in responding to those needs. The person receiving care will see a familiar face, which can be very important for someone whose world may otherwise be quite confusing. And because people with Alzheimer's become disoriented as to time, it is best to have the same aides work at the same time each day. A patchwork schedule can contribute to a patient's disorientation.

Alzheimer's Support Groups and Day Care

Coping with the early stages of Alzheimer's can be emotionally trying for the person with the disease. People with early-stage Alzheimer's still have most of their mental faculties. They are often painfully aware of the onset of the disease, the problems they are having, and, worst of all, what the future might hold. Losing their cognitive abilities is distressing, embarrassing, and frightening.

The early and middle stages of Alzheimer's are also physically and emotionally exhausting for family members, who have to manage not only their own fears, anxiety, and sadness over their loved one's condition, but also must arrange and provide care.

Fortunately, there is an extensive network of support groups for people with Alzheimer's and their families. People with Alzheimer's can share their fears, frustrations, angers, and coping devices with others who are in a similar stage of the disease. Family members can share experiences and ideas with others who face the same daunting caregiving tasks.

Some support groups are only for people with Alzheimer's. Others are for family members only. And still others are for both. Some support groups also offer adult day care, which provides companionship and perhaps some therapeutic classes for the person with Alzheimer's—and a welcome break for family members.

To find out about Alzheimer's support groups near you, contact the Alzheimer's Association or the Alzheimer's Disease Education and Referral Center. (See "Information and Referrals About Alzheimer's," above.)

Sundowning

Many people with Alzheimer's become particularly disoriented, anxious, and agitated as day turns to night and natural light is replaced by the dark and electric lights. No one knows exactly why this phenomenon, known as "sundowning," occurs. But, if you must cope with sundowning, you can do two things to minimize its effects. First, ask the family member or outside caregiver with whom the patient is most comfortable to be "on duty" during those hours. This can help diminish the patient's disorientation. Second, alter household lighting to avoid abrupt changes in light as night falls. For example, you can install and use dimmers on overhead lights and lamps, turn on lights before it gets dark, and avoid high intensity bulbs. Because shadows are also known to disorient those with Alzheimer's, you might also try to eliminate patterns of bright light and dark.

Wandering

One of the most common and frightening symptoms of early- and middle-stage Alzheimer's is the phenomenon of wandering. Even a patient who is usually competent and clearheaded can have a lapse in concentration, wander out of the house or away from a companion on an outing, and quickly become lost and disoriented.

You can do several things to manage with this problem. Make sure the person with Alzheimer's engages in lots of physical activities, including regular walks and other outings, to reduce restlessness and the inclination to wander. You can also remind any caregiver or family member who takes the patient on an outing to stay alert. Some also find it helpful to talk regularly to the person with Alzheimer's about where he or she is—this helps patients orient themselves and reassures them that they are where they should be (that is, at home or in another safe place).

Because you may not be able to curtail entirely a patient's inclination to wander, make sure to keep all doors leading to the outside locked.

You can also install door alarms and other security devices. You might also let your neighbors know that the elder could wander off, so they will know to alert you if they see the elder heading out alone. Finally, the Alzheimer's Association has a program called "Safe Return" which helps identify and return Alzheimer's wanderers. Some local police agencies have similar identification programs.

Don't Ignore Other Ailments

Sometimes, family members caring for someone with Alzheimer's dismiss the elder's complaints about physical ailments as just another of the disease's delusions. But, caregivers have to bear in mind that people with Alzheimer's are no less susceptible to physical ailments than other people of the same age. So, when someone with Alzheimer's complains about a physical symptom—even if the complaint isn't entirely clear—make sure to have a physician look into the matter. Remember, Alzheimer's patients depend on their caregivers to communicate their problems to physicians. If you ignore physical complaints, you might allow what could have been a minor, treatable problem to become more serious—or even terminal. What's worse, your delay might force the elder to suffer through physical pain that could have been alleviated.

Safety

Making a home safe for an elder who is frail or has mobility problems is generally a simple matter of eliminating loose electrical cords, installing hand rails, and rearranging furniture and other obstacles. But, for someone with Alzheimer's, the task is much more difficult. An elder with Alzheimer's has to be protected not only from obvious hazards, but also from his or her own thoughtless acts. For example, someone with

Alzheimer's might momentarily forget that an iron or a stove might be hot or that a knife is sharp.

An Alzheimer's patient's tendency to wander and frequent wakefulness at night when caregivers are sleeping can magnify these safety concerns. An elder who is disoriented, lacks judgment and coordination, and wanders around the house in the dark can easily come to harm.

The best way to protect against injuries is to be extremely vigilant. But no caregiver can watch every move an Alzheimer's patient makes, particularly at night. This makes preventive measures very important. Because an elder with Alzheimer's has reduced balance and coordination, your home should be cleared of tripping hazards—such as cords and loose rugs—and sharp, protruding corners that could cause serious injury in a fall.

Some other things that can make your home safer for someone with Alzheimer's include:

- deadbolt or inaccessible locks or gates, not only to the outside, but also to stairways and to areas of the house that should be off-limits without supervision

- protected access—child-proof locks, for example—to sharp or otherwise potentially harmful appliances, objects, and substances, particularly in the kitchen, bathroom, and garage

- lowering hot water settings to avoid scalding

- night-lights in the person's bedroom and other rooms accessible at night, to permit safe movement

- extra lighting and contrasting floor colors at doorways, stairways, and landings, to make it easier to see the difference in surface, and

- motion sensors and door alarms, to alert caregivers when the elder moves around at night.

Home Care in an Organized Senior Residence

Those in the early stages of Alzheimer's can also receive home care in an independent living senior residence, sometimes called a "retirement home." (See Chapter 3). This option works well for single people with Alzheimer's, as well as for couples in which only one spouse or partner has the disease.

Some single people in the early stages of Alzheimer's can get by safely on their own but cannot fully manage the daily running of a household. If these elders do not have an adult relative with whom they can or want to live, an organized senior residence can provide a number of advantages. Similarly, a spouse who provides care for an Alzheimer's spouse may find it difficult to manage both caregiving and housekeeping responsibilities. If your home is large, open, or isolated, you may find it especially hard to care for a spouse. Moving together into an independent living residence for seniors may considerably improve the situation.

Because independent living units are usually small apartments or rooms, they are physically easier to manage than larger apartments or houses. Also, these living units are designed to make life easier for older people, with built-in safety features and easy-to-use appliances. Senior residences often offer meals in a common dining room, which can eliminate the hassle and dangers of cooking and cleaning up.

Independent living residences do not offer personal assistance with the activities of daily life, nor do they provide round-the-clock supervision. But they do have some staff on hand all the time. The staff and other residents provide not only a social community, but also a kind of neighborhood watch—they can provide physical and emotional support while keeping an eye out for trouble. A single person may feel more secure in such a community. And a caregiver spouse won't have to provide constant care and companionship, because there will always be familiar faces nearby.

Although an independent living senior residence offers many advantages, an elder with Alzheimer's may also need outside home care as time goes on. As the disease moves into its more difficult stages, a person with Alzheimer's may need more help than the community alone, or a caregiver spouse, can provide. Most independent living residences are used to having outside home care aides regularly work with residents. In fact, most residences have a formal or informal referral service for home care aides—and work with those aides to make life easier for residents. However, some independent living communities restrict access by outside care aides, or do not permit residents to remain if they are not able to function independently. If you are considering an independent living community for yourself or someone else with early-stage Alzheimer's, make sure its rules permit continued residence and unlimited outside home care as the disease progresses.

Residential Care Facilities for Alzheimer's

There are many types of residential facilities for older people who are no longer able to live independently and who cannot or do not want to rely on home care. For example, assisted living residences provide a small amount of daily assistance plus round-the-clock monitoring. Long-term care facilities—also called board and care homes, residential care facilities, custodial care facilities, sheltered care residences, or the like—provide 24-hour personal assistance but not much nursing or other medical care. And nursing facilities provide round-the-clock personal assistance plus nursing and other medical care. These facilities can eliminate or limit an elder's need for outside assistance, reduce the physical space and daily tasks the person with Alzheimer's and caregivers have to navigate, and provide a community of people offering round-the-clock companionship.

As someone's Alzheimer's symptoms become more severe, caring for that person at home can become extremely difficult. If you use a lot of paid outside assistance, care may quickly become prohibitively expensive. For these reasons, most people with middle- to late-stage Alzheimer's eventually move to an assisted living, residential care, or nursing facility. And many of those people later have to move to a higher level of care, either within the same facility or in a different setting.

The same nursing home or assisted living facility that provides excellent care for someone with physical frailties will not necessarily work well for someone with Alzheimer's. So, many nursing facilities and assisted living facilities now have units or sections specially designed and staffed to care for people with Alzheimer's. The design of the unit may include extra safety features and elements to minimize confusion. Staff may have specialized training, some of it required by state law. Many facilities also have memory classes and other activities designed for people with Alzheimer's. Even if there is no special unit in a facility you're considering, you should make certain at the very least that it has staff with Alzheimer's care training. Of course, the facility's location and cost are also important considerations, but within your area and budget, you should look for facilities that make special accommodations for Alzheimer's residents.

Below are some of the special factors you should consider when choosing a residential care facility for someone with Alzheimer's. Use the information here to supplement the more general discussion of residential facilities in Chapters 3 and 4.

Help From a Geriatric Care Manager

Geriatric care managers are professional advisers who help seniors and their families arrange long-term care. They know most of the agencies and facilities in a given geographic area and can help arrange complicated combinations of home health and personal assistance care. They are particularly useful to people who are trying to arrange care for someone from long distance. They can also help people find a residential facility for someone with Alzheimer's. Particularly in urban areas where there may be many residential facilities, a geriatric care manager who has experience placing people with Alzheimer's may know which facilities do well with Alzheimer's residents (and which ones do not). Read more about geriatric care managers in Chapter 1.

Physical Space

You should always look for a facility that is roomy and comfortable. But for someone with Alzheimer's, a facility's design and layout can be equally important. If the person is physically active, as many people with middle-stage Alzheimer's are, the facility must provide space to move about freely, without a sense of confinement. But, because Alzheimer's patients often wander and become disoriented, the space must also be safe and constraining. Some facilities combine space and constraint by using a circular design for hallways, which permits Alzheimer's patients to walk about in any direction, for as long they want, without being stopped or confused by dead ends or doors. When combined with a protected inner courtyard or patio for fresh air and a bit of greenery, these circular designs allow someone with Alzheimer's to feel a sense of movement and visual variety without risk. Avoid facilities with intersecting corridors, locked doors, and dead ends, where someone with Alzheimer's can quickly grow frustrated and disoriented.

Other Residents

Some long-term care facilities advertise a separate "special care unit" or "Alzheimer's care unit" exclusively for people with dementia. If a separate unit truly is designed and operated for dementia sufferers, its special features and staff may provide distinct advantages for those with Alzheimer's.

But a separate unit does not guarantee high-quality care. Unfortunately, some special units or wings offer nothing more than a higher price. And in some facilities, Alzheimer's residents are segregated into a separate unit merely because it is easier for the staff to control them there—and to prevent them from mixing with other residents.

Facilities that admit only Alzheimer's residents can provide some advantages. The staff can organize meals, activities, and care, including the monitoring of nighttime wandering—solely with Alzheimer's residents in mind. And, because they only care for people with Alzheimer's, the staff are likely to develop good skills in handling the particular difficulties Alzheimer's presents. Also, some Alzheimer's-only facilities have programs of Alzheimer's education, family counseling, and support groups that might not be available at other facilities.

But facilities that mix Alzheimer's residents with those who are only physically limited also offer some benefits. People in early- and middle-stage Alzheimer's often benefit from contact with non-Alzheimer's residents. The conversation and activities of these other residents can help people with Alzheimer's remain oriented, alert, and calm. However, if there is a mix of residents in an open facility (one that permits its non-Alzheimer's residents to go in and out freely), make sure that the facility pays close attention to the safety and security of Alzheimer's residents. Some open facilities rely solely on the watchful eyes of staff to monitor the movements of Alzheimer's residents. Others add closed-circuit monitors, door alarms, or sensors—used with a wristband or other device—to alert staff when an unattended Alzheimer's resident wanders at night or attempts to leave the facility.

Staff Skills

Perhaps the single most important quality to look for in a residential care facility is the staff's skills in dealing with Alzheimer's. Unfortunately, it can be difficult to gauge staff skills during brief visits to a facility. Therefore, you should try to visit a facility several times before you make your choice.

Be sure to visit at different times of the day, including meal times. Meals are the highlight of the day for most residents—how well the staff help residents in the dining room will make a big difference in how happy residents are. Try to make a night visit also—night is a particularly difficult time for people with Alzheimer's, and the facility may have different people staffing the night shift.

Your initial visit to a long-term care residence will almost certainly be conducted by the facility director, administrator, general manager, or other top-level official. This person may have a very impressive professional resume. He or she may also be charming and helpful both to you and to the residents you encounter on your tour. Except in a very small facility, however, this administrator is likely to spend much more time dealing with paperwork and staff than directly caring for residents. Of course, if the administrator is obviously awkward or callous in direct contacts with residents, this is a bad sign; such an attitude can easily rub off on the rest of the staff.

Your main focus should be on how the line staff—the personal care aides—interact with the residents. They are the facility employees who will spend the most time with residents. Are they calm and soothing with residents or cold and abrupt? Do they treat the residents like children or respectfully as adults? Do they acknowledge resident comments and requests and offer solutions—or do they simply try to quiet or distract residents? Do they have good language skills, either in English or a resident's other first language?

Make sure you see how the staff does with Alzheimer's residents, not just residents who are physically limited. And try to observe them with the most seriously ill Alzheimer's residents—this will be your best measure of staff attitudes and capabilities. Do the Alzheimer's residents seem comfortable with the staff? If a resident is distressed or disruptive, as people with middle-stage Alzheimer's often are, how well do staff members respond?

Family Participation

In either an assisted living facility or a residential care facility, regular visits from family members can greatly improve an Alzheimer's resident's comfort and sense of well-being. Some facilities make family visiting easy and encourage participation in a resident's care. They maintain avenues of communication for family members, readily accepting family comments and requests and willingly acting on them. Other facilities, however, set limits on visits and treat family members as aliens who must be tolerated but should not be encouraged.

You may have trouble getting a sense of a facility's attitude toward family members during your first visits. Try to see how family members of current residents interact with the staff. Do family members move about the facility easily, or do they seem like uncomfortable guests? Do they know staff members by name, and vice versa? See if the facility will give you the names and phone numbers of some immediate family members of current residents with Alzheimer's. If so, give them a call and find out how their relatives have been doing at that facility.

Special Programs for Alzheimer's Residents

Alzheimer's residents can benefit from programs designed to address symptoms particular to the early and middle stages of the disease. Special arts and crafts work, reading, word games, and outings can help residents stay mentally alert. Memory enhancement programs can slow memory loss. Resident participation in room and hallway decoration can help keep the resident oriented within the facility. The facility can offer physical exercises tailored to people with relatively healthy bodies but poor balance or coordination. And staff can pay special attention to residents during the hours around sunset, to minimize the effects of sundowning.

Incontinence

Almost everyone with middle-stage Alzheimer's disease becomes incontinent to some degree. At first, they will have only occasional loss of bladder control. Later, they are likely to develop nearly total incontinence. This presents several problems. It is embarrassing to the person with Alzheimer's. It is unpleasant for other residents and staff. It can be physically uncomfortable. And, if it is not properly attended to, it can present health problems.

For all these reasons, you should try to get a sense of how a facility handles residents' incontinence. A facility cannot be expected to keep a resident completely clean every moment. But some things can be done to help minimize incontinence, particularly in its early stages. Does the staff try to help residents control the problem, if possible? And when incontinence is beyond control, does the staff regularly monitor and clean residents—day and night—so that they are reasonably comfortable?

Medication and Other Medical Care

Find out whether the facility is licensed—usually this means it has a registered nurse on duty—to administer drugs by injection and to deliver other types of non-self-administered medical care. People with Alzheimer's are not immune to other ailments and may need regular medical attention. Assisted living residences and small long-term care facilities might not have staff who can administer such medical care. If you are looking for a facility for someone who has a physical condition that may soon require regular medical intervention, make sure the facility can deliver it.

Also, look into the facility's policy on using medications to control Alzheimer's symptoms themselves. There are drugs that can help control the anxieties, aggressiveness, agitation, and sleeplessness of people with Alzheimer's. The proper use of these drugs can make life more comfortable for the resident. And, facility staff may legitimately need to use accepted Alzheimer's medication to help control the extreme behavior of some residents in the later stages of the disease. But, who decides what drugs, what doses, and what frequency? Ask the director about the facility's policy (it should be in writing) on the use of behavior-controlling medication. To what extent is a resident's personal physician consulted regarding medications? What about family? And does the facility keep a written record of each administration of these medications, including dosage and frequency? ●

Hospice Care

Medical care during the final stages of life is often invasive and traumatic, forcing a patient to move from home to hospital to nursing facility and back again, over and over. This usually results in unnecessary pain and discomfort but no significant benefit. And, lost in the medical shuffle is comprehensive care for the patient's overall well-being—control of pain and other symptoms and a comfortable, peaceful setting for patient and family.

Hospice responds to this problem of end-of-life care. Hospice provides a special kind of care designed for people who are in the last six months of a terminal illness, though sometimes it provides care for longer. Hospice replaces regular medical care. Instead of continuing with futile efforts to cure a disease or attempting to briefly prolong life, hospice offers a coordinated plan that pays special attention to a patient's comfort, including carefully calibrated relief from pain and other symptoms. This can mean a considerable improvement in a patient's quality of life during the last stages of a terminal illness—with a focus on the patient rather than on the disease. It can also bring great relief to the patient's family and other caregivers.

Hospice offers physician, nursing, and home health care as well as drugs, medical equipment, counseling, and homemaker services. It also directly addresses the needs of a patient's family or other nonpaid caregivers, including respite care which offers caregivers some temporary relief from their responsibilities.

Hospice does not provide a residence or living arrangement. Instead, caregivers deliver hospice care wherever a patient lives, whether at home or in an assisted living or nursing facility. Hospice's comprehensive comfort care sometimes makes it possible for a patient to leave a hospital or nursing facility and return home to be cared for there. Conversely, someone who lives at home can be moved to a hospice inpatient facility, or to a special hospice section of a hospital or nursing facility, during short periods of respite care.

Medicare pays for almost all of hospice care—the patient has only small copayments. Medicaid and most private health insurance also offer hospice coverage. Because of this nearly total coverage by Medicare or other insurance, hospice should be considered—at the appropriate time——by anyone who receives long-term care and is nearing the end of life.

Medicare Eligibility for Hospice Care

Coverage for hospice care is offered under Medicare Part A (Hospital Insurance). Anyone enrolled in Medicare Part A is eligible for Medicare hospice coverage if they also meet all of the other conditions discussed in this section.

Medicaid and Private Insurance Also Cover Hospice

Medicare covers almost all hospice care for people age 65 and over. If you do not qualify for Medicare, you may still receive hospice care through Medicaid (Medi-Cal in California) or private health insurance if you have it. Both the Medicaid program and almost all private health insurance policies provide the same kind and levels of hospice coverage, under the same eligibility rules, as Medicare does.

Final Six Months of a Terminal Illness

To qualify for hospice care, your primary care doctor, or other physician in charge of your treatment, must certify that you have a terminal illness and probably have less than six months to live. This assessment of your condition must also be verified by the medical director of the particular hospice agency you choose, though this is usually just a formality.

The six-month certification requirement means that many people do not take advantage of hospice care as soon as they might. It is sometimes difficult for a doctor to put a time frame on a patient's survival. This may be due to the unpredictable nature of some illnesses and to the way in which different patients respond differently to a disease or condition. But it can also result from a doctor's reluctance to say openly that the patient has only a relatively short time to live. Or it may be that the patient, or the patient's family, does not want to accept the doctor's prognosis and refuses to pursue the opportunity to receive hospice care.

Communicating With Your Physician About Hospice

There are two difficult aspects to choosing hospice care. One is that both the patient and a doctor must admit that the patient probably has only six months to live. The other is deciding that hospice care is preferable to further treatment. To address these issues, have a direct, one-on-one conversation with the primary care or other treating physician. To get your doctor's undivided attention for such a conversation may require you to set up a special appointment with the doctor solely for that purpose. It may also mean excluding family members if you feel that either you or your doctor might not speak freely enough if someone else is present. On the other hand, you may want to have a family member or someone else present, to ask questions you fail to ask and to confirm to you later what you and the doctor discussed.

Giving Up Potentially Life-Prolonging Treatment

The second requirement for hospice care is that you agree, in writing, to end Medicare coverage for treatment of your terminal illness. Essentially, by choosing hospice you make a trade: You give up further medical attempts to cure or delay the progress of your illness. And in exchange, you receive coordinated care specifically designed to make the final months of life as comfortable and pain free as possible for you and your family.

You May Still Receive Treatment for Other Problems

If you choose hospice care, you give up Medicare coverage for regular medical treatment of your terminal illness. However, you remain covered by Medicare for treatment of any other illness or condition. For example, if you elect hospice because of cancer, you no longer have Medicare coverage for chemotherapy or any medication or procedure used to treat or slow that cancer. But you are still covered for treatment of any noncancer condition, and for any new problem that arises, such as the flu or a broken bone.

Deciding to give up treatment can be extremely difficult for both patient and doctor. Even if doctors say the odds are extremely slim of further treatment prolonging life, many people have great difficulty giving up that faint chance. Many doctors, too, have a hard time stopping treatments. In the American medical system, doctors are trained to make every effort to prolong patients' lives. But doctors tend to pursue these often invasive, discomforting, and painful efforts no matter how poor the odds and with little concern for how miserable the treatments make the patient. So, it may be necessary for you to be the one to suggest to the doctor that further treatment efforts are no longer in your best interest.

You May Return to Regular Medical Treatment at Any Time

The decision to forgo treatment and choose hospice care instead is extremely difficult. But, it is not necessarily a final decision. If you change your mind any time after you have elected hospice, you may immediately go back to regular Medicare or other insurance coverage for treatment of your disease. This may be because the progress of your disease has slowed, or it has gone into remission. Perhaps there is a different treatment that you want to try. Or, you may simply have a change of heart. The reason does not matter, because you do not have to give a reason. You simply have to notify the hospice program, which, in turn, will notify Medicare or another insurer, that you are ending your hospice care and returning to your previous coverage. If you later decide to return to hospice, you may do so as long as you once again meet all the requirements as discussed in this section.

Care Only From Approved Hospice

If you choose Medicare hospice care, you may receive that care only from one Medicare-approved hospice program. This has two different implications. First, it means that you may not receive care from two different hospice programs at the same time. And, it means that if you also receive home health care which includes some of the same services the hospice program care plan provides, you may have to give up some of those services from the home health care agency. In particular, hospice, rather than the home care agency, will direct your overall care. Medical personnel from the hospice—doctors, nurses, therapists—will make specific decisions about your care, rather than personnel from the home health agency. The extent to which nonhospice home health aides, homemakers, and other assistants may work with you depends on whether they conflict—either in time spent with you or in duties performed—with similar help provided to you by the hospice.

For the most part, the hospice program will take charge of decisions about your care. However, it will consult with your treating physician to design a plan of care for you, and your own doctor may continue to treat you for conditions other than your terminal illness.

Services Provided by Hospice

Hospice provides a coordinated program of care which may include any of the services discussed below, depending on the needs of the individual patient and of his or her primary caregivers. Hospice services focus primarily on the patient's comfort and secondarily on the peace of mind of the patient and family.

Medical Personnel

In consultation with your primary treating physician, a hospice physician oversees the development of a care program for you. After your hospice plan has been put into place, you will probably not see much of either your primary care physician or the hospice physician unless a problem occurs which cannot be handled by other hospice staff. However, your own physician will still handle treatment of any other medical condition that needs attention.

Specially trained nurses often play an active role in hospice care. You are likely to see a nurse frequently during the initial stages of setting up your hospice care plan. Nurses may visit regularly during the course of your care, though the number and length of those visits will depend on the amount of skilled attention you need. Hospice nurses are always on call to visit you if your condition changes or if management of your symptoms needs adjustment.

Hospice patients also receive care from physical, speech, and occupational therapists, as needed. The therapists do not offer long-range programs designed to return a patient to full physical capability. Rather, they help the patient maintain mobility, flexibility, and physical ability so that, for as long as possible, the patient may perform the activities of daily life and communicate with loved ones and caregivers. Dieticians are also available to help patients cope with digestion and nutrition difficulties caused by illness and medications.

Aides and Volunteers

Much direct hospice care comes from home health aides. These aides are trained to monitor symptoms, make a patient comfortable, and administer drugs. They come as often as needed—in the last stages of illness, that may be every day. Hospice programs try to send the same home health aides to the same patient, allowing patient and aides to develop a level of comfort and understanding with each other.

Many hospice agencies also make use of trained volunteers. These volunteers may provide limited homemaker services and they may help with transportation, shopping, and other errands, depending on the patient's needs and the ability of nonhospice caregivers to meet those needs. Volunteers also sometimes provide unofficial respite care, spending short periods at the patient's home while a regular caregiver temporarily goes elsewhere.

Counseling and Social Services

Counseling of various kinds is available through hospice for both patient and family. Social workers are available to help you and your family deal with health care, insurance, financial, and end-of-life decisions and paperwork. Specially trained counselors are also available to help you and your family deal with emotional issues surrounding terminal illness.

Medication

Hospice provides a patient with all the drugs needed to be comfortable. These include medicines for relief from pain and control of other symptoms, as well as drugs that can help with sleep, mobility, and digestion. Because hospice focuses on pain and symptom relief, it may provide a better and more carefully administered drug regimen than regular Medicare coverage provides under the care of your treating physicians. And because you will no longer be taking the medicines that attempt to treat disease, hospice medical personnel may find it easier to provide you with effective pain and symptom relief. These outpatient medications are available to you directly from the hospice, without the need to go through a pharmacy or to use Medicare Part D or other prescription drug insurance.

Equipment and Supplies

Hospice directly provides you with any needed medical equipment, such as a hospital bed, wheelchair or walker, or special bathing aids, without having to go through a medical appliance provider. Hospice similarly provides all medical supplies, without the need to get a doctor's prescription or to go through a pharmacy.

Respite Care

One of the special features of hospice is respite care. Patients receiving long-term care at home usually depend on family and other nonpaid caregivers to provide most of their day-to-day care. But those caregivers often suffer from both physical and emotional exhaustion. Respite care can give those caregivers short breaks, allowing them to deal with things other than care for the patient, or simply to get extra rest.

If you live at your own home or at the home of a family member, you will probably be moved for the respite care period to a hospice residential facility or to the special hospice section of a hospital or nursing facility. Respite care is also available if you live in assisted living or other long-term care facility. If so, you might remain where you are, with the respite provided by hospice aides, assistants, and volunteers spending extra time there with you.

Respite care is available for up to five days at a time. There is no limit to the number of times you may receive respite care. However, a request for respite care must be approved by the hospice agency, which will not permit frequent, repeated periods of respite care to turn hospice into an everyday, round-the-clock personal care service.

How Hospice Operates

Hospice care begins when you choose and enroll with a specific hospice care agency. The agency works with your treating physicians and your family or other caregivers to set up a hospice plan for your care. Hospice care continues for up to six months, and sometimes longer. During that time, the agency monitors and adjusts your care as your needs change.

Choosing a Hospice

Several sources are available to help you find a Medicare-certified hospice agency that provides care in the area where you live.

The first source for a referral may be your treating physicians. They will be familiar with one or more hospice agencies, and one of your doctors may recommend a particular agency. Be aware, however, that doctors have little contact with hospice agencies once hospice care begins, so their actual experience with how well an agency cares for patients may be limited.

If you are in the hospital or a skilled nursing facility at the time you want to choose a hospice, the hospital or facility discharge planner will have contact information about hospice agencies in your area. If the hospital or facility refers you to only one agency, however, you may want to have your family or other caregivers investigate others, too. Hospitals and care facilities sometimes have a contractual relationship with a particular hospice agency, but that does not necessarily mean that agency is the best one for you.

If you live in an assisted living or other long-term care facility, that facility will have a relationship with one or more local hospice agencies. Using one of these agencies is usually a good idea because the hospice agency's staff will have experience with the staff and ways of doing things where you live, improving the likelihood that the two providers will work smoothly together. However, you should be permitted to use a different Medicare-certified hospice agency if you choose to.

You can get free referrals to all the Medicare-certified hospice agencies that serve your geographic area by contacting your state's nonprofit hospice organization. See the appendix of this book for hospice resources.

Once you choose a hospice agency, you need to formally enroll in it. To enroll, your treating physician will fill out and submit a Medicare document which officially confirms the prognosis that you probably have six months or less to live. Additionally, you must sign a document in which you give up regular Medicare coverage for treatment of your terminal illness. Patients whose physical or mental condition prevents them from signing the document may be enrolled in hospice by the person who has power of attorney or other authority over the patient's health care decisions (see Chapter 10).

Switching to Another Hospice

It sometimes happens that you or your family are not comfortable with the hospice provider with whom you initially enroll. It may be that its service is not to your liking. Or you or a family member may have a personality conflict with one of the hospice staff. If for any reason you are unhappy with the hospice provider you first choose, you are allowed to switch at any time to another Medicare-approved hospice agency. However, you may make only one such switch during any period of care. If you leave hospice altogether but return to it for another period of care later on, you may choose a different hospice provider from any that you had before.

A Care Plan

Once you enroll with a particular hospice agency, the agency sets up a care plan for you. This involves agency consultations with your treating physicians about your condition. It also includes an assessment of the environment where you will receive care, including the physical facilities and the family or other caregivers who will be providing most of your day-to-day care. Most importantly, it includes extensive conversations with you, about your needs and wants, about what you do not need or want, and about things the hospice can make available to you.

Initially, there may be flurry of activity as you are visited by nurses, aides, counselors, social workers, and volunteers. The amount and frequency of continuing visits from these various agency staff depends on the plan the agency develops. It also depends on your continuing to make your needs and wishes known to the agency.

Your care plan is not set in stone. It can and should be adjusted as your needs change. Your comfort, especially relating to pain relief and symptom management, is the primary job of hospice. So, hospice should continually monitor your need for medication and other symptom relief and adjust it according to your changing condition. It should also monitor your living situation and provide supplemental care—such as housekeeping, help with diet, transportation, shopping and errand services—as needed.

Regular Periods of Evaluation

Hospice is available if you have received a prognosis of less than six months to live, but it is not provided on an open-ended basis for the entire six months. Instead, hospice is provided in segments. After an initial 90-day period the agency and your physician assess your condition and determine whether you still need hospice. This determination depends on whether your survival prognosis, as determined by your treating physician, remains six months or less. After a second 90-day hospice period, your treating physician makes another prognosis. After that, the periods are 60 days.

You May Leave Hospice and Return to It Later

After you have begun hospice care, your prognosis may change, you may again wish to try treating your disease, or you may no longer believe that you have less than six months to live. In any of these circumstances, you may want to give up hospice care and return to regular Medicare coverage and medical treatment. You may do so at any time. And leaving hospice does not affect your right to return to it later. Later, if you meet all the qualifying conditions, you may again choose hospice and receive its care under the same terms as if it were your first time.

There is no limit to the number of 60-day periods of hospice you may receive. Although hospice is intended to care for a patient for six months or less, a person's condition does not always follow this script. It is not unusual for patients to live well beyond their six-month prognosis. If that happens to someone who has already received six months of hospice care, hospice coverage continues. Continuing hospice care then depends only on the treating physician's continuing prognosis that the patient has less than six months to live. The treating physician reevaluates this prognosis every 60 days.

Payment for Hospice Care

One of the great advantages of hospice is that you get very intensive care for very little money. Medicare pays the hospice agency directly for almost the entire cost of your care. (Medicare can afford to do this because choosing hospice requires that you give up expensive treatments and hospitalizations associated with serious illnesses.) You are responsible for only two payments directly related to hospice:

• The hospice may charge you up to five dollars for each drug prescription or product you receive to help control your pain and other symptoms, or to otherwise make you comfortable.

• If you receive respite care as an inpatient in a hospice residential facility, hospital, or nursing facility, you are responsible for 5% of the amount Medicare pays for that inpatient care. So, for example, if Medicare pays the facility $200 per day for your inpatient respite care, you are responsible for ten dollars per day (5% x $200 = $10).

There may be several other costs during hospice. Most people with Medicare receive Part A (Hospital Insurance) coverage for free. But if you are someone who has to pay for Medicare Part A coverage, you must continue to pay for it while you receive hospice care. Likewise, if you receive Part A coverage through a Medicare Advantage managed care plan, you must continue to pay your premiums in order to maintain enrollment in Part A.

You will also probably want to keep up your Medicare Part B (Medical Insurance) coverage, whether through original Medicare or with a Medicare Advantage plan. Part B coverage helps pay for doctor visits and other outpatient care. You will still need this coverage while in hospice if you continue to receive medical care for conditions other than your terminal illness. Likewise, you may want to continue coverage under a private Medigap supplemental insurance plan, if you have it. This plan helps pay for the portions of Part B medical expenses which Medicare does not pay. Under either regular Part B coverage or a managed care plan, you will continue to be responsible for copayments and deductibles for any nonhospice care you receive.

Finally, you may want to continue paying for your Medicare Advantage managed care plan or for your Medigap insurance policy, in case you leave hospice care and return to regular Medicare coverage. If you give up your Medicare Advantage managed care plan or Medigap policy when you enter hospice, you may have a hard time regaining them when you return to regular Medicare coverage. ●

7

Medicare and Veterans Benefits

The cost of custodial care nursing facilities averages over $5,000 per month—with some costing more than $10,000 per month. And these amounts are increasing much faster than the general cost of living. Home health care, too, can cost many thousands of dollars a year if you need skilled or frequent services. Who pays for all this? For the most part, the answer is you—at least until almost all your money is gone, when Medicaid may begin to pay. (See Chapter 8.)

Many people believe—incorrectly—that Medicare covers nursing facility care. The truth is that Medicare pays only for short-term skilled nursing facility care, which amounts to only about 10% of all nursing facility costs nationwide. Medicare does not cover long-term nursing facility, assisted living, or other residential care. Medicare's coverage of home care is also extremely limited, paying only for short-term home health care while someone recovers from an illness, an injury, or surgery. Private long-term care insurance may pay some of the cost of nursing facility care, but even if you have such insurance, you may wind up having to pay much out of pocket. (See Chapter 9.)

Medicaid provides the only comprehensive coverage of long-term care. This federal government program for low-income people, administered by the states, pays for almost half the nation's total nursing facility costs and for much home care as well. But, as discussed later in Chapter 8, a person is not eligible for Medicaid coverage unless he or she has extremely low income and has used up almost all personal assets. In other words, if you have money saved when you begin long-term care, you must pay the bills yourself until your money is nearly gone; only then will Medicaid begin to pay.

There is no easy way out of this financial crunch. Once you actually need long-term care, the best way to protect your assets is to get only the services or level of care you really need from the most cost-efficient provider. (See Chapters 1 through 4.) But you should also be aware of how much and under what rules Medicare, the Department of Veterans Affairs (VA), and Medicaid may pay for long-term care, so that you can get the most from these programs. And, even long in advance of your need for long-term care, you may be able to take some steps to protect some of your assets. Long-term care insurance is one avenue to consider. (See Chapter 9.)

This chapter explains what coverage Medicare provides for nursing facility, home, and hospice care, and what assistance the VA provides—both direct care and monthly benefit payments—to certain veterans.

Medicare Coverage for Long-Term Care

Most Americans age 65 and older are eligible for Medicare coverage, but few understand how it works. Medicare is a federal government program created to assist older Americans with medical costs. The program is divided into two parts. Part A is "hospital insurance," which covers some of the bills for a stay in a hospital or a skilled nursing facility. Part B is "medical insurance," which pays some of the costs of doctors and outpatient medical care. If you are 65 or older and eligible for Social Security retirement, survivor's, or dependent's benefits, you are automatically eligible for Part A coverage. For a monthly premium, anyone 65 or older can enroll in Part B coverage, whether or not they are eligible for Part A.

Medicare Eligibility

Even people who are not eligible for Social Security benefits may be eligible for Part A Medicare when they reach age 65. For a complete discussion of Medicare eligibility, see *Social Security, Medicare & Government Pensions*, by Joseph Matthews with Dorothy Matthews Berman (Nolo).

One of the worst misconceptions about Medicare is that it covers nursing facility care. In fact, Medicare nursing facility coverage is severely limited, which means most people must pay for virtually all long-term care out of their own pockets.

Because home health care can be considerably cheaper than nursing facility care, it would seem sensible for the government to encourage home care by covering a sizable portion of the cost. Unfortunately, it does not. Medicare pays much less for home care than such logic might lead you to expect. And it pays nothing at all for custodial care in nursing facilities or other residential long-term care facilities.

It's important to know what long-term care Medicare pays for so you can get the most out of available coverage. But it's just as important to find out what Medicare does not pay for, so you can be prepared either to gather the funds elsewhere or obtain most of your care and coverage from other sources.

Skilled Nursing Facility Care

Part A of Medicare covers a small amount of skilled nursing facility care. Specifically, it pays for:

- up to 100 days per benefit period—that is, per continuous period of treatment—in a skilled nursing facility

- a semiprivate room (two to four beds); if you want a private room, you must pay the difference in cost yourself, unless the private room is medically necessary as prescribed by a doctor and approved by the facility and the Medicare intermediary—an insurance company that administers Medicare funds in your state

- daily, regular, skilled, and special nursing as medically necessary, but *not* a private-duty nurse

- skilled rehabilitation services—such as physical, occupational, or speech therapy—if medically necessary, as long as you are showing improvement, and
- medications, medical supplies and equipment, and dietary requirements as supplied by the facility.

What Isn't Covered by Medicare Part A

Medicare part A does not cover:

- custodial care (nonmedical assistance with normal daily activities such as eating and bathing), unless it is part of skilled nursing care in a skilled nursing facility
- nursing care or therapy provided in a facility that is not certified by Medicare as a *skilled* nursing facility, or
- doctor's care while you are in a nursing facility. However, Medicare Part B Medical Insurance covers doctor's care in a nursing facility under the same terms as any other medical care.

Requirements for Coverage

Unfortunately, Medicare's conditions for coverage of nursing facility costs eliminate far more types of care than they cover. When you also consider that Medicare partially pays for only 100 days of care in total, it is easy to understand why Medicare covers only about 10% of all nursing facility costs.

Here are some Medicare coverage requirements:

- **Immediate prior hospital stay.** Medicare pays for your stay in a skilled nursing facility only if you have first spent at least three consecutive days (not counting the discharge day) in a hospital. You must be admitted to the nursing facility within 30 days of your discharge from the hospital.

- **Daily skilled nursing care or therapy.** Medicare pays only for the skilled nursing care or rehabilitative therapy you need and receive every day. If you receive such care intermittently, you do not qualify for Medicare coverage.

- **Prescribed by a physician.** Your daily skilled nursing care or therapy must be "medically necessary"—that is, it has to be specifically prescribed by a doctor.

- **Medicare-approved skilled nursing facility.** You must receive care in a *skilled* nursing facility certified by Medicare. Medicare checks on the quality of care in each nursing facility and certifies only those that meet its standards. Ask to see the current Medicare certification documents of any nursing facility you are considering. Medicare also won't cover care that is, or could be, received in a lower-level facility.

- **Only while condition "improving."** Even though Medicare covers up to 100 days in a skilled nursing facility, and even though you may need daily skilled care for each of those days, Medicare will cover you only as long as your condition is "improving." Once Medicare determines, after a review, that your condition has stabilized, it will no longer pay for skilled nursing facility care—no matter how serious your condition remains or how much skilled nursing care you continue to need.

- **Approval on review.** Even if your doctor prescribes "medically necessary" skilled nursing care for you in a skilled nursing facility and continues to certify that your condition is improving, this does not guarantee that Medicare will provide nursing facility coverage. The doctor's opinion must be approved by both the nursing facility's utilization review committee—facility doctors who review patient conditions—and by the Medicare "intermediary."

How Much Medicare Pays

During the first 100 days of coverage, Medicare covers these amounts for skilled nursing facility care:

- **Days 1 to 20.** You are responsible for paying up to your yearly Medicare Part A deductible, if you have not already reached it. Once you have paid the yearly deductible, Medicare pays all your covered nursing facility charges.

- **Days 21 to 100.** After the first 20 days of coverage, Medicare pays all covered charges except what is called a "coinsurance" amount, for which you are personally responsible. In 2012, that coinsurance amount was $144.50 per day; the figure goes up slightly each year.

- **Days 101 on.** After 100 days in a skilled nursing facility, you are on your own. Medicare pays nothing toward your stay there.

Home Health Care

Although Medicare coverage for home care is extremely limited, it does provide substantial payment for the most expensive part of home care—skilled nursing or therapy—during the time immediately after an illness or injury, when you are most likely to need it.

Services Covered by Medicare

The home health care services Medicare covers are listed below, limited by the conditions discussed in the following section:

- skilled nursing
- physical and speech therapy as needed during recovery while your condition is improving, and
- supplemental care. If (and only if) you receive skilled nursing or physical or speech therapy, Medicare may also pay for limited visits by a home health care aide to help you with personal care—usually only if there is no one else at home to help. Medicare may also

cover required medical social services, some medical supplies or equipment provided by the home care agency, and the services of an occupational therapist to help you relearn daily household tasks.

What's Not Covered

Medicare home health care does not cover custodial personal care, drugs, meals, or homemaking services.

Restrictions on Coverage

As with nursing facility care, a number of restrictions limit home health care coverage. Medicare covers care only during periods of recovery from acute illness or injury or following a change in condition while you are learning how to administer drugs or otherwise care for yourself.

To qualify for Medicare coverage, your care must be:

- **For a part-time need for skilled care.** It must be "medically necessary" for you to receive skilled nursing care or rehabilitative therapy on a part-time-only basis. Full-time nursing care at home is not covered. Note that this is the opposite of the requirement for covered care in a skilled nursing facility.

- **Doctor prescribed.** A physician must have ordered the skilled care.

- **Only during recovery.** Care is covered only while you are recovering —that is, while your condition is improving. As soon as your condition has stabilized, as determined by a Medicare review, coverage ends.

Medicare Pays for Hospice Care at Home

Medicare's coverage of home health care is limited in several ways. Most significantly, it is available only while a patient is recovering from an illness or injury. Once the patient is stabilized, Medicare no longer pays for home care, even if the person now needs care on a long-term basis.

Medicare also has hospice coverage, however, which provides home care for someone who is not recovering. In fact, hospice home care has the opposite requirement from regular Medicare home care coverage—for Medicare hospice coverage, the patient must have been diagnosed with a terminal illness and be expected to live only another six months or less.

If someone is eligible for hospice, they can receive extensive care at minimal cost. Hospice can offer home care for people who otherwise might not be able to afford it and allows some people to leave a hospital or nursing facility so they can be cared for at home. It also offers respite care, which gives a patient's relatives or other caregivers a break from their responsibilities. For a complete discussion of hospice, see Chapter 6.

- **For an injury, illness, or a medical condition.** Your need for care must be the result of a specific injury, illness, or medical condition. If you need home care because of general frailty, Medicare will not pay for it.

- **While you are confined to home.** Care is covered only while you are confined to home (except for brief, infrequent occasions out, usually related to receiving medical care). Medicare considers you to be "confined to home" if you are unable to leave home without difficulty and without the assistance of another person or a medical device such as a wheelchair. Confined to home does not necessarily mean bedridden, however.

- **Provide by an approved agency.** Care must be provided by a Medicare-certified home care agency or other provider. This sometimes eliminates independent nurses and therapists. Always ask the home care agency or other provider to show you its Medicare certification documentation before beginning care.

How Much Medicare Pays

In general, Medicare pays 100% of the "approved costs" of covered services provided by a certified home care agency or other provider. "Approved costs" are the standardized charges Medicare decides are appropriate for specific services, based on a national cost average. You are personally responsible for the cost of any services that aren't covered, such as homemaking or unapproved personal care from a home care aide.

No matter what the home care provider might normally charge for the covered services, it must accept as payment in full whatever Medicare decides is the approved cost. The home care agency will submit all bills for covered services directly to Medicare. You don't have to be involved in the paperwork.

In some situations, it may not be clear whether Medicare will cover a particular service. In that case, the home care agency or other provider must notify you of the problem, in writing, before it provides the service. If it notifies you of a problem and you accept the service anyway, you are personally responsible for the bill if Medicare denies coverage. If it does not notify you in advance, the provider cannot bill you.

Long-Term Care Coverage by HMOs and Medigap Insurance

Many people have private health insurance that supplements their Medicare coverage, commonly called Medigap. Many others get supplemental coverage through membership in an HMO or other managed care plan. Most Medigap and managed care plans cover no more of nursing facility or home health care costs than Medicare. If Medicare does not cover it, a Medigap policy or managed care plan usually does not cover it either. And Medigap or managed care payments plus Medicare's payments may still leave some part of the bills unpaid—even for covered care.

A few managed care plans offer extra home care and nursing care coverage beyond what Medicare covers. This coverage is not for long-term care, but it may pay for a few extra weeks. Given the cost of nursing facility and home care, even a few extra weeks of coverage is worth collecting.

Veterans Benefits for Long-Term Care

The Department of Veterans Affairs (VA) provides two different types of long-term care support for certain veterans, and some assistance to surviving spouses. First, the VA offers direct care in its own facilities or through its own care programs. This includes nursing home residence, community residential care, home health care and personal home care, and hospice. Second, the VA provides money—monthly benefit payments, grants, and loans—to help support certain veterans with disabilities and low-income surviving spouses.

Direct Long-Term Care From the VA

For many veterans, the VA provides space in its nursing homes and community residential facilities, as well as long-term "extended care" in a veteran's home.

Eligibility for Direct Long-Term Care

Eligibility for direct long-term care from the VA depends on a combination of the veteran's physical condition, the source of any disability (service connected or not), and financial position. Among those eligible for VA nursing home or other extended care, depending on their care needs, are veterans:

- with service-connected disability ratings (or combined disability ratings) of 70% or higher
- who have service-connected disability ratings of "permanent and totally disabled"
- with 60% service-connected disability ratings who are unemployable
- with service-connected disabilities that result in the need for nursing home care, as determined by VA physicians, or
- who require nursing home care for any disability (not service connected) and who have very low income and few assets.

Other veterans may also be eligible for nursing home and other long-term care, determined a case-by-case basis, with priority given to those with service-connected disabilities and those who need care for post-acute rehabilitation, spinal cord injury, or hospice.

For more information about eligibility for VA nursing home and other extended care programs, contact the VA's Office of Geriatrics and Extended Care at www.va.gov/geriatrics or toll-free by phone at 800-827-1000.

Nursing Home Residence Through the VA

The VA provides long-term nursing home care through various types of facilities. The VA operates its own nursing homes, and it contracts with private nursing homes (called "community nursing homes") to care for veterans when no VA facility is available in the area. The VA can also pay a portion of the cost of residence in state veterans homes for veterans who aren't eligible for care in a VA nursing home. A veteran can qualify for residence in a VA or community nursing home only if VA physicians certify that he or she has a physical or mental impairment serious enough to require nursing home-level care.

VA Community Living Centers and Residential Care Program

In addition to nursing homes, the VA also operates what it calls Community Living Centers. These provide a combination of short-term residential and ongoing community care for veterans with chronic conditions, including Alzheimer's and other dementia. The centers can also accommodate veterans who need rehabilitation following an acute health episode, or short-term services, such as respite care or intravenous therapy. The centers also provide hospice and other palliative care at the end of life. Care from a Community Living Center is usually limited to no more than 100 days, though a center can provide longer-term care for veterans who require lengthy rehabilitation or are unable to obtain a place in a VA or community nursing home and lack a clinically appropriate alternative.

Community Residential Care is another long-term residential program from the VA. It provides room and board, plus some personal care assistance, for veterans who do not require nursing home care but who are not able to live independently and who do not have family able to provide the needed care.

VA Home Care and Other Nonresidential Community Care

The VA operates home care and other long-term nonresidential care programs for veterans who do not need nursing home-level care or who are able to live at home if they receive regular assistance with the activities of daily living. Based on the veteran's needs, as determined by a Geriatric Evaluation and Management team from the VA, the veteran can receive:

- **Home health care.** This is long-term nursing and other basic medical care, provided to chronically ill veterans in their own homes.

- **Homemaker/home health aide services.** These are personal care, minor health-related assistance, and limited homemaking services provided by a home care agency and paid for by the VA.

- **Adult day health care.** These programs provide meals, companionship and activities, supervision, health maintenance, and some rehabilitative services in a group setting during daytime hours, either at the VA's own or a community facility.

- **Hospice/Palliative Care.** This is pain relief and other comfort-oriented care, along with supportive services, for veterans in the end-of-life stages of an incurable disease. It can include respite care, which allows for short-term inpatient care for the veteran in a VA hospital or nursing facility, which gives temporary relief from care responsibilities to the veteran's spouse or other caregiver.

There may be some costs to a veteran for extended care services, with copayments for some programs and services of up to $100 per day, though usually the cost is much less. The copayment amount depends on the type and expected length of the care or service provided, the veteran's VA health system priority group, and the veteran's income and other personal finances. To learn more about how these copayments are calculated, see the VA's Web page Determine the Cost of Care at www. va.gov/healthbenefits/cost.

How to Apply for VA Extended Care Coverage

To apply for a place in a VA nursing home or for other long-term care, a veteran fills out the Application for Extended Care Services (Form VAF 10-10EC), which can be found at www.va.gov/vaforms. Veterans who are already receiving VA compensation or VA medical treatment for a service-connected disability need not file this separate application.

If you need help with this application, or with any VA-related question, you can contact your local VA Vet Center or Veterans Benefits Administration office. To find the center or office nearest you, visit the Department of Veterans Affairs website at www2.va.gov/directory/guide/home.asp or phone the VA toll-free at 800-827-1000.

VA Payments to Veterans and Survivors Who Need Care

The VA has a number of programs that can provide direct financial support to a veteran, his or her spouse, and survivors. Even if a veteran did not claim—or was denied—benefits based on medical condition in the years immediately following service, his or her advanced age, deteriorated physical condition, or low income might now make him or her eligible for financial aid.

Service-Connected Disability Compensation

Many VA benefits are payable only if a veteran has a service-connected disability. Officially, a "disability" means a physical, mental, or emotional condition that limits or prevents a veteran from performing some normal, everyday activities. "Service-connected" means the condition first occurred when the veteran was in the military, though the condition did not have to actually disable the veteran during the time he or she was in the military. This last part of the rule, about when the condition became disabling, can be very important to many veterans. That's because a condition that began decades before in the military might only become disabling as the veteran ages. If so, the veteran may qualify for service-connected disability benefits even though the condition has only recently become disabling.

Any veteran who has a service-connected disability may be eligible for a monthly disability compensation payment. When a veteran applies for disability payments, the VA examines the veteran's medical history and current condition, then assigns his or her condition a rating, with the lowest rating (least disabled) being a 10% disability and moving up in severity in 10% increments. The amount of monthly compensation received depends on the disability rating:

- The lowest rating (10% disability) pays slightly over $100 per month.
- The highest rating (100% disabled) pays over $2,500 per month.
- A veteran who is housebound or needs regular in-home care (called "aid and attendance") can receive an additional monthly payment.
- If an older veteran has a 30% or higher rating, his or her spouse is also eligible for benefits.

VA Pension for Older, Wartime Service Low-Income Veterans

A veteran may be eligible for a monthly VA pension if he or she:

- is at least 65 years old
- has a low income
- had 90 days or more of active military service, and
- at least one day of active service was during a "period of war" (which is defined as World Wars I and II, the Korean War, the Vietnam War, and the Persian Gulf War), though the veteran need *not* have been in actual combat.

The amount of a VA pension depends on the veteran's financial need. It can be over $900 per month for an individual and over $1,200 per month for a couple. If the veteran is permanently housebound, the monthly individual benefits could be over $1,100 per month. If the veteran needs regular in-home assistance, the individual pension may be over $1,500 per month, with more for a spouse.

VA Grants to Modify a Home or Car

The VA offers veterans with a service-connected disability Specially Adapted Housing Grants to help pay to modify homes, adapting them to help compensate for physical limitations. The grants may also be available even if the veteran does not own the home he or she lives in. A similar grant is available for some veterans to modify their cars.

VA Benefits for a Veteran's Surviving Family Members

The VA makes several benefits available to a deceased veteran's surviving spouse. There are also benefits for the surviving, low-income parents of certain veterans. These survivors benefits are described here.

Death pension for surviving spouse. A veteran's spouse with very low income may qualify for a pension, but only if he or she did not remarry after the veteran's death. The veteran must have had at least 90 days of active military service, with at least one day during a period of war. The pension is small, only going up to slightly over $600 per month; the actual amount depends on financial need. The amount can be slightly higher if the surviving spouse is housebound or needs regular in-home assistance.

Dependency and Indemnity Compensation (DIC) for surviving spouse and low-income parents. The surviving spouses of certain veterans are entitled to DIC pensions of at least $1,000 a month, and up to more than $2,000. DIC is also available to a veteran's surviving parents if they have very low income. For a survivor to qualify for DIC, the deceased veteran must have:

- died while on active duty

• died from an injury or disease incurred while on active duty or on inactive duty training, or

• had a 100%-rated service-connected disability for at least ten years prior to death, or for at least five years from the date of discharge from the military to the date of death.

Applying for VA Benefit Payments

The simplest way to get more information about VA pensions and other cash benefits is to visit the VA's website www.va.gov or call the VA toll-free at 800-827-1000. Advisers there can answer questions, direct you to a local VA office, and even start a benefits application for you. You can start an application for some benefits directly online at the VA website's online application page at www.va.gov/onlineapps.htm. Or you can get help from a VA benefits counselor in person at a local VA benefits office. To find a veterans benefits office near you, go the VA website's office locator page at www2.va.gov/directory/guide/home.asp or phone them toll-free at 800-827-1000. ●

Medicaid Coverage for Long-Term Care

Medicaid (called Medi-Cal in California) is a federally funded program, administered by the individual states, that helps pay for medical care for financially needy people. For low-income older people who qualify, Medicaid supplements Medicare to cover many of the costs of long-term care—including home care and almost all types of long-term residential facility care for an unlimited time. The Medicaid program pays for about half of the country's total nursing facility costs.

To qualify for Medicaid, an elder must have a low income and very few assets. Unfortunately, this means that many people are not eligible until they have spent almost all their savings paying for residential facility or home care themselves. Medicaid allows you to keep more assets if one spouse remains at home while the other lives in a long-term care facility.

Because Medicaid pays a lower rate than that charged to privately paying residents, some facilities either do not accept Medicaid residents or put them in less desirable rooms. So, if you are dependent on Medicaid when you look for a long-term care facility, your choices may be limited. If you become eligible for Medicaid after you are a resident (because your funds diminish), the facility is legally prohibited from discharging you, but it might move you to a different room. Before choosing any long-term care facility, find out the details of its Medicaid policy.

Eligibility for Medicaid

Each state has its own Medicaid eligibility standards—check with your county's social services agency to get the rules for your state. Federal government standards require your assets and income to be below certain levels (with special rules for nursing facility residents). These rules differ greatly for married couples and unmarried individuals. Medicaid defines the term unmarried to include divorced people and widows or widowers.

Help From SHIP

Every state has a State Health Insurance Assistance Program (SHIP) which provides free assistance for people trying to qualify for Medicaid. The state program may go by one of several different names—SHIP, Health Insurance Counseling and Advocacy Program (HICAP), Senior Health Insurance Benefits Advisors (SHIBA), or the like. Whatever the name, the program provides free counseling to seniors about Medicaid and related long-term care and medical coverage matters. SHIP's trained staff can counsel you about your state's Medicaid eligibility standards—and the documents you need to prove your eligibility. To find the SHIP office nearest you, visit the website of the National SHIP Resource Center at www.shiptalk.org or phone the Eldercare Locator at 800-677-1116.

Home Care: Income and Asset Limits

You are eligible for Medicaid assistance for care you receive in your home only if your income and assets (such as savings, investments, and property) fall within guidelines established by the federal government. Some states have stricter rules—and some are more liberal. To find out your state's income and asset limits, contact your local county's department of social services or welfare department.

Income Limits

Medicaid figures out your income by adding up the money you receive from Social Security and other government benefit programs, wages or self-employment income, interest and dividends from savings or investments, rents, royalties, pensions, annuities, and gifts. If one spouse in a couple is still working and earning income, about half of that money does not count against the other spouse—that is, Medicaid will not

A Note on Financial Planning

As discussed below, Medicaid is a program intended to help people who have low income and few assets. Its rules severely restrict how much of your savings you can keep and still be eligible for coverage. These rules also prevent people from getting around the eligibility requirements by simply moving their money around.

However, a few options are available to people who are likely to need Medicaid coverage for long-term care but have slightly too many assets to qualify for Medicaid—or who want to try to keep at least some of their assets to pass on to their survivors. This usually requires advance planning, and the older person may have to give up control over some assets. Even with these drawbacks, however, you should consider whether one or more of these options might work for you—and what you need to do now to plan for the future. (See "Strategies to Protect Your Assets," later in this chapter.)

consider about half of the working spouse's income when figuring out the income of the other spouse.

Once your income is tallied, states use the total in one of two ways to decide whether you are eligible for home care coverage. Some states offer Medicaid only to those who qualify as "categorically needy." This term simply means that your income and assets, without considering your medical bills, are low enough that you fit into the "category" of people eligible for Medicaid. A person whose actual monthly income is less than $800 to $1,500 may qualify for home care coverage under this type of system. For married couples, the income limit is higher—roughly $1,200 to $1,600 per month. Because state rules vary—and because they can be quite complicated—you should apply for coverage even if your income exceeds these figures by a small amount. (See "Finding Out About Medicaid in Your State," below.)

Other states provide Medicaid home care coverage to those who qualify as "medically needy." This category includes a person whose income is over the state's general Medicaid eligibility limit, but whose medical expenses would reduce his or her income below that limit (subtracting medical expenses from income in this way is referred to as "spending down"). This type of system is more generous to people who have high medical expenses.

Even with the two ways of measuring Medicaid eligibility, there is considerable variation in the rules from state to state. If you have few cash assets and income of less than $1,500 per month, or you have income over that amount but are facing home care bills that would leave you with less than $1,500 per month income to spend on other things, you should apply for Medicaid coverage in your state.

Asset Limits

People who live at home, rather than in a long-term care facility, may have nonexempt assets worth no more than $2,000 ($3,000 for a couple). These figures vary a bit from state to state. Also, some states permit people to qualify for Medicaid home care services if paying their medical expenses themselves would force them to spend their assets down to a level below these eligibility limits. You must check with your local county social services office to find out the specific limits in your state, and whether they have spend-down rules regarding eligibility for home care.

Fortunately, a number of assets are exempted from these eligibility figures—that is, their value doesn't count toward the eligibility limits. These exempt assets are:

• a car (up to a certain value limit, in some states)

• furniture and other household goods

• personal effects

- your home of any value, if you and your spouse, or you and a minor, blind, or disabled child live in it, and

- your home, if you live in it alone (or with someone other than your spouse or minor, blind, or disabled child), if your equity in the home is $500,000 or less. In some states, this equity limit goes as high as $750,000. If your equity in your home exceeds your state's limit, you are not eligible for Medicaid coverage of home care.

How to Calculate Income and Assets

Medicaid has a number of rules for deciding which assets and income to consider in determining eligibility:

- The assets and income of children, grandchildren, or other relatives do not count toward Medicaid limits, even if they live in the same household as the elder applying for Medicaid—unless they provide regular financial support to the elder. Regular financial support is not limited to money but can include food and clothing or other personal items.

- If a married couple live together, both of their incomes and assets are counted toward the Medicaid limits (except as explained in "Income Limits," above).

- If a couple is divorced or legally separated and living apart, only the income and assets of the spouse applying for Medicaid are counted, including any actual support received from the other spouse.

- If an unmarried couple lives together, only the income and assets of the person applying for Medicaid are counted, including any direct financial support received from the other partner.

Paying Family Caregivers

Family members do most of the work for people who are cared for at home, even if there is also paid home care help. There are two circumstances in which you may be able to pay a family caregiver for that work, while you continue to qualify for Medicaid coverage of home care:

- If you would like to qualify for Medicaid home care coverage but have slightly too many assets, you may want to consider paying that family caregiver for his or her work, in addition to what you pay to nonfamily caregivers, if any. This would not only give the family member some pay, but over time, the money you use for that pay can reduce your assets down to the qualifying levels for Medicaid coverage of home care, meaning that you could get Medicaid to pay for additional home care help. To ensure that Medicaid considers this pay to a family member as legitimate, you should carefully follow several steps:

  1. Call around—to other people getting care, and to local home care agencies to find out how much their aides are paid for the exact same kind of work your family member performs for you.

  2. Draw up a simple written agreement—it doesn't need to be in any special form or require any legal lingo—that specifies the work your family member is to do, how often, and how much the pay will be (in line with what you've found out about the normal rate of caregiver pay where you live). You should both sign and date the agreement (sometimes referred to as a "caregiver contract" or "personal care contract").

  3. Pay the family member by check, keeping an ongoing record of how much time he or she works and how much you pay.

- Once you qualify for Medicaid coverage of home care, find out from your Medicaid caseworker whether your state has a program in which Medicaid pays your family caregiver. These programs are often called Cash and Counseling, but sometimes have other names. If your state's Medicaid program does have one of these family caregiver payment programs, don't expect it to pay a lot—both the pay rate and the number of hours will be limited. Still, it's nice to have a family caregiver getting paid for work that someone else might otherwise do, or that the family member would do for free.

Medicaid May Pay for Assisted Living

In many states, Medicaid or a Medicaid-related program may pay part of the cost of assisted living for some Medicaid-eligible residents. Usually covered through a program called Home and Community Based Services (HCBS), these payments usually cover only the cost of personal care services provided in the facility, not the full cost of residence. However, some programs also limit the total amount the facility can charge a resident. In some states, eligibility is open to anyone who qualifies for Medicaid benefits and needs assisted living care. In other states, however, eligibility is limited to those whose condition would otherwise qualify them for nursing facility care.

For a complete discussion of assisted living as an alternative to nursing facility care, see Chapter 3. To find out whether Medicaid covers assisted living in your state, see "Finding Out About Medicaid in Your State," later in this chapter.

Income and Asset Rules for Long-Term Care Facilities

Once a resident of a Medicaid-certified long-term care facility has qualified, Medicaid pays virtually all facility costs for as long as a person remains there. But as with home care, a long-term care facility resident is only eligible when his or her assets are below a certain level. Until then, the resident must pay. Once Medicaid begins paying, almost all of an individual's and much of a couple's income will go to the facility to reduce the amounts Medicaid pays.

Because Medicaid rules for long-term facility residents are quite different for unmarried individuals and married couples, this section is divided in two parts. The first section explains the income and assets that a single person who enters a long-term care facility can retain. The second section explains the income and assets that each member of a married couple can retain when one spouse enters a long-term care facility.

Unmarried Individuals

Keep in mind that for Medicaid purposes, "unmarried" includes a person who is divorced or whose spouse has died. Also, the federal government does not recognize the marriage or domestic partnership of same-sex couples. So, even if you have legally married your same-sex partner in your state, or a foreign country, Medicare still considers you to be unmarried.

If your marital status changes after you qualify for Medicaid, the Medicaid limits on your income and assets will also change.

Income Eligibility Limits

About 30 states have no limits at all on the income an unmarried long-term care facility resident can have and still be eligible for Medicaid coverage. However, as discussed below, the resident will have to pay virtually all of that income to the nursing facility, with Medicaid paying the balance of the cost.

The rest of the states have eligibility income limits, which vary from about $500 to the low $2,000s per month. An unmarried long-term care facility resident in one of these states whose income is over the limit does not qualify for Medicaid coverage at all.

To find out about your state's eligibility rules, contact your local social services or welfare office (see "Finding Out About Medicaid in Your State," below).

Income Retained by the Resident

If an unmarried long-term care facility resident qualifies for Medicaid, all of that person's monthly income will go to the facility (and Medicaid will pay the balance of the bill), except:

- a small monthly amount for personal needs—books and magazines, grooming, and toilet articles—ranging from $30 to $70, depending on the state

- any income the resident spends directly on Medicare premiums, deductibles, and copayments, medical insurance, and out-of-pocket medical expenses not covered by Medicare or Medicaid, and

- in about 30 states, $150 to $600 a month for upkeep and repairs on the resident's private home; this home maintenance allowance continues for up to six months if the resident's doctor gives a written prognosis that the resident is expected to be able to return home within six months after entering the facility.

Asset Eligibility Limits

Medicaid will cover an unmarried person's stay in a long-term care facility only if that person's savings and other assets are below certain limits. If your assets exceed these limits, you will qualify for Medicaid coverage only after you have paid enough for facility coverage out of your own pocket—referred to by Medicaid as "spending down"—to reach these limits. Medicaid asset limits are:

- no more than $2,000 in savings or other liquid assets, such as stocks or certificates of deposit (this limit varies slightly from state to state)

- household and personal items, usually limited to several thousand dollars in value

- one automobile, up to a certain value limit, in some states

- one wedding and one engagement ring of any value

- a burial plot and up to $1,500 in a separately maintained fund for burial costs

- a life insurance policy with a face value of no more than $1,500, and

- a home, under limited circumstances. Some states won't count your home in determining Medicaid eligibility for long-term care facility coverage if you indicate on your long-term care facility admissions

How Does Medicaid Know What Assets You Own?

A natural question arises when people read that Medicaid coverage is available only to people whose assets are below certain levels: How does Medicaid know what my assets are?

The answer is that Medicaid workers ask you—and examine your financial records. When you apply for Medicaid, you must fill out extensive application forms that ask you to list all of your assets. You must also show the Medicaid eligibility workers copies of all ownership documents, bankbooks, and the like. If there are any large or regular withdrawals from your assets in the 60 months prior to your application, you will have to show where that money went and why. (See "Medicaid Rules on Transfer of Assets," below.) Remember, too, that Medicaid will have your Social Security number, so it can cross-check many financial transactions. Medicaid eligibility workers can also pay home visits.

If you fail to report income or assets and are caught by Medicaid, you run the risk of being denied coverage, being forced to repay any money already paid on your behalf, and even getting hit with additional penalties and fines.

form that you intend to return home, and your doctor certifies in writing that you are likely to recover sufficiently to eventually leave the facility and return home. Some states also add a six-month or 12-month time limit. However, if your equity in your home is over $500,000 (up to $750,000 in some states), you will not be eligible at all for Medicaid even if you and your doctor certify that you will return home to live.

Even if your state's Medicaid program allows you to keep certain assets while you live in a long-term care facility, that won't protect your assets after you die. Medicaid may seek reimbursement from any of your remaining assets for payments it made on your behalf (see "Medicaid Will Seek Reimbursement," at the end of this section).

Note that Medicaid rules do not permit you to simply give away assets to relatives or friends and then qualify for coverage. The few permissible methods to protect some assets are discussed in detail later in this chapter.

Married Couples With One Spouse in a Long-Term Care Facility

While many states do not set income limits for unmarried people entering a long-term care facility, different rules apply to married couples.

Whose Income Counts for Eligibility?

Most states use a "name-on-the-check" rule to determine whether income received by a married couple is counted against the Medicaid eligibility of the spouse in the long-term care facility. This rule basically says that if the income is received solely in the name of the at-home spouse, it is not counted toward the state's maximum income limit for the facility spouse's Medicaid eligibility.

Two states—California and Washington—have "community property" rules that can help a facility resident spouse qualify for Medicaid coverage even though the name-on-the-check rule would deny eligibility. If the facility resident spouse in a community property state receives income in his or her name that is over the state's Medicaid limit, Medicaid will look at the at-home spouse's income as well. If one-half the total community property income (the combined income of both spouses) is not over the limit, then the facility resident spouse will qualify for Medicaid.

Three other states—Indiana, Nebraska, and West Virginia—also count the at-home spouse's income over certain limits as part of the facility resident spouse's income when calculating eligibility.

Income Retained by Each Spouse

Of income received in his or her own name, the facility resident spouse may keep between $30 and $70 per month for personal use, plus amounts to pay for Medicare, other medical insurance, and medical expenses not covered by Medicare or Medicaid. The rest of the facility resident spouse's income goes to the facility, except for any amount necessary to give the at-home spouse a minimum allowance.

The at-home spouse is allowed to keep all income in his or her own name. If more than half the couple's joint income is in the facility resident spouse's name, the at-home spouse is allowed to keep some of that income up to a basic living allowance of between $1,839 and $2,841 (in 2012; higher in Alaska and Hawaii), when combined with the at-home spouse's own income. The specific amount varies from state to state and goes up every year. Some states also have an additional monthly allowance of $500 to $600 specifically for housing costs. Check with your local social services agency to find out your state's limits.

Assets Retained by Both Spouses

The name-on-the-check rule does not apply to assets—savings, property, and investments, for example. Formerly, if a couple transferred all their assets to the sole name of the at-home spouse, the facility resident spouse might qualify for Medicaid. No longer. Medicaid now looks at the combined assets of both spouses, regardless of whose name is on the asset. The combined assets a couple may retain and still qualify for Medicaid coverage of the facility resident spouse are:

- the home in which the at-home spouse lives, regardless of its value
- a "community spouse resource amount" equal to one-half the value of the couple's nonexempt liquid assets (such as cash, bank accounts, and bonds) for the at-home spouse to use, in an amount between $22,728 and $113,640 (in 2012)—the maximum amount varies from state to state and both amounts increase yearly with the cost of living
- one automobile, regardless of its value
- furniture and household goods, regardless of value
- one wedding and engagement ring each, regardless of value
- life insurance with cash value of $1,500 for each spouse, and
- two burial plots and a separate savings account of up to $1,500 per person for burial costs.

You should establish the total value of your assets through bank records or other documentation when the facility resident spouse enters a facility, so that you can claim and retain everything to which you are entitled.

Medicaid Will Seek Reimbursement

A Medicaid recipient and his or her spouse may retain a certain amount of assets—including a home of any value if at least one of them lives in it—while Medicaid pays for long-term care. However, Medicaid has a right to seek reimbursement from the property of the Medicaid recipient for everything Medicaid spends on long-term care after the recipient turns age 55.

Medicaid cannot force the sale of a home while either a spouse, or a minor or disabled child, lives in it. But it can seek reimbursement from the estate of the Medicaid recipient once the recipient and his or her spouse have both died. Those who take title to the property after the second spouse's death must either pay off the Medicaid amount or sell the property and have Medicaid collect its reimbursement out of the proceeds of the sale.

However, with some advance planning, it may be possible to protect the value of the property from some of Medicaid's reimbursement right. (See "Strategies to Protect Your Assets," below.)

What Medicaid Pays For

What Medicaid covers and how much it pays varies by state. In some states, Medicaid charges additional fees such as:

- **An enrollment fee.** Some states charge a small, one-time-only fee of a few dollars when you first enroll in Medicaid.

- **A monthly premium.** States are allowed to charge a small fee to "medically needy" Medicaid participants—those who would not normally qualify because of their income or assets, but who become eligible because paying their medical bills would drop their income or assets below the eligibility levels. The amounts of these premiums vary but are usually only a few dollars a month.

- **Copayments.** States may charge a copayment—as Medicare does for the first few days of nursing facility care—which is a fixed amount for each covered service you receive. States can only charge those who qualify for Medicaid as "medically needy" (see above) or receive "optional" services (those the state program decides to cover, even though federal law doesn't require it).

In general, though, Medicaid pays for extensive home care and the full cost of long-term facility care as long as either is necessary.

Medicaid-Certified Providers Only

Medicaid pays only for covered services performed by a Medicaid-certified provider. Some home care agencies and long-term care facilities do not meet Medicaid quality standards and therefore are not certified to participate in the program. Also, because Medicaid pays less than what agencies or facilities charge private consumers, some providers choose not to participate in the Medicaid program. However, once a facility has accepted a resident who pays privately, it must allow that resident to remain if the resident switches to Medicaid coverage. Finally, many individual home care providers choose not to seek Medicaid certification because they want to be paid in cash.

It is important to find out whether a facility, agency, or individual care provider participates in Medicaid before you obtain service. This is particularly true for long-term care facilities. Even if you are not initially dependent on Medicaid, you should find out the facility's policy on Medicaid patients. Some facilities maintain different, less desirable rooms for Medicaid patients. Switching to Medicaid later may affect the quality of care you receive.

Facility Must Keep You If You Begin Medicaid Coverage

Many people enter a long-term care facility as privately paying residents, but later run out of money and become eligible for Medicaid. Because Medicaid pays less than the facility could charge a privately paying resident, a facility might prefer to move out those who become eligible for Medicaid and move in waiting residents who can pay their own way. But federal law forbids that.

Facilities that participate in the Medicaid program may not discharge a resident who becomes eligible for Medicaid. A facility may not avoid this law by withdrawing from the Medicaid program. No one who resided in a facility while the facility participated in the Medicaid program may be discharged if he or she later becomes eligible for Medicaid, even if the facility drops out of the Medicaid program.

The only people not covered by these legal protections are residents of facilities that never participated in Medicaid, or people who move into a facility after it has dropped out of the Medicaid program.

Home Care Coverage

Medicaid does not usually have stringent rules about either the kind or duration of home care services it covers. This is very different from Medicare, which has strict limitations on home care coverage. In most states, Medicaid pays most of a certified home care agency's reasonable costs, even if care is primarily custodial, and covers many services by nonagency providers (as long as they are Medicaid-certified). In some states, Medicaid also pays for extra-duty nursing, rehabilitation therapies provided outside the home, prescribed medications, and medical supplies. To find out whether Medicaid covers a particular service in your state, check with both the provider of the service and your local social service office.

If Medicaid covers a service and the provider accepts payment from Medicaid, the provider cannot then charge you for any amounts over that payment. But, of course, the provider can and will charge you for services not covered by Medicaid.

Long-Term Care Facility Coverage

Medicaid, unlike Medicare, can be a lifesaver when it comes to long-term care facility bills. In general, Medicaid pays for all levels of care in certified facilities for an indefinite period of time.

Levels of Care Covered

In all states, Medicaid covers residence in certified skilled nursing facilities. Unlike Medicare, however, this coverage does not require a prior hospital stay.

Also, unlike Medicare, Medicaid covers the full cost of long-term residence in custodial care nursing homes. This means that Medicaid covers the situation that most commonly exhausts a family's savings: a long-term stay in a custodial care facility where the resident receives primarily nonmedical personal care. Be aware, however, that not all nursing homes accept Medicaid payment for their residents. And many nursing homes that accept Medicaid-paid residents do so only for a limited number of their beds.

Medicaid covers residence in a certified long-term care facility indefinitely. Again, this is very different from Medicare, which limits this care to 100 days. However, if you are in a skilled or intermediate care facility, Medicaid may review the level of care you are receiving. If Medicaid determines that the higher level of care is no longer medically necessary, it can require you to move to a custodial care facility if you want Medicaid to keep paying for your care.

Medicaid Coverage for Some Assisted Living Facilities

In recent years, assisted living facilities (ALFs) have become an increasingly popular alternative to nursing homes for people who need regular assistance and monitoring but not constant, close attention. ALFs are less institutional and less expensive than nursing homes, and provide more private living space. For many years, Medicaid would pay for nursing home care but not for assisted living. Initially, that was because assisted living was not a closely regulated industry, and the Medicaid program was not sure what it would be paying for.

Recently, however, Medicaid has recognized that ALFs can be a better and less expensive way to care for people who otherwise would have to enter a nursing home. So, the federal Medicaid program has authorized states to approve ALFs for Medicaid coverage. Not all states have done so, however. And even those states that have approved assisted living coverage in principle have been slow to certify specific ALFs for Medicaid payment. Also, many ALFs choose not to participate in Medicaid or offer only a few living spaces to Medicaid-covered residents.

Despite these limitations, if you might be eligible for Medicaid nursing home coverage but are considering assisted living as an alternative, check to see which facilities in your area—if any—are approved for Medicaid funding.

How Much Medicaid Pays

Some state Medicaid programs pay only a certain percentage of the cost of care. Check in advance with both the facility and your local Medicaid social worker to determine what Medicaid will cover and how much it will pay.

In general, Medicaid pays a nursing or other qualifying residential facility a daily rate that covers medical and personal or custodial care, rehabilitation therapies provided by the facility, and room and board. For anything Medicaid covers, the facility must accept Medicaid's payment as payment in full. The facility cannot bill you any additional amounts for covered services. Among the personal care items for which the facility may not charge extra to a Medicaid resident are nonprescription drugs, incontinence supplies, razors, soaps, tooth care items, and services such as laundry and basic hair and nail grooming. In some states, more items and services are covered. You can get a full list of what is covered from the facility, the facility's ombudsman, or the social services office that administers Medicaid in the county where the facility is located.

Finding Out About Medicaid in Your State

Protect Your Assets

Before you apply for Medicaid, consider taking steps to help protect some of your assets from nursing facility and other costs. Asset protection is discussed later in this chapter.

To qualify for Medicaid, you must file a written application to the agency that handles Medicaid on the local level, usually the county department of social services, health department, or welfare department. If you are already hospitalized or in a long-term care facility, ask the institution's medical social worker to assist you in obtaining and filling out the applications.

You should bring some financial documents with you when you apply. Even if you do not have all of the following documents, go ahead and begin the application process. The Medicaid eligibility workers can help you get whatever papers and documents are necessary, including:

- recent interest and dividend statements, your previous year's income tax return, and recent pension and Social Security benefit papers or deposit slips indicating your current income

- papers showing all of your financial assets, such as bankbooks, insurance policies, stock certificates, and car registration (if you used the assets worksheet in Chapter 1, bring documents relating to all the assets you listed there)

- rent receipts, lease agreement, or canceled rent checks if you are a renter, or your mortgage payment book and latest tax assessment on the property if you're a homeowner

- your Social Security card or number

- if you live with your spouse, information about his or her income and separate assets, and

- medical bills from the previous three months. If you are planning on home care or residence in a care facility in the near future, bring medical records or reports that confirm your condition will require that type of care; if you don't have records or reports, bring the names and addresses of doctors who are treating you.

A Medicaid eligibility worker will interview and assist you in filling out your application. Write down his or her name and telephone extension in case you have specific questions during the application process.

You may have to make several visits and wait through some delays in processing your application while the proper documents are located and reviewed. Normally you will receive a decision within a few weeks; the law says the agency must make a decision within 45 days after your application is complete. If you don't hear from Medicaid within 30 days after completing your application, call the Medicaid social worker who interviewed you and ask what's going on.

Social service and Medicaid agencies are very overworked; sometimes a person's application gets delayed in the shuffle. Stay on top of things so your application isn't delayed any more than necessary.

The Retroactive Coverage Rule

If you become eligible for Medicaid, you may be covered for home care or long-term care facility costs incurred since the beginning of the third month before you filed your application. You must present proof that you incurred covered costs during that time. Make sure to tell your Medicaid eligibility worker when you apply that you want retroactive coverage.

If You Are Denied Medicaid Coverage

If you are notified that you do not qualify for Medicaid, or that coverage is denied for a particular service, facility, or time period, you have a right to what is called a "fair hearing" to determine if the decision is correct. If you receive notice of a decision that you think is wrong, inquire immediately at the office where you applied about the procedure in your state for getting a fair hearing.

The rules for a fair hearing vary. In general, you are permitted to have a friend, relative, social worker, lawyer, or other representative appear with you and testify about your financial situation, medical condition, or expenses if such evidence would be helpful. The hearing itself is informal—you will be able to explain your position in your own words, without having to worry about legal technicalities or jargon. If your medical condition or need for treatment is in question, a detailed letter from your doctor would be of great help. The hearing officer who makes the decision is a Medicaid eligibility specialist rather than a judge.

Although the odds of getting a Medicaid denial reversed at a fair hearing are not in your favor, reversals do happen. And the amount of money at stake is large enough to make it worth the effort. Even if the fair hearing officer decides against you, there may be procedures in your state for further appeal. You will probably receive information about that appeal along with the fair hearing decision. If not, check with your local social service office.

Get Free Assistance From Your Local Ombudsman

If you are entering a nursing or personal care facility and are having trouble either being accepted for Medicaid or getting Medicaid to cover that facility, contact your state's long-term care ombudsman. The ombudsman program is financed by the federal government. Its purpose is to assist people with problems relating to nursing facilities. There is no charge for using its services. You can find a local ombudsman office by searching online or in the white pages of your telephone directory. Your area, state, or local Agency on Aging or the central ombudsman office for your state can also refer you to the ombudsman. (See the Resource Directory in the back of this book.)

Medicaid Rules on Transfer of Assets

Because a person is only eligible for Medicaid when his or her assets are reduced to minimum levels, which vary depending on your state's rules, your marital status, and the type of care you need, a person (and spouse) must personally pay all long-term care costs—for home care or a long-term care facility—until assets have been spent down to Medicaid levels.

To avoid spending all their savings on long-term care before Medicaid began coverage, many people used to give away assets—or at least transfer legal title—to children or other relatives, and then they applied for Medicaid. But Medicaid rules now severely restrict such transfers as they apply to nursing home coverage. There is no simple way to keep your assets in the family and also qualify for Medicaid coverage of nursing home care. Long-range planning may permit someone to qualify for Medicaid while his or her assets remain with family members, but only if the Medicaid applicant has relinquished personal control over the assets.

Before learning about the few ways to protect family assets through long-term planning, you have to understand the basic rules Medicaid uses to judge whether a transfer of one type of asset or another is proper.

Penalized Transfers

There is one basic Medicaid rule limiting your ability to transfer assets: Any money or other asset transferred out of your name during the "look-back period" is an invalid transfer for the purpose of Medicaid coverage for a nursing facility, if you are age 55 or older. An invalid transfer results in a penalty period during which you are not eligible for Medicaid. Medicaid calculates this penalty period by dividing the amount transferred by the average monthly nursing facility cost in your state.

The look-back period is 60 months from the date of your Medicaid application. If there is an invalid transfer during that time, the period of ineligibility begins from the date of your application. Also, the purchase of an annuity or a transfer of funds to a trust may be considered a transfer of funds (see "Transfers to a Trust," below).

Asset Transfer Rules Don't Apply to Home Care

The rules discussed in this chapter about transfer of assets and qualifying for Medicaid apply to nursing home or assisted living coverage, not to home care. For home care, the question is what assets are now actually available for your use—Medicaid doesn't concern itself with when you gave assets away and to whom. Even if you are receiving Medicaid coverage for home care, however, it is good to familiarize yourself with these rules regarding asset transfers and residential care facilities. That's because, while you may not need nursing home or other residential care now, you might someday. And since that someday might be within the Medicaid five-year look-back period, these rules may become extremely important to you.

EXAMPLE: Alton gave $50,000 to his daughter in March 2011. A year later, in March 2012, he entered a long-term care facility and applied for Medicaid. Not counting that $50,000, he was eligible for Medicaid. Because the transfer was within the 60 months prior to his applying for Medicaid, that transfer could be penalized. The average monthly stay in a long-term care facility in Alton's state costs $5,000. That means the penalty is ten ($50,000 divided by $5,000) months of no coverage. The transfer was made more than ten months before, but under the current rule, the penalty starts not from the transfer date but from the date Alton applied for Medicaid. So, he would not be eligible for Medicaid coverage for the first ten months of his stay in the long-term care facility.

A Question of Ethics

This section of the book discusses ways in which Medicaid rules permit people to transfer assets to become eligible for Medicaid coverage and to protect assets from Medicaid reimbursement. In other words, these rules permit people to keep their money, yet have their long-term care costs paid for by the government as if they were broke.

These rules—and the way some have chosen to apply them—have rankled many. Medicaid was enacted as a safety net for the poor. Many elderly people truly become impoverished because of their high medical costs. Medicaid saves their dignity and prolongs their lives by guaranteeing a decent level of care. But this care comes at a cost to taxpayers—a cost that our society has declared a willingness to pay. However, the public hasn't yet voiced support for assisting the elderly who have assets. A truly compassionate society might provide free long-term care for all its citizens, but ours has not shown a willingness to pay—through taxation—for this.

Despite recent changes tightening up the rules, some people with sizable assets are still able to skirt around the edges of the law and get Medicaid to pick up the tab for their long-term care. Following the rules carefully makes this legal. Whether it is entirely ethical—that is, whether it is a violation of the spirit of the Medicaid law and the position of those who have refused to support long-term care for all—is a different question, and one which each person who considers these rules must answer privately.

Transfers to a Trust

In an attempt to get around Medicaid eligibility rules, some people place some or most of their assets in a trust and then claim that the assets no longer legally belong to them. Congress responded to this maneuver by creating rules about transferring assets to a trust. Under these rules, assets transferred to a trust are still considered, for Medicaid eligibility purposes, to belong to the transferring person for 60 months after the date of trust. So, the use of a trust as an asset protection device for Medicaid eligibility purposes works only with long-term planning. Most people don't want to restrict the use of their assets for such a long time. Nevertheless, this type of trust might be a valuable planning device if you or a spouse have a slowly deteriorating condition that is likely, in the long run, to require extensive and expensive nursing facility care.

Other Medicaid rules govern the structure of the trust itself. First, the trust must be irrevocable. That means the person who put the money in trust cannot later change his or her mind and take the money back. Also, in general, neither the income from, nor the assets of, the trust may be available for use by the person applying for Medicaid. In other words, the person creating the trust must give up control over the money put into the trust.

If you are considering using a trust to preserve assets and then qualify for Medicaid long-term care coverage, consult with an experienced elder law attorney. Because of the 60-month rule, the further ahead you do this, the better. You can get a referral to elder law attorneys through any of the organizations listed in the "Legal Assistance" section of the Resources Directory in the appendix to this book.

Permissible Transfers

Medicaid permits some exceptions to this 60-month rule. These exceptions differ considerably depending on marital status. And they vary greatly depending on whether an asset is exempt or nonexempt.

Unmarried Individuals

An unmarried person can transfer the assets listed below without any eligibility penalty.

Home. A home can be transferred:

- to the Medicaid applicant's minor child (through a custodianship or trust arrangement) or to the applicant's blind or disabled child of any age
- to the applicant's child of any age, if the child has lived in the home for two years prior to the parent's entry into a nursing facility and cared for the parent, allowing the parent to remain at home rather than enter a nursing facility during that time, or
- to a brother or sister who already has some ownership interest in the property and has lived in the home for at least the previous year.

Other Exempt Assets. You may transfer to anyone, at any time, your car (in some states, only up to a limited value), personal or household belongings, your engagement or wedding rings, or other exempt assets.

Nonexempt Assets. You may transfer any asset, at any time, to your minor, blind, or disabled child. You may also transfer any asset at any time to any person if you can prove to Medicaid that you made the transfer for some reason *other* than to qualify for Medicaid eligibility, such as to help a relative in need.

Married People Entering a Long-Term Care Facility

Medicaid rules give married couples an advantage over unmarried people by permitting an at-home spouse to retain some liquid assets and income. The rules also provide an additional benefit by allowing the couple to change the title on their home when one spouse enters a long-term care facility.

Home. A married person can transfer title to a home to his or her spouse before or after entering a long-term care facility. Although the home is exempt as long as the spouse is living in it, it may be best to transfer title to the at-home spouse, who can then transfer the home to children or others in case the at-home spouse should die first. A married person can also transfer title to the home to any of the people an unmarried person can transfer to, as described above.

Other Exempt Assets. A married person can transfer exempt assets to anyone at any time.

Other Assets. You can transfer any assets, at any time, to your minor, blind, or disabled child. Any asset can also be transferred to anyone at any time if the person making the transfer can prove that the transfer was for some purpose other than to qualify for Medicaid eligibility. To qualify for this exception, you will need convincing proof that you made the transfer for a valid reason—for example, to help a brother or sister keep a failing business or to pay a child's medical costs that aren't covered by insurance.

Before applying for Medicaid, a spouse may transfer any nonexempt asset to his or her at-home spouse, but only if the at-home spouse does not transfer it to anyone else within 60 months for less than its true value. For example, nonexempt assets cannot be transferred to the sole name of the at-home spouse and then given immediately to the children.

Strategies to Protect Your Assets

This section discusses two separate but related questions.

Transfers for Eligibility. If you have too many assets to qualify for Medicaid, are there lawful ways to transfer some of those assets so that you become eligible for Medicaid?

Transfers for Asset Protection. If you can qualify for Medicaid, are there lawful ways to transfer some assets so that they are out of reach when Medicaid seeks reimbursement after your death?

Each of the options discussed in this section has some drawbacks, and not all of them will be available to everyone. Carefully read through the rules to decide whether any of these options might be right for you.

Medicaid May Recover Cost of Care

Medicaid has the right to collect the entire amount it has spent on long-term care—whether home care or care in a long-term care facility—for anyone age 55 or over. It recoups this money out of any assets in the Medicaid recipient's estate at death. If assets have been lawfully transferred out of the Medicaid recipient's name before death, without violating Medicaid's transfer rules, those assets cannot be taken for Medicaid reimbursement.

Usually, the largest asset from which Medicaid can seek reimbursement is the recipient's home. Medicaid can place a lien on the property and collect on the lien whenever the property is sold, if the recipient:

- is in a long-term care facility
- is not expected to return home as certified by a physician, and
- has no spouse, minor or disabled child, or sibling who has an equity interest in the property and lives in the home.

However, if the recipient, spouse, or minor or disabled child, or sibling with an equity interest in the property is living in the home, or if the recipient intends to return to the home, the rule is different. In these situations, Medicaid cannot place a lien on the home but must wait to collect its reimbursement out of the recipient's estate.

The amount to which Medicaid is entitled as a reimbursement may be decreased if the Medicaid recipient had secured a state partnership long-term care insurance policy. You can read more about these policies later in this chapter.

Transfers Earlier Than the Look-Back Period

Although many people need long-term care as the result of an accidental injury or the sudden onset of illness—a stroke or heart attack, for example —many others need care because of a slowly deteriorating physical or mental condition. If you are gradually heading toward the need for long-term care, one of the ways you may financially plan for it is to divest yourself of assets that might make you ineligible for Medicaid. Any asset you transfer before the beginning of the look-back period prior to applying for Medicaid will not be considered in determining your eligibility.

As long as you do it well ahead of time, you can transfer liquid assets to your children or others whom you would eventually want to give them to anyway. For many, the main problem with this approach is that when you give away assets, you lose control over them. If you later need the funds or change your mind about giving them away, you must depend on the cooperation of those to whom you gave the assets. And, you risk the possibility that they will have already spent, invested, or otherwise used them.

Tax Consequences of Property Transfers

Transferring your home or other valuable assets may have unforeseen gift tax and income tax consequences. You may need to consult with a tax specialist to understand these consequences—and figure out how to minimize any undesirable tax consequences.

Investments in Your Home

Because Medicaid rules often exempt a home of any value from asset eligibility limits, concentrating your assets in your home is a good way to protect them. Investing in your home may help you qualify for

Medicaid. And, if you follow some of the other steps discussed here, you can also protect the value added to your home from Medicaid claims for reimbursement. Both unmarried individuals and couples can use this strategy, but the rules are different for each and must be carefully followed.

Assuming you don't have other immediate needs for your savings or investments, you could put those assets into your home by:

- paying off your outstanding mortgage
- making home improvements or large-scale repairs, or
- buying a new home or condominium for more money than your present home is worth (for the home to be protected, you or your spouse must live in it).

Home Investment by Unmarried Individuals

The rules governing an unmarried individual's ability to affect Medicaid eligibility and reimbursement by investing in a home depend on whether the person lives in the home or moves into a long-term care facility. In either case, you may require some assistance from a lawyer or tax accountant familiar with Medicaid procedures. A brief explanation of possible options follows.

Long-Term Home Care. As long as an unmarried individual continues to live at home, Medicaid will pay for long-term home care regardless of the value of the house. So, if you have too many nonexempt assets to qualify for Medicaid, investing the excess assets in your house would permit you to qualify.

States Without a Strict "Return Home" Rule. Medicaid rules in some states permit unmarried long-term care facility residents to exempt their homes—meaning that the value of their homes does not disqualify them from Medicaid coverage. This is true even if the individuals are unlikely to return to live in those homes. The only requirement is that the individual entering a facility must state on the admission form that he or she intends to return home. If you live in a state with such a rule, you may be free to invest assets in your home, thereby making them exempt. Check with the local department of social services, health department, or welfare department to find out the current rule in your locale.

Exempt Child or Sibling. If your adult child or sibling lives in your home and would qualify the home as an exempt asset, you may want to invest further in the home.

Transfer to Nonexempt Adult Child. Even if it would not qualify the house as an exempt asset, you may still want to consider investing assets in the house and transferring title to a son or daughter. This requires you to give up control over the property, so you must trust your child to manage it according to your wishes. Also, you should do this only if you want the home to belong to that child after your death.

If you transfer your home to your child, you won't have to sell the home to pay your nursing facility bills. If you transfer the home before the beginning of the look-back period prior to applying for Medicaid for long-term facility coverage, the value of the home will not affect your Medicaid eligibility at all. If you transfer it within the look-back period before entering a long-term care facility, your eligibility will be delayed for a period equal to the value of the home divided by the average monthly long-term care facility cost in your state. (See the explanation of the Medicaid look-back rule above.) For example, if the equity in your home is $100,000, you could be denied Medicaid coverage for 18 months to three years, depending on the cost of care in your state. One month of coverage will be denied for roughly every $3,500 to $4,000 of equity.

Home Investment by Couples

A home is a particularly good place for a married couple to invest savings or other assets. Even if one spouse enters a long-term care facility, as long as the other spouse lives at home, the home is completely exempt from Medicaid eligibility limits—no matter how much it is worth.

Investing in the home may only be the first step toward protecting those assets. If one spouse enters a long-term care facility, he or she could transfer sole title to the property to the spouse who remains at home. The spouse at home could then transfer the property to children or others (but not back to the spouse in the facility). The transfer can be made by immediate gift or by a provision in a will or living trust under which the property will not actually transfer until the at-home spouse's death.

This transfer protects against the possibility of the at-home spouse dying first. In that case, if the spouse in the facility still held title to the property, the value of the home would be used to reimburse Medicaid for all the money it had spent on care for the facility spouse.

Also, once the home is in the sole name of the at-home spouse, he or she may be able to make good use of the equity by, for example, selling the home and using the money. There are also other equity conversion devices an at-home spouse can consider. Reverse annuity mortgages, for example, allow a homeowner to use the home's equity as collateral for a loan; the lender then makes monthly or lump sum payments to the homeowner.

To know what effect transfer of title, sale of your home, living trusts, or equity conversion devices might have on your tax liability and Medicaid eligibility, you should seek the advice of a lawyer, accountant, or business advisor who is familiar with both Medicaid rules and tax laws.

Investing in Other Exempt Assets

A home is not the only asset automatically exempt from Medicaid eligibility limits. Those listed below are also exempt. Up to each state's limits, you can invest in these assets without affecting your Medicaid eligibility:

• an automobile (in some states, only up to a limited value)

- furniture and household goods (of any value in some states; only up to a certain dollar limit in others)

- one wedding and one engagement ring per person of any value (individual or couple)—they don't have to be the original engagement or wedding rings; so you can buy a new ring at any time, and

- a burial plot and separate burial fund up to a cash value of $1,500 for each spouse.

Transferring Nonexempt Assets to At-Home Spouse

Although transferring nonexempt assets from a spouse in a long-term care facility to an at-home spouse will not prevent Medicaid from counting those assets toward its eligibility limits (unless they are then transferred to others before Medicaid is applied for), such a transfer can save a lot of money if the at-home spouse dies before the spouse in the facility.

When one spouse is a resident in a long-term care facility, Medicaid counts the joint assets of the couple and allows the couple to keep one-half of those combined assets—in some states up to $113,640 (in 2012). But an unmarried facility resident can keep only about $2,000. If the at-home spouse dies, the spouse in the facility becomes an unmarried individual who can only keep $2,000, and the $113,640 (in 2012) the couple had been allowed to keep then automatically goes to pay long-term care facility bills.

A couple can avoid losing most of this benefit by taking two simple steps. First, the facility spouse transfers the $113,640 (in 2012) into the sole name of the at-home spouse. Then, the at-home spouse makes a will or creates a living trust that leaves the money to the children or to anyone other than the spouse in the facility. If the at-home spouse dies first, the money goes to the children or other named beneficiary and not to the long-term care facility.

Transferring Exempt Assets

Exempt assets—such as your home, car, or household goods—may be transferred to children or anyone else even within the 60-month Medicaid no-transfer period. But if assets are exempt, why bother to transfer them? Look back at the Medicaid rules for exempt assets and you will see that the exemptions for a married couple with one spouse in a long-term care facility are far more generous than for an unmarried individual. But if the at-home spouse dies, a couple's exempt property— home, car, household goods of any value, and up to $113,640 (in 2012) in savings—instantly becomes an unmarried person's nonexempt property—and so, a source for paying facility bills. To protect against that, some people transfer title to exempt property as well.

Medicaid Annuities

One recent wrinkle that lawyers and accountants have come up with to help some people protect a certain amount of assets is called the "Medicaid annuity," a financial instrument something like an insurance policy. The annuity pays a monthly amount—low enough to stay under Medicaid eligibility limits—to the person who buys it. In this case, the person receiving the monthly annuity payments would be the spouse who remains living at home (called the "community spouse" in Medicaid lingo). If the annuity meets all Medicaid specifications, the amount the couple spends for it is no longer considered part of the couple's estate for Medicaid eligibility purposes, even though the annuity was purchased within the five-year look-back period.

The following rules and costs of these Medicaid annuities make them suitable only for people with substantial assets who cannot distribute the money in other ways:

• The annuity must be irrevocable. That means that once you buy it, you cannot cancel it and get the money back. If the spouse in the nursing home dies, there is no longer any reason to keep the money tied up in the annuity but no way for the at-home spouse to regain use of the funds.

- The annuity must be nonassignable, which means the monthly income can't be transferred to someone else if and when the at-home spouse dies.

- The state must be named as the beneficiary of the annuity after the at-home spouse. In other words, if the at-home spouse dies before the end of the annuity term, the remainder of the money goes to the state, not to the family or anyone else.

- Setting up the annuity usually requires the services of a lawyer or tax accountant who specializes in such trusts. Of course, he or she will require a substantial fee to do so.

- The insurance or other financial company that sells the annuity will also charge a fee.

Medicaid and Divorce

It may seem strange to think of divorce in connection with long-term care. Unfortunately, however, the Medicaid income and assets limits have forced more than a few couples to divorce for solely economic reasons. If all other methods for transferring or otherwise protecting your assets are unavailable, or continuing income presents an eligibility problem, you may at least want to consider the unpleasant alternative of divorce. Remember, though, that changing your Medicaid status requires only the formal, legal divorce. A couple need not stop living together, but they must separate their bank accounts and joint income, change title to property, and otherwise shift their financial interests to reflect separate lives. Any asset they continue to own or control jointly will be considered part of the Medicaid applicant's assets.

This situation often arises when a couple must choose either to enter a long-term care facility and be covered by Medicaid or to remain home without coverage. About 30 states have no income eligibility levels for

Medicaid coverage of residential facility care; the other states have income levels of $700 to the low $2,000s per month for eligibility, but allow the at-home spouse to keep all income in his or her name. And all states allow the at-home spouse of a facility resident to keep between $22,728 and $113,640 in savings or other assets.

For nonresidential facility care, on the other hand, all states place severe limits on the amount of income and assets a couple can have and still qualify for Medicaid coverage. A couple may thus be forced to choose either to get care at home and be disqualified from Medicaid, or to get divorced. A divorce permits the working spouse to keep all of his or her income without disqualifying the other spouse, and protects at least half of the couple's assets without limit. The spouse (now ex-spouse) needing care can then remain at home and receive Medicaid-covered home care.

A couple may face the same difficult choice even when one spouse is already in a long-term care facility. If a couple has considerably more in savings and other nonexempt assets than the Medicaid rules of their state would permit them to keep, a divorce settlement that gives more assets to the at-home spouse than Medicaid would have allowed the couple to keep may protect some of those savings.

These are all matters that depend on both the specific Medicaid rules and the divorce laws of your state. If divorce seems like the best last resort for you, consult a lawyer who is familiar with both sets of laws.

Long-Term Care State Partnership Insurance Protects Assets

To get more people with assets to insure against the possibility of long-term care, some states encourage people to buy special state-certified (called "state partnership") long-term care insurance policies. Almost every state offers some extra asset protection to a person who buys such a policy. In exchange, the state promises to allow the insured person to keep more assets than normal under the state's Medicaid rules, if and when the person's insurance benefits run out and the person applies for Medicaid nursing home, home care, or (in some states) assisted living coverage. (These policies do not, however, affect rules relating to income limits for Medicaid long-term care coverage.) Also, the protected amount will not be sought by Medicaid as reimbursement from the person's estate after death.

State partnership policies offer some of the best terms available for home, community, and sometimes assisted living coverage. They also are required to offer inflation protection and nonforfeiture provisions. State partnership policies come in two basic types—dollar-for-dollar and total asset policies.

Dollar-for-Dollar Asset Protection Policies

In states with state partnership long-term care insurance programs, all insurance companies sell dollar-for-dollar policies that cover assets equal to the amount of benefits paid under the policies. When the benefits of such a policy run out, the insured person can receive Medicaid coverage while keeping savings or other assets worth whatever the insurance policy had paid out in total benefits.

EXAMPLE: Mrs. Garcia, a widow, purchased a dollar-for-dollar state partnership long-term care insurance policy. The policy paid $150 per day for two years of nursing home care, for a total of $109,500. After her insurance benefits ran out at the end of the two years, Mrs. Garcia qualified for Medicaid coverage of her continuing nursing home stay even though at the time she applied for Medicaid nursing home coverage she had $100,000 in savings. Medicaid covered her nursing home costs and did not touch her savings, either during her lifetime or after.

Total Asset Protection Policies

Some state partnership programs allow insurance companies to offer total asset protection long-term care policies. With these policies, Medicaid will cover long-term care costs once a policy has fully paid all benefits allowable under the policy terms, regardless of a Medicaid applicant's assets. (There is still an income limit, however.) Further, the Medicaid program will not seek reimbursement of any costs from the estate of the policyholder. These total asset protection policies are much more expensive than dollar-for-dollar policies, in part because they are required to cover a longer period of care—for example, a minimum of three to four years of nursing home care, as opposed to only 18 months to two years with a dollar-for-dollar policy.

Switching From an Existing Policy to a Partnership Policy

Many states have only recently adopted state partnership long-term care insurance programs. In some of these states, it may be possible to switch an existing long-term care insurance policy to a state partnership policy. The ability to switch, and the terms and cost of the new policy, depend on both the rules of your state program and the participation of the insurance company for your existing policy. If you are interested in exploring the possibility of switching your existing long-term care policy to a state partnership policy, find out what your options are by contacting the insurance agent who handled your original policy or the consumer assistance office of the insurance company.

Additional Benefits and Risks

In addition to their asset-protecting terms, most policies offered under these state partnership programs have other beneficial features. They must offer—at some additional cost—home and community care coverage in addition to institutional care. Most of these policies also offer good benefits, inflation protection, and level premiums. (See Chapter 9 for an explanation of these terms and their importance in choosing a policy.)

But, as with all long-term care insurance, if you are considering a state partnership policy, you must compare its terms to those offered in other policies. Although these Medicaid partner policies generally offer good terms and some asset protection, for most consumers, they also present the same basic risks as do other long-term care policies. The first and foremost of these risks, as explained in Chapter 9, is that any long-term care policy is a gamble. These partnership policies, like all others, are expensive. Over the years, you pay significant premiums to protect against the chance that you will someday need substantial long-term care.

The likelihood that you will need a two- or three-year period of care in a long-term residential facility, however, is only about 30% for women and 15% for men who reach age 65. Only about 10% to 15% remain in a facility for more than three years. The numbers of people who need some sort of long-term home care is greater, but the average cost of such care is significantly less than the cost of institutional care. If it turns out that you do not need long-term care at all, or need it only for a relatively short time, all the money you spend on years of insurance premiums will have been wasted.

A second risk is that you will not be able to afford to continue paying premiums and therefore will lose your coverage. Even state partnership policies are expensive. If your income drops in your later years, the premiums may become too much for your budget. If so, you may decide you have to drop your coverage just as you reach the years when you are most likely to need it. And the years of premiums you have already paid would wind up being nearly a total loss, depending on the level of reduced benefits or the nonforfeiture provision in your policy. (See Chapter 9.)

Another risk with an asset-protecting policy is that the cost of long-term care in some urban areas may eat up most of your assets before Medicaid ever kicks in to cover you. For example, if you have a policy that pays $100 per day in long-term care facility costs, but the facility you choose charges $175 per day—as many do—the uncovered part of your costs ($75 per day) would mount up to $82,000 in three years. If you have well over $100,000 in assets to protect in addition to your home, the policy might work to preserve a portion of those assets. However, if you have less than $100,000 in assets other than your home, the policy would allow you to save very little—even though you will spend a tremendous amount in premiums over the years.

For some people, a major drawback with these asset protection policies is that they do not protect income. If you expect to have substantial income while you receive long-term care, that income will be unprotected and may disqualify you from Medicaid—even though your assets would otherwise be protected. A Medicaid recipient may keep only a small amount of income—$30 to $75 per month for a residential facility resident, and $500 to $600 per month for someone receiving home care—even with a state partnership policy.

These state partnership policies also present the risk that, if you wind up receiving care in another state, that other state's Medicaid program will not honor the agreement with the state where you bought the policy. The policy itself will remain enforceable—that is, the insurance company must pay benefits—but the asset protection provision will have gone out the window because you will be bound by the new state's Medicaid rules. This presents a particular risk if you are in your fifties or sixties when you buy a policy, because you may not know whether you will remain in the same state for the next 20 to 30 years. It may also be risky if most or all of your supporting family—siblings, children, and adult grandchildren—live in other states. If so, you might want to move to receive care near your family.

Finally, all the other pitfalls of long-term care insurance apply to Medicaid partner policies as well. These problems are discussed in Chapter 9. Before making a decision, read that chapter carefully and examine and compare all the terms of an asset-protecting policy just as you would any other long-term care policy. ●

Long-Term Care Insurance

L ong-term care insurance (LTCI) is frequently a hot topic—particularly in the media—for two reasons: Americans are living longer, meaning more people are likely to need care in later life; and the cost of that care is rising faster than the cost of living. LTCI is one approach to this problem. But LTCI is a gamble, and an expensive one, and less than 10% of all older people in need of long-term care actually buy this insurance.

If you are considering buying LTCI, this chapter can help you decide whether to do so, and if you do, what to look for in a policy.

The Truth About Long-Term Care Insurance

The long-term care insurance industry capitalizes on media attention to long life, the exorbitant cost of care, and fear of not being able to afford care as we age. The industry advertises LTCI as protection against what it hints is inevitable—that everyone will need long-term care, particularly in a nursing home, and that the costs will wipe out a family's life savings.

However, the truth about LTCI is different from what the industry wants you to believe:

- A good LTCI policy is costly, and you will likely have to pay the premiums for decades.
- Most LTCI policies contain extensive restrictions and conditions that significantly limit coverage for care.
- Most importantly, because most people will never need a long stretch of intensive, paid long-term care, the odds are high that you will never collect much from an LTCI policy.

Is Long-Term Care Insurance Right for You?

There is no simple answer to whether LTCI is a good choice for you. You have to consider its cost over many years, the likelihood that you'll need enough paid care to make it worthwhile, and the specific policies available to you. If you are considering buying an LTCI policy, read through this chapter first. As you do, keep in mind the three essential facts about LTCI described below:

It's added security, *not* investment. For reasons explained in this chapter, buying LTCI is not a good purely *financial* choice: The odds are small that you will actually need and collect benefits for long enough to justify the cost of premiums. But, if you can afford a good policy, it can provide you and your family with extra *security* against the relatively small but real possibility of high long-term care costs.

Benefits are for way down the road. Fifty percent of all claims on LTCI policies are not made until the insureds are in their eighties. And another 40% of claims are made by people in their seventies. So, if you are a middle-aged person when you buy LTCI, you are protecting against a situation that is most probably 20 or 30 years away. With most policies, that means you have to pay—and be able to afford—the premiums for all those years. It also means you must get a policy with good inflation protection, so that if and when you finally claim the policy benefits, they will have kept up with the cost of care.

You won't be on the street without it. LTCI is about helping you save your assets, *not* about keeping you from being tossed into the street. For people who run low on funds, Medicaid (called Medi-Cal in California) pays the full cost of nursing home care—in all, Medicaid pays more than half the nation's long-term nursing home costs. (See Chapter 8.)

Health Reform's LTC Insurance Plan Indefinitely Delayed

Part of the Affordable Care Act, the health reform law passed in 2010, was authorization for a new government-administered long-term care insurance program called CLASS (Community Living Assistance Services and Supports). The program was designed to support private long-term care insurance offered to workers, on a voluntary basis, through their employers. The idea was to greatly expand the number of people who have long-term care insurance, thereby reducing the number of people who come to rely on Medicaid to pay their nursing home and other long-term care costs.

The law stated that the CLASS program had to be entirely financially self-sustaining, and after almost two years of administrative struggling and political wrangling about how to set up the program, in October 2011, the Department of Health and Human Services (HHS) acknowledged that it was unable to structure a workable program under current regulations. So, for now the program is on hold. The law authorizing it is still in force, and HHS is trying to develop new regulations that might someday bring the program back to life. Those regulations are scheduled to be released for early consideration in October 2012, but there is no guarantee that HHS will make this deadline, and no assurance that the regulations will lead to a workable program in the foreseeable future.

Myths and Realities of LTCI

LTCI insurance provides some protection against the cost of paid long-term care. A long stay in a nursing home is the scenario most people worry about, though LTCI can also cover home and assisted living care. But what are the actual odds of a long nursing facility stay? And what about the other statistics that get thrown around in the media and insurance industry reports? Before you decide whether to buy an LTCI policy, take a good look at the following figures that may help you get a clearer picture of the actual financial risk you face and whether LTCI is the right approach for you:

- **Some insurance industry statistics claim that 65% to 70% of all people over 65 years old will "need care."** But *how much* care are you likely to need? According to other, nonindustry studies, 80% of all long-term care is informal, unpaid home care. And of paid care, less than 20% is for nursing home costs. In fact, only 3.6% of people 65 and over were in nursing homes in 2004 (when the National Nursing Home Survey was conducted), which was *down* from 4.2% in 1985.

- **The insurance industry claims that women over 65 "use" long-term care an average of 3.7 years, and men "use" care for an average of 2.2 years.** But these statistics do not say how much care is used or what type of care. In fact, most nursing facility stays are far shorter than these numbers. The median nursing home stay for all ages (65 and over) is less than 1.5 years, decreasing with the greater availability of other types of care. And for people admitted to a nursing home when they are age 75 or older, nearly 80% stay less than one year.

- **The insurance industry sells its policies with the "promise" that the benefits will be there when you need them.** However, history tells a different story. For example, during the mid-2000s, about 25% of all LTCI benefit claims in the largest single market, California, were denied—meaning the insurance company refused to pay anything.

These figures don't necessarily mean that LTCI isn't a good idea for you. However, they do mean that if you buy an LTCI policy you might never collect much, if any, of its promised benefits. Again, this points to the fact that if you can afford LCTI, you should consider it as extra protection for your assets, not as something to count on.

Some Common LTCI Scenarios

To illustrate the risks and rewards of LTCI, here are a few common scenarios. Let's assume Mary bought an LTCI policy at age 55. The policy provides benefits of $200 per day for nursing home care and $100 per day for home care, for up to three years. Mary pays $200 per month for this policy. (For simplicity's sake, we won't consider here any rise in premiums. And we'll use current dollar figures for both the cost of care and the policy benefit amounts.) Here are some possible scenarios for her care during the last year or years of Mary's life.

Mary dies at age 65, 75, or 85 having used three months of Medicare-covered skilled nursing home care and hospice, but no other home or nursing home care. In these scenarios, Mary paid $24,000 (ten years), $48,000 (20 years), or $72,000 (30 years)—unless she had paid for a cap on premium years, but this would have boosted the monthly premium amount—in LTCI premiums. But she would have received no benefits at all. Any of these three scenarios would have been a very bad trade-off for Mary.

Mary uses a year of LTCI-covered home care, beginning at age 75. Mary paid $48,000 (20 years) in premiums and got $35,000 in benefits. Still a bad trade for Mary.

Mary uses two years of home care at age 75. Mary paid $48,000 (20 years) in premiums and got $70,000 in benefits. This seems to be a good trade-off for Mary, but in fact she could have done better by just putting that $200 per month in a long-term savings or other secure account (at 3% to 4%) for those 20 years, at much less risk.

Mary uses a year of home care at age 75, followed by a year of nursing home care. Mary paid $48,000 (20 years) in premiums and got $105,000 in benefits. This would have given Mary a slightly better return than banking her $200 per month.

Mary uses a year of home care, beginning at age 75, followed by two years of nursing home care. Mary paid $48,000 (20 years) in premiums and got $175,000 in benefits. This is a scenario in which Mary's LTCI policy paid off.

Mary uses a year of home care at age 85, followed by a year of nursing home care. Mary paid $72,000 (30 years) in premiums and got $105,000 in benefits. She could have done better by just putting that $200 per month in the bank for those 30 years, with much less risk.

Mary uses a year of home care, beginning at age 85, followed by two years of nursing home care. Mary paid $72,000 (30 years) in premiums and got $175,000 in benefits. This is a scenario in which Mary's LTCI policy was slightly better than banking the money.

Mary uses three years of nursing home care, beginning at age 85. Mary paid $72,000 (30 years) in premiums and got $210,000 in benefits. This is a scenario in which Mary's LTCI policy paid good dividends.

Finding Long-Term Care Policies

If you are shopping for an LTCI policy, do not choose solely based on what's offered by a single insurance agent or broker. Different brokers and agents represent different companies, and you should consult with more than one. Also, some agencies and organizations provide free information about LTCI policies sold in your state. If you gather general information from these sources, you can then contact the insurance company directly to get details about a particular policy. These informational sources include your state government's department of insurance. (See the "Government" section of your local telephone directory, or go to www.consumeraction.gov/insurance.shtml to search a list of all state departments of insurance.)

State Partnership Policies Help Protect Assets

In most states, special asset-protecting LTCI policies are available. These "state partnership" policies allow a person to keep a greater measure of personal assets than Medicaid (called Medi-Cal in California) normally allows while the insured person qualifies for Medicaid long-term care coverage (in addition to what the LTCI policy pays). In Chapter 8, we described the Medicaid asset protection aspects of these special long-term care policies. If you are shopping for an LTCI policy, ask the insurance broker or agent you're dealing with whether your state offers state partnership policies. If so, make sure that any policy you buy qualifies as a state partnership policy.

Remember, though, that a state partnership policy is not automatically a good investment for you. Don't purchase one unless it also meets other requirements for a good policy, as described in this chapter.

LTCI for Federal Employees and Retirees

The Office of Personnel Management of the federal government, in partnership with a private insurance company, sponsors LTCI at group rates. The insurance policies under this "Long Term Care Partners" program are available to federal employees, retirees, and certain immediate family members. The premiums may be slightly less expensive than for similar retail policies. However, the insurance itself operates just like any other private policy, with all the risks and limitations described in this chapter.

To find out about these policies, go to the website of the U.S. Office of Personnel Management (www.opm.gov/insure) or the Federal Long Term Care Insurance Program (www.ltcfeds.com).

Warnings About Insurance Practices

Shopping for any kind of insurance can be a daunting task. You have to read the fine print, compare the rates and benefits of different policies, and figure out which policy will best meet your individual needs. Here are a few additional things to keep in mind when you're researching long-term care insurance.

Beware of Pretty Promises

Don't be blinded by the first numbers you get from insurance advertisements, agents, or brokers. And don't be fooled by the boldface promises of a glossy brochure. Too often, a company flashes what seems like high benefits for low premiums, plus a promise that the premiums will never rise. Unfortunately, the fine print always permits the insurance companies to increase premiums one way or another—and they will. (See "The Cost of Premiums," below.) And what seem like high benefits today may be far from adequate when you finally need them. (See "Benefits Amounts and Length of Coverage," below.)

Beware of Brochures and Agents

Insurance brochures and advertisements are often misleading and always incomplete. These devices are intended to get you interested in insurance policies and convince you how great they are—not to explain their pitfalls or even accurately explain how they work. And brochures are generally not detailed enough to bind an insurance company to anything in particular, so you cannot rely on their glossy promises.

Insurance agents, too, are in the business of selling policies—not of warning you why you should not buy one. Although most agents are conscientious about not selling a policy they know is not right for a customer, some will say things carelessly during the course of trying to make a sale. Other agents may sell you a bad policy simply because they do not know better. LTCI is relatively new and policies change rapidly, so many agents simply do not have much experience with particular policies and coverage.

In general, an insurance agent—as opposed to a broker—represents only one company or group of companies. He or she may know that company's policies fairly well, but cannot compare their premiums and coverage to those offered by another company's policies. If you have received information from one company's agent, even if the agent has shown you all of that company's policies, be sure to investigate several other companies' policies as well. Also, do not rely on what an agent tells you about how a policy works. If you are going to rely on something the agent tells you, insist that you see the promise in writing on the policy itself or from a company representative in official company correspondence addressed to you.

An insurance broker, as opposed to an agent, works independently and can offer policies from a number of different companies. A broker can probably show you a somewhat wider selection of long-term care policies than could an agent who works for only one company. However, a broker may not know very well how all the different policies operate. And a broker cannot make binding promises on behalf of the insurance company. If the broker contends that a policy operates in a certain way, be sure you see it in writing on the policy or in official correspondence from the insurance company to you.

Beware of Mail-Order and Limited-Time-Only Policies

You have probably seen these advertising catchphrases before: Limited Offer! Once-in-a-Lifetime! When this offer expires, you'll never get the same chance again! One Month Only!

These one-time-only offers are usually misleading nonsense. The best advice may simply be to avoid buying any policy touted in an advertisement that uses an exclamation point. If it is a reputable insurance company with a legitimate policy to offer, the same or similar terms will be available to you at any time (except for premium increases as you grow older). No matter what the advertising says, don't be rushed into buying anything.

Check the Company's Reliability Rating

Even the best-sounding insurance policy won't be much good if the company that issued it has gone bankrupt by the time you try to collect your benefits 20 or 30 years down the road. At best, you might collect far less than you bargained for if another insurance company takes over from the one you originally contracted with; at worst, you might wind up with nothing at all.

A rating of the financial health of individual insurance companies is offered by several services: A.M. Best Insurance Reports (www.ambest .com), Standard & Poor's (www.standardandpoors.com), Moody's (www.moodys.com), and Weiss Ratings (www.weissratings.com). These ratings are also available at most local libraries, on the phone with any of these companies, or with your state's department of insurance.

Insurance companies are rated with financial strength "grades" A through F. You should not buy a policy from any company that does not receive at least a B+ rating from two or more of these rating services.

Examine the Policy Itself

When you consider a particular LTCI policy, don't be content just to look at a summary of it. Examine the entire policy—and not in the insurance agent's or broker's office. Take it home so that you can study it carefully and have family, friends, or a financial advisor check it with you.

After reading the policy carefully, ask the agent or broker any questions you have about any aspect of the policy—premiums, coverage, exclusions, or benefits. If the broker cannot point to a place in the policy itself that answers your question, you need to request a response in writing, signed, directly from the insurance company itself. If you choose to purchase a policy based on such an extra written explanation, make sure that the written explanation is attached to and made an official part of your policy.

Group LTCI

Your employer, union, trade association, or professional organization may offer you the chance to buy group LTCI rather than buying an individual policy. In a group insurance policy, the group (called the "master policyholder"), rather than the individual, has the direct contractual relationship with the insurance company. Policy terms are established jointly by the group and the insurance company. As a result, you may have fewer options to choose from than you might get in an individual policy.

Group policies usually offer one advantage over individual policies: Because of the group's greater purchasing power, the initial policy premiums are generally lower than they would be for an individual policy.

But group policies also carry their own hidden risks. Over the years, the group will be free to decide—in negotiations with the insurance company—how much premiums will rise. The group may make decisions that favor newer or younger members over older ones. Or, the group may even decide to terminate the policy altogether. The insurance company is free to cancel group coverage, something it cannot do to an individual policy. Depending on the policy's terms, those covered by the group policy may then have to continue as individual policyholders at higher premiums.

If you are considering a group long-term care policy, study its terms very carefully. Pay special attention to what rights you have if the group or the insurance company cancels the policy.

Eligibility for LTCI

Wanting to buy LTCI and being able to afford basic coverage may not be enough to get you a policy. That's because insurance companies weed out people they decide are most likely to need a lot of expensive long-term care or to need care soon and deny them coverage or charge them high premiums for it.

When you apply for a policy, the insurance company is likely to ask for "underwriting." This means you will have to provide information not only about your current health but also about your medical history. You may even be required to undergo a physical exam and "cognitive testing" to determine if the insurance company believes you are at increased risk of developing Alzheimer's or dementia.

Depending on its interpretation of your medical history and condition, plus your age, the insurance company might decide not to sell you a policy at all. Over 40% of LTCI applicants in their seventies are denied a policy; 20% of people in their sixties are denied; and 10% of people in their fifties. Even if an insurance company does not deny you a policy, they might charge you a considerably higher premium because of your health history. (See "The Cost of Premiums," next.)

The Cost of Premiums

When you consider the cost of any LTCI policy, you must consider your financial position at two different stages in your life. First, look at the premiums you'll have to pay compared with your income and assets during your working years. And then, because you probably will have to keep paying premiums into your seventies and eighties, you must also look at your likely income if and when you stop working full-time.

In your calculations, you must also factor in the likelihood that your premiums will rise 10% to 25% during the life of the policy. This is true despite an insurance company's advertising that it won't raise your rates. The fact is, they won't raise your rates individually, but at some point they probably can and will raise rates for all similar policyholders —which means that your premiums will go up. So, remember that not only the initial premium, but also the terms under which premiums may be raised, are important (see "Premium Hikes," below).

The Five-Percent-of-Income Guideline

Consumer and financial experts generally agree that LTCI is too risky unless you can pay the monthly premium with no more than 5% of your income. When calculating this 5% figure for future years, bear in mind that your premiums are likely to rise 10% to 25% over the life of the policy, while at some point—for many people, when they formally "retire"—your income will probably drop.

In general, if you expect to have substantial assets and income—over $500,000 in assets in addition to your home, and over $50,000 per year in income (in today's dollars)—when you reach your eighties, then a long-term care policy with good benefits and compound inflation protection might continue to be comfortably affordable for you.

Initial Cost of Premiums

From one insurance company to another, there may be considerable difference in premium amounts for virtually the same policy—another reason to shop around. For different policies and coverage, the cost of initial premiums varies greatly—from $100 to $500 or more per month—depending on a number of different factors:

- **Your age when you first buy the policy.** Policies tend to be about 10% higher if you buy them in your fifties rather than your forties, then roughly 10% higher for each five-year increment between age 65 and 75.

- **Your overall health and health history.** Insurers rate applicants—usually putting them into one of four categories—based on their and their families' health history. They charge higher premiums for people whose condition or history indicates either that they are more likely to need care early, or they are likely to need care for a long time (such as for dementia).

- **The different types of care covered.** The more types of care—home care, assisted living, adult day care, and nursing home—that could be covered by the policy, the higher the premium. (See "Kinds of Care the Policy Will Cover," below.)

- **Where you live.** The cost of long-term care varies greatly from state to state, and from urban to suburban to rural locations. Insurance companies vary their rates depending on where you live now, because that is their best guess of where you are likely to receive care later.

- **The amount of potential benefits.** The higher the daily benefit you choose, the higher your premium. Also, the longer the coverage could last—two years, three years, five years, indefinitely—the higher the premium. (See "Benefit Amounts and Length of Coverage," below.)

- **Inflation protection.** The care you are insuring for may be ten, 20, or 30 years away. And the cost of care when you need it is likely to be much higher than it is today. So, almost as important as the amount of your benefits is having inflation protection, which will raise your benefit amounts over the years. Inflation protection increases your premiums. Good inflation protection increases them even more, but it is essential. (See "Inflation Protection," below.)

- **Marital status.** Married couples can get two breaks on the cost of their premiums. If one spouse is relatively healthy and considerably younger, the premium for the other spouse might be lower (because the younger, healthy spouse is likely to help care for the older spouse). Also, if both spouses buy the same policy, there is usually a discount of 10% to 20%.

- **Other terms and conditions.** Other terms and conditions in your policy can mean higher or lower premiums. These terms include the length of the elimination (waiting) period before benefits are paid, length of exclusion (another waiting period) for preexisting condition, benefit payout flexibility, and refund provisions. (These terms and conditions are discussed later in this chapter.)

A Cap on the Length of Premium Payments

If you buy an LTCI policy at a fairly young age and then have the good fortune of living a long and healthy life, you might wind up paying your LTCI premiums for 30 years or more—whether or not you ever collect on them. One way to avoid this possibility is to buy a policy that caps the number of years you would be obligated to keep paying premiums. Caps are available from some companies at 15, 20, 25, or 30 years.

Of course, if the company offers a cap, you'll pay more in monthly premiums—the earlier the cap, the greater the rise in premiums. Still, if you are healthy now and have a family history of long life, you may want to figure that longevity into your LTCI plans by buying a policy that includes a premium cap.

> ### LTCI May Be Tax Deductible
>
> A certain amount of LTCI premiums may be tax deductible as medical expenses—if your total medical deductions exceed 7.5% of your gross adjusted income. Also, benefits paid to you under an LTCI policy are not taxed as income.
>
> However, these tax advantages apply only to policies that are considered Qualified Long Term Care Insurance (QLTCI), under guidelines established by the federal government. If you enrolled in your policy before 1997, it is automatically considered a QLTCI for tax purposes. If you enrolled after January 1, 1997, the policy must meet the federal requirements.
>
> The maximum amount per year of QLTCI policy premiums that can be deducted as a medical expense depends on your age. The amounts change every year—check the instructions on your federal tax return for the current figures.

Premium Hikes

No matter what an advertising brochure seems to indicate, an insurance company always retains the right to raise premiums—or at least to ask state regulators for permission to raise premiums on all policies of a certain type—in one way or another. There are two common ways policies allow for premium increases.

Attained-Age Provisions. One of the ways insurance companies entice customers to a particular policy is to offer very low initial premiums but have these premiums rise automatically when the insured person attains certain age levels—usually 70, 75, 80, and 85. Also, some of these policies don't say precisely how much the premium will increase when you reach these ages. In that case, a premium might rise so much that you would be forced to drop your coverage—wasting all the money you've paid in premiums up to that point, just when you are most likely to need its benefits.

Level Premiums. With level premiums, insurance companies promise that your premiums will be raised only if they are raised by the same percentage for all other holders of the same policy. Unlike attained-age increases, an insurance company must get the approval of your state's insurance commission to raise level premiums. Insurance commissions routinely grant these across-the-board increases, so be prepared to pay higher premiums—perhaps 10% to 25% higher—in future years even with a level-premium policy.

"Noncancelable" Group Policies Are Not as Good as They Sound

Some insurance companies advertise their group LTCI policies as "noncancelable," meaning that the insurance company cannot raise premiums and cannot cancel an individual's coverage unless he or she fails to pay those premiums. While this sounds like a great deal, the reality isn't nearly so terrific. Despite these limitations, insurance companies retain the right to terminate the entire group policy. Or, the group itself may end the relationship with the insurance company.

When an insurance company terminates a group policy, people who were covered under the policy are allowed to convert to individual policies offering identical or equivalent coverage. But the new policy premiums are then calculated on an individual basis, not at the previous group rate. And the insurance company then has the same right to raise those premiums as it has for any other individual policy.

Kinds of Care the Policy Will Cover

The long-term care you may one day need could take one of several forms—and over time, perhaps more than one form. Initially, you might only need help at home from time to time, provided from family and friends (80% of all long-term care is like this). Or you might need regular but not daily help—some of it paid, some not—at home with certain routine activities of daily living. At some point, you might require 24-hour monitoring, though not much actual hands-on care, provided by an assisted living or similar residential care facility. Eventually, you might need the intensive monitoring and care of a nursing home.

Almost all basic LTCI policies offer some amount of home care and nursing facility care. Most also offer coverage for assisted living and adult day care, though you may have to pay extra for it. (These are relatively new developments—in the past, many policies did not cover home care without added premiums, and very few policies covered assisted living.)

When you consider long-term care insurance, look for policies covering the broadest types of care that might be useful to you. Most people want coverage for all possible types of coverage, since it's difficult to know what might be needed someday. But you may be able to reduce your premium by choosing a policy that covers some types of care but not all. (See the discussion of types of care, below). For each type of care, you must also determine how much in benefits you will pay for, how the benefits will be paid, and how long they will be paid.

Custodial Care Nursing Homes

Unless you are interested in a policy that only covers home, your primary concern may be finding coverage for a long, expensive stay in a nursing home.

Look for a policy that broadly defines what is a nursing facility. A policy should specifically state that it will pay nursing home care benefits for care in any "custodial care" facility licensed by the state. Avoid any policy that will pay for care only in facilities that are certified by Medicare. Many custodial care facilities do not provide skilled nursing care and, so, do not need Medicare certification.

Beware of any policy requirement about the size of the facility. Some policies will not cover care in a facility with less than a certain number of beds, usually 20 or 30. But there are many fine small residences, and there is no reason a smaller facility cannot provide excellent care. There may be more of these smaller residences to choose from near you, and such a residence might be best able to meet your needs.

Assisted Living Facilities

One of the most important recent developments in long-term care has been the rise of assisted living residences (sometimes called residential care or extended care facilities) as an alternative to nursing homes. (See Chapter 3.) They provide part-time personal assistance and monitoring for people who need some help with the activities of daily life but do not need the intensive care and monitoring of a nursing facility. They are also considerably less expensive than nursing homes. Recently, LTCI has begun to recognize this trend by including assisted living coverage in policies.

One of the first things to investigate about any policy is whether (and under what terms) it covers assisted living residences. Find out what specific conditions, including any state certification a facility must have, under which a policyholder may qualify for coverage. The policy should use the same triggers for benefits to start for assisted living as it does for a nursing home. In this way, your decision about moving to an assisted living facility or to a more restrictive, institutional, and expensive nursing home can be based on your personal needs and preferences, not on whether your insurance policy will cover you.

Home and Community Care

Most LTCI policies provide coverage for home care, and many also include care provided at nonresident community care facilities (often called adult day care). Because good home care and community care have become common in most places, it makes good sense for most people to look for a policy that covers these services as broadly as possible.

As discussed in Chapter 2, home care can mean a wide variety of services, including fairly intensive nursing and physical or speech therapy, help with activities of daily living such as bathing, eating, or moving about, and homemaker services such as housecleaning, shopping, and laundry. In an LTCI policy, look for the widest variety of coverage possible. There are a number of coverage issues to consider:

- Most home care policies cover skilled nursing care, other professional medical services, and nonmedical personal care, provided by a licensed home care agency. Personal care includes help with the activities of daily living, such as eating, bathing, dressing, using the toilet, and moving around. It may also cover what are sometimes called "instrumental" ADLs, such as monitoring medications.

- Some policies also provide limited coverage of some personal care or homemaker services, such as light housecleaning, grocery shopping, meal preparation and clean-up, phone calls, and paperwork. But many policies cover such services only if they are provided by a certified home health agency aide who is also providing other home care duties.

- Good home care policies also provide for respite care and hospice care, in addition to what is covered by Medicare (see "Supplements to Home Care" in Chapter 2).

- Also look for policies that cover care at licensed community care facilities, such as adult day care centers. This can be a crucial supplement to paid home and family care, allowing you to regularly get out of the house and see people in a safe, structured environment while your family members are at work, and for less cost than an individual home care aide.

Get Coverage for Independent Home Care Aides

You can get high-quality, flexible, and less costly personal care at home from independent aides who do not work for a home care agency. (See Chapter 2.) Therefore, it's important to get home care coverage that pays for independent aides, as well as care from a certified home care agency. There are three different types of coverage that could pay for independent home care aides, some more flexible than another:

- One type of policy requires only minimal qualifications, such as state or county certification as a home care aide, in order for you to receive benefits to pay the aide. Many independent aides will fall within such policy guidelines. But many others—usually the least expensive and sometimes the easiest to work with—are not certified, and so this type of policy would not pay for them.

- A better type of coverage pays home care benefits no matter who— except family members—provides the care as long as it is part of a formal plan of care developed by your physician or by a home care agency. This includes adult day care as well as in-home care.

- The best policy of all has what's called "indemnity" home care coverage. It pays the policy's daily home care benefit for care provided by *anyone*, including unlicensed aides and family members. With this type of coverage, once you meet the policy's conditions for home care coverage, the daily benefit amount is paid directly to you—and you can use it to hire whomever you choose, at whatever rate they agree to.

When Narrower Coverage May Be Enough

Generally, most people should look for an LTCI policy that covers a wide range of care, because you don't know now what kind of care you will need down the line. However, under some circumstances, it may make sense to buy a less expensive policy that covers fewer areas of care.

Home Care Coverage Without Residential Care

In some situations, you may want to consider an LTCI policy that covers *only* home and community care, without any residential facility coverage. (This is particularly the case if you live in an area with good home and community care services available.) Here are some examples of those situations:

- You are part of a couple, you are considerably older or more physically limited than your spouse, and she or he is capable of caring for you at home if the need should arise.

- You have a large, supportive family who live nearby and would fill in whatever care is needed beyond paid care.

- You have one or more adult children who are committed and able to take you into their home to care for you if that need should arise, and you prefer that arrangement to living in an assisted living or nursing facility.

   Remember, though, that you are insuring for a need that may not arise for 20 or 30 years, and it is difficult to predict what your situation— including your spouse's health and your family's ability to help out—will be at that time.

Residential Coverage Without Home Care

Some people may want a policy that provides residential facility coverage, but not home care. If you are unmarried, do not have younger family members close by who will give you substantial help if you stay at home, or live in an area with few home or community care services available, home care might *not* be a realistic alternative for you. In that case, there is probably little point in paying much extra for its coverage.

However, if the cost of adding home care is not too great, the extra coverage is usually worth it. That is because by the time you need long-term care, home and community care may have become a viable and more attractive alternative for you.

Benefit Amounts and Length of Coverage

If you are purchasing LTCI to protect your income and assets from the high cost of long-term care, it makes sense to buy coverage only if the benefits will be high enough and last long enough to defray a lot of those costs. If your benefits cover only a small percentage of your long-term care costs, those costs will eat up your savings anyway—and you will have spent money on years of premiums for nothing. So, as a rule, policies with small benefits (under $100 per day for residence facility care; under $50 per day for home care) and a limited coverage period (less than two years) are of questionable value.

Benefit Amounts

Long-term care policies pay a fixed dollar amount of benefits for covered care. Benefits vary from $50 to $500 a day, depending on how much you pay in premiums. A policy may pay the same daily benefit amount for any type of care, or it may set up a two- or three-tier system, with different amounts for different types of care. A common policy set-up has home care being paid for at 50% or 75% of the daily rate for nursing home care. The best arrangement is to have a flexible benefit payout, in which you determine how much (up to a daily maximum) the policy pays for each type of care *at the time you receive that care.*

Flexible Benefit Payout

If you have coverage for both residential facility care and home care—or for nursing home, assisted living, and home care—it is a great advantage to have a policy that will pay benefits in any combination, sometimes called a "pool of coverage." This allows you to use your benefits for one level of care, then switch to another level and use whatever total amount of benefits remains unpaid.

For example, take a policy with a maximum benefit of $219,000—$200 per day for three years of nursing home care, $100 per day for six years of home care. Flexible benefit terms would allow three years of home care benefits $109,500 ($100 per day for 1,095 days) and leave the remaining $109,500 for nursing home care ($200 per day for 547 days).

Also, look for flexibility regarding how the policy measures home care benefit amounts. Will the policy pay by the week or month rather than by the day? This could save you money if you don't get care every day but the daily costs exceed your daily benefit amount. For example, if you receive $100 per day worth of home care three days a week, a policy that pays $75 per day would leave you with $25 per day unpaid for each of the three days of care. But if your policy would pay $525 weekly (up to the same amount as seven days at $75 per day), then the policy would cover the full amount of your $300 per week home care costs.

Length of Coverage

The length of time for which benefits might be paid can vary widely, from one year to an open-ended "no lifetime maximum." For example, a policy paying $200 per day for three years of nursing home care, or $100 per day for six years of home care, would have a potential for $219,000 in total benefits. The actual amount you wind up receiving depends on how long you qualify for care, whether your policy has benefit flexibility, how long the "elimination" or waiting period is, and what kind of inflation protection is built into the policy.

How Much Coverage You Need

The point of long-term care insurance is to protect against the financial consequences of an extended need for care, particularly in a nursing facility. For this reason, you need to pay attention to the minimum and maximum benefit amounts and the time periods that will apply.

Nursing Home Care

For nursing home care, the average annual cost nationally is about $80,000, or roughly $220 per day; it is lower or higher in some states and in urban areas versus rural ones. Before you buy a policy, get a sense of the average annual nursing home costs near you by checking with a half dozen or so nursing homes in your area. Then, gauge your policy benefit amount based on these figures. Of course, there is no guarantee that you will be in the same area if and when you need nursing home care years from now. So, keep these guidelines in mind:

- **Daily benefits.** A good policy will cover $150 per day minimum and $400 per day, maximum.
- **Length of coverage.** The minimum should be two years. Three to five years will be a sensible term for most people. More than five years coverage, or "unlimited lifetime coverage," on the other hand, means paying a very high premium for an unlikely scenario.

Home and Community Care

The amount of benefits needed for home care is very hard to judge. Unlike the fixed costs of nursing home care, the cost of home care depends on how much paid care you use (in addition to care provided by family and friends). For example, three days a week of a two-hour visit by a $20-per-hour aide costs $120 per week—a daily home care benefit of $50, or a weekly benefit of $250, would cover that cost entirely. On the other hand, eight hours a day, five days a week for the same aide would cost $160 a day, or $800 per week—for that, you would need a much larger policy benefit.

If you have an extensive, committed family who could and would provide you with substantial unpaid home care, you might be able to remain at home even though you need substantial paid care, too. In that case, a relatively high home care benefit—$200 per day, $1,000 per week—makes sense (if you can afford the premium). But if considerable family care is unlikely, then there is less need to pay for high home care benefits. That's because once you need a lot of care, without family support it would become too expensive to get at home even with high insurance benefits.

As discussed above, the best option is flexible benefits, in which you decide at the time you need care how much of your total benefits you want to spend on home care and how much to hold in reserve for nursing home or other care. Also, look for "indemnity" home care coverage—once you qualify for benefits, an indemnity policy pays the set daily benefit amount directly to you, and you can use it to pay anyone you want, at any pay rate.

Usually, people choose a longer period of benefits for home care than for nursing home care—often twice as long. This makes sense because people who can manage on home care tend to live longer than people who must enter a nursing home. But this is an average, not a prediction (or a rule), so benefit payout flexibility remains the best choice.

Inflation Protection

A benefit of $200 per day for nursing home care is a reasonable amount, given today's average nursing home cost of about $80,000 per year. But you are not buying a policy to protect yourself against today's long-term care costs. Instead, you are buying a policy to protect against the costs of care ten, 20, or 30 years from now. Because the cost of long-term care widely outpaces the overall cost of living, custodial care in a long-term care facility could easily cost $400 per day ten years from now. In 20 years, who knows how high the cost will be? If your benefits then are still only $200 daily, the uncovered costs would eat up your personal assets at lightning speed, and the insurance benefits you've paid for all those years would not protect them.

The only way to shield yourself from skyrocketing care costs is to make sure your long-term care policy has good inflation protection built into it. The emphasis is on *good,* because inflation protection comes in several different forms, and some are definitely better than others:

- **Added coverage purchase.** This type of provision permits you to purchase added coverage every few years, raising your benefit amounts. But the added coverage would come with new premiums—based on your increased age plus any other rate increases—that you may not be able to afford.

- **Simple automatic increase—cost of living.** Many policies offer benefits that increase by each year's national cost-of-living increase. However, these policies use the original benefit amount to calculate the percentage increase each time. These policies are better than the added coverage purchase option because your benefits go up automatically without requiring higher premiums.

- **Simple automatic increase—set amount.** These policies offer benefits that increase each year by a fixed amount—usually 5%. These are a little better than the cost-of-living increase policies because for the past few years, the cost-of-living has increased less than 5% per year. These policies, too, use the original benefit amount to calculate the percentage increase each year.

- **Compounded automatic increase.** These policies automatically increase benefit amounts each year by a set percentage, or by the cost-of-living, but they compound the increases each year rather than always using the original benefit amount as a base figure. Over ten, 20, or 30 years, this compounding will increase your benefits substantially. Of course, because automatic compounded inflation protection is so much better for the insured, premiums for such coverage are usually higher than with noncompound increase provisions.

- **Time-limited protection.** Most policies put a time limit on the yearly inflation benefit increase. The limit is usually ten to 25 years from the date the policy begins, or when the insured reaches a certain age, usually 80 or 85. If you buy the policy when you are in your fifties or sixties, make sure you get the longest possible period of inflation protection.

Good inflation protection may raise the initial cost of a policy by 25% or more. But without good inflation protection, the lower premium—and the policy it pays for—may be a total waste of money.

Shared-Care Policy for Couples

A recent innovation in LTCI policies gives greater flexibility to couples when they buy a policy that covers both spouses. Most LTCI companies now sell "shared-care" policies, in which spouses can pool together their benefits. So, for example, if each buys four years of coverage, they actually have a pool of eight years from which they can draw benefits in any combination. One spouse might use only a year of benefits, which would leave seven years of benefits for the other spouse. This arrangement is often beneficial for a woman in a couple, since women tend to live, and to need long-term care, longer than men do. It also tends to benefit the younger partner in a couple. That's because the survivor has no partner to provide unpaid care, and so usually needs paid care sooner.

Shared-care policies cost a bit more than traditional policies. But they allow the couple to buy a policy with a shorter benefit period—for a lower premium—because of the likelihood that one spouse will need less, leaving a longer period of benefits for the other.

Triggers That Start Your Benefits

Most policies will not begin paying benefits unless and until a physician certifies that your physical or mental condition has reached a certain level. This is often called a "benefit trigger." What the benefit trigger is—and what physician decides whether you meet it—plays a large role in determining whether and when you actually receive benefits.

Performing Activities of Daily Living

The benefit trigger most commonly used in long-term care policies is "inability to perform without assistance" some specified number of activities of daily living (ADLs). Each insurance policy includes its own list of five to seven ADLs, including:

- bathing
- eating
- dressing
- using the toilet ("toileting")
- walking ("ambulating")
- getting in and out of bed or a chair ("transferring")
- taking medication ("medicating"), and
- continence.

The policy pays benefits only when you need assistance to perform a specified number of the ADLs listed in the policy. When choosing a policy, consider the following:

- Some policies pay benefits if you need assistance with only two ADLs; other policies require three. Some policies will pay for home care once you need assistance with two ADLs, but won't pay for nursing home care until you need assistance with three. Obviously, the fewer ADLs necessary to qualify, the better for you.
- Consider a policy that requires you to need assistance with three ADLs only if there are at least seven ADLs on the total list.

- Bathing and dressing are almost always among the first ADLs with which people need help—so they should both be included in the list of qualifying ADLs.

- Make sure that you will be considered unable to perform an ADL without assistance even if you can perform it sometimes, but not without supervision.

- A policy should state that benefits will be paid if you have a "cognitive impairment" (diminished mental capabilities) that prevents you from regularly performing the requisite number of ADLs, even though you are physically capable of performing them. This is a crucial policy term because many people end up needing long-term care because of Alzheimer's disease or dementia rather than for physical disability.

- Do not buy a policy in which benefit payments are triggered only by "severe" cognitive impairment. This is a tough standard to meet.

Medically Necessary Due to Illness or Injury

In some policies, benefits are triggered only if you need care that is "medically necessary due to an illness or injury." "Medically necessary" is sometimes defined to mean that your medical condition will deteriorate if you do not receive the recommended level of care.

Avoid these policies for several reasons. First, simple frailty, sometimes combined with some disorientation or memory loss, is the most common reason elders require long-term care. If this is your situation, you may not be able to pinpoint a specific illness that has caused your condition. Second, your inability to perform several ADLs may make your life very difficult even though your medical condition is no longer deteriorating—and therefore, not triggering coverage. Third, it is often difficult to determine when an illness ends. If you originally need care because of an illness, the insurance company might eventually claim that the illness has ended—and, therefore, that your care is no longer covered. Because of all these serious problems, some states have gone so far as to outlaw policies that contain this "medically necessary due to illness or injury" trigger. If it's still legal in your state, don't buy a policy with this type of trigger.

As Determined by a Physician

Some policies will pay benefits only after a physician certifies, in writing, that the insured cannot perform the specified number of ADLs without assistance. Other policies require a physician or licensed home care agency to prepare a plan of care that describes the patient's needs and prescribes the type and amount of care needed. In either case, the policy should permit your personal physician, rather than a doctor appointed by the insurance company, to make the initial determination that you qualify for care. However, almost all policies include a provision that allows for a second opinion by a doctor appointed by the company.

Cognitive Impairment

Most states now require all long-term care policies to provide benefits to those who require care for Alzheimer's disease, as diagnosed by a physician. This sounds like a valuable consumer protection—except that there is no clear medical test to determine when someone has Alzheimer's disease rather than some other form of mental disorientation. Therefore, regardless of whether Alzheimer's is specifically mentioned, a good policy must include the inability to perform a number of ADLs because of cognitive impairment as a benefit trigger.

Coverage Conditions and Exclusions

The biggest risk with an LTCI policy is the great likelihood that you will pay premiums for many years but never require care for a long enough period to collect much in benefits. However, many of these policies also present other barriers to or delays in collecting benefits. The conditions and exclusions in LTCI policies sometimes eliminate or seriously delay coverage for the very people who need it most. You must consider these conditions—particularly the most common ones discussed below—very carefully when shopping for a policy.

Standard Elimination or Waiting Period

Almost all LTCI policies have an initial waiting period immediately after you file a claim for benefits. During this "elimination" period, no benefits are paid—you are responsible for paying all your long-term care costs. Elimination periods range from ten days to a year. Generally, the longer the elimination period, the lower your premiums. An elimination period of six months to one year may reduce your premiums by as much as one-third.

In many instances, an elder only needs care—either at home or in a nursing facility—for a short period of time. So, in this situation, a long elimination period would mean no benefits at all. However, the real purpose of an LTCI policy is not to cover a short period of care but to prevent the impoverishing costs of a long period of expensive care. Therefore, purchasing a policy with an elimination period of 90 days to six months probably makes good sense if it results in substantial premium savings. This is particularly true if you are buying the policy when you are in your fifties or early sixties and therefore will probably be paying the premiums for a long time.

Prior Hospital or Skilled Nursing Facility Stay

One of the insurance industry's cruelest tricks during the early days of LTCI was to hide in the small print the condition that benefits would be paid only if care began within a short time—usually seven to 30 days—after the insured spent at least three days in a hospital or skilled nursing facility (SNF). Sometimes, long-term care does immediately follow a hospital or SNF stay. However, most long-term custodial care is for chronic illness, frailty, Alzheimer's disease, or other physical or mental impairment, and does not follow an acute medical episode requiring a three-day or longer stay in a hospital or SNF.

Most states have now banned this prior-stay condition. However, in about a quarter of the states, such provisions are still legal. It is up to you as a consumer to spot such a provision in any policy that is offered to you. Ask the insurance agent or broker whether such a provision exists in any policy you are considering—and don't buy any policy that includes it.

Permanent Exclusions for Certain Conditions

Many policies permanently exclude coverage if you enter a nursing home or begin receiving home or community care as a result of specified illnesses or medical conditions. This means that you receive no benefits, no matter how long you receive care, if you need the care due to one of the specifically listed excluded conditions.

Conditions most commonly excluded are mental illness and alcohol or chemical dependency. But, a few policies also exclude coverage for HIV-related illness, nervous disorders, and even certain heart diseases, some forms of cancer, and diabetes. If your need for long-term care arises from any excluded condition, your policy will not pay any benefits toward the cost of that care.

If you already know that you have suffered from one of the excluded conditions listed in a particular policy, this policy obviously won't work for you—assuming some company would even sell you a policy. But you should also avoid any policy that has a long list of exclusions even if you have never had any of the listed illnesses or conditions. You may not need the policy coverage for many years—and in those intervening years, you may develop one of the excluded illnesses or conditions.

Preexisting Condition Benefit Delay

Some long-term care policies delay covering care if it is the result of an illness or condition that was diagnosed or treated within a certain period of time—usually six months to two years—before the start of the policy. This device works by delaying coverage—meaning the insurance company pays you no benefits at all—for a certain time after you begin receiving long-term care. If this period is relatively short (one to three months), you don't lose too much in benefits. Look for a policy with no delay at all. If you must accept a preexisting condition delay, look for a combination of the shortest prepolicy period and the shortest delay.

Useful Added Policy Provisions

Many policies offer added terms or provisions that can make them a bit more attractive or secure. Some of these provisions may make your premium slightly higher but are worth the cost. Others are simply included at no extra cost in certain policies.

Step-Down Provisions

One of the major problems with LTCI is that at some point policy-holders may have trouble continuing to make premium payments, especially if they don't need benefits for 20 or 30 years. Premiums rise over time, incomes drop, and other expenses may take over most of an elder's expendable income. Because of this slow deterioration in many older people's finances, over half of those holding LTCI policies bought in the mid-1980s to the early 1990s had to allow their coverage to lapse.

To help reduce the odds of this happening to you, look for a policy that allows you to step down your coverage. With a step-down provision, the amount of the daily benefit the policy will pay, the level of care it will cover, or the length of coverage is reduced from the amount for which you originally signed up. In exchange, the insurance company lowers your premium by a certain percentage. This may make it possible for you to keep the policy in effect—although for a diminished benefit—if you have trouble continuing to pay the original premium.

Policies with step-down provisions sometimes permit you to step up as well—to increase potential benefits in exchange for a higher premium. However, many policies require a step-up to be underwritten—meaning that you must still be in good health to move to higher benefits. A step-up provision may be of particular interest to someone who is young and doesn't want to take on high premiums until he or she is sure that the financial future will be rosy enough to pay for them, but who wants to leave open the option to pay for higher benefit protection.

Waiver of Premiums

A waiver of premiums provision allows you to stop paying premiums after you begin collecting benefits, or after you have collected benefits for a certain period of time. Without this important provision, much of the benefits you receive may just go back to the insurance company in the form of continuing premium payments.

Waiver of premiums often applies to nursing home or assisted living benefits only, not to home care. A few policies offer premium waivers as soon as benefits begin, although most require that you continue paying premiums for 30 to 90 days after you begin receiving benefits. As with most other policy terms, the better the waiver of premiums provision, the higher your initial premiums will be.

Some policies also offer a survivorship premium waiver. This means that if a couple with a joint policy has paid premiums for a certain amount of time—ten, 15, or 20 years—without collecting benefits, a surviving spouse no longer needs to pay any premiums if one spouse dies.

Refund or Nonforfeiture Provisions

There are several reasons why you might end your long-term care policy before you receive all or any of its benefits—a change in your financial picture, a sharp increase in premiums, a change in your health. If you end your policy, what happens to all those years of premiums you paid?

If you drop your coverage before full benefits have been paid, a few long-term care policies provide that a small percentage of your premiums will be refunded. These provisions are only offered in some policies, and often they apply only if the policy has been in effect for a long time—ten, 15, or 20 years. A nonforfeiture provision probably offers the most benefits to someone who is relatively young when first buying the policy and who is, therefore, more likely to pay premiums for many years before requiring care. Even in that case, though, such a provision doesn't provide much financial protection, so it should not be a major consideration when you choose a policy. But if you are trying to decide between two policies that are close in most important respects, the existence of one or another of these refund provisions might tip the balance.

Reduced Paid-Up Provisions

Reduced paid-up provisions allow you to drop your coverage—that is, stop paying premiums—but still collect reduced benefit amounts if and when you qualify for them, once you have paid premiums for a set number of years (usually 20 or 25).

Death Refunds

Death refunds provide that a small percentage of the premiums paid (less any benefits paid) will be returned to the insured person's estate, if an insured dies before a certain age (usually 65 or 70).

Survivorship Provisions

Survivorship provisions give some protection to a surviving spouse when both spouses have purchased a joint LTCI policy. With a survivorship clause, if one insured spouse dies, the surviving spouse may stop paying premiums after a set number of years, with the insurance remaining in effect. This can be very important if the death of one spouse drastically reduces what had been the couple's income. ●

Protecting Choices About Medical Care and Finances

Whether you are reading this book for yourself or helping an elder make choices about long-term care, it's important to plan for the time when someone else must step in to help with medical and financial decisions. In particular, there are two types of simple legal documents that everyone should make while they are able to do so: health care directives and durable powers of attorney for finances.

A health care directive allows you to state your wishes for medical care in the event that you are unable to speak for yourself. You can also name a trusted person to make sure your wishes are carried out—and to make other crucial medical decisions for you. If you become incapacitated, the person you name can then work closely with your health care providers to ensure that you get the kind of care you would want.

A durable power of attorney for finances lets you name someone to manage your finances if you are no longer capable of doing so. This person can pay your bills, collect and deposit any income or benefits due to you, and take care of any other financial matters that must be handled.

Unfortunately, if you are caring for an elder who is already mentally incapacitated, it is too late to prepare these documents. (The elder must be of sound mind to make them.) However, it is possible to go to court and ask that you or another trusted relative or friend be named to make decisions on the elder's behalf. You'll find a brief discussion about these procedures—known as conservatorship or guardianship proceedings—at the end of this chapter.

Health Care Decisions

Years ago, the U.S. Supreme Court recognized that every individual has the constitutional right to control his or her own medical treatment. Today, every state provides standard methods and forms you can use to express your health care wishes in advance, and to name someone to make decisions for you if you are unable to communicate.

When Your State Form Is Not Enough

When it comes to health care directives, there are many differences in the terminology, forms, and formats used from state to state. A few state laws require you to use a specific form for your directive to be valid. Regardless of your state's requirements, your goal is to make sure your directions to doctors and other health care providers are clear. If you feel strongly about a particular kind of care but your state's law or form doesn't mention it, you should add that specific request to your directive. You can simply write your added requests on the form and ask that they be respected and followed, as is your right under the U.S. Constitution.

Putting your wishes for health care in writing can help alleviate your fears that unwanted medical treatment will be administered to you or that desired treatments will be withheld. Your documents can also relieve family members from having to make agonizing decisions about your medical treatment. This can be particularly important when family members might not agree about what care you should receive. Also, doctors and hospitals have their own rules and beliefs about what constitutes proper medical care. Even if your family knows your wishes and tries to have them followed, medical personnel are not necessarily bound to follow them unless you have completed and signed valid health care documents.

This section explains the basics of health care directives and tells you how to make them.

Types of Health Care Directives

There are two documents that allow you to set out your wishes for medical treatment. Both are grouped under the broad label health care directives. The first is a living will—a written statement you make directly to health care providers setting out the types of care you do and do not want if you become incapacitated. You can use your living will to say as much or as little as you wish about the kind of care you want to receive. (This is covered in more detail below.)

The second document, a durable power of attorney for health care, lets you name someone you trust to be your health care agent (sometimes called an "attorney-in-fact" or "health care proxy"). It's this person's job to make sure that doctors and other health care providers give you the kind of care you've requested.

In some states, both of these documents are combined into a single form, often called an advance directive.

Planning for Incapacity: Vocabulary

Several terms used in this chapter sound similar but have distinct meanings, and some terms vary by state. Here's a chart to help you keep the terms straight.

Term	Also Called	What It Means
Health Care Declaration	• Living will • Directive to physicians • Health care directive • Medical directive	A legal document in which you state your wishes about life support and other kinds of medical treatments. The document takes effect if you can't communicate your own health care wishes.
Durable Power of Attorney for Health Care	• Medical power of attorney • Power of attorney for health care • Designation of surrogate • Patient advocate designation	A legal document in which you give another person permission to make medical decisions for you if you are unable to make those decisions yourself
Advance Health Care Directive		A legal document that includes both a health care declaration and a durable power of attorney for health care. It is currently used in more than one-third of the states
Health Care Agent	• Attorney-in-fact for health care • Patient advocate • Health care proxy • Surrogate • Health care representative	The person you name in your durable power of attorney for health care to make medical decisions for you if you cannot make them yourself
Durable Power of Attorney for Finances		A legal document in which you give another person authority to manage your financial affairs if you become incapacitated
Attorney-in-Fact for Finances	Agent for finances	The person you name in your durable power of attorney for finances to make financial decisions for you if you cannot make them yourself
Springing Power of Attorney		A durable power of attorney that takes effect only when and if you become incapacitated

What You Can Cover in Your Health Care Directives

You have many options and a great deal of flexibility when providing instructions for your medical care. In fact, some people feel unsure about how to complete their health care documents because they are faced with big choices—and unfamiliar terminology. But filling out the forms is not as difficult as it may seem at first. Here's some guidance to help you complete both your living will and your durable power of attorney for health care.

What to Include: A Checklist

Following is a list of the most important things you can accomplish by making health care directives. You aren't required to address every issue but, if you like, you are allowed to:

- appoint your health care agent—that is, the person who will make decisions for you if you are unable to speak for yourself
- name the doctor you'd like to supervise your care
- specify whether or not you want your life prolonged with medical treatments and procedures
- identify specific medical treatments and procedures that you want provided or withheld—for example, a respirator or artificially administered food and water
- state any general feelings or wishes you have about your care, such as where you would like to be cared for or any special directions that may affect your comfort or awareness—for instance, whether you want full doses of pain medication even if it makes you unconscious or unaware of family or friends, and
- provide instructions for donating your organs, tissues, or body after death.

Your Living Will

When you make your living will, you'll be asked to express your wishes about many types of end-of-life medical care. Whether your preferences are simple or quite detailed, you should give some attention to the issues discussed here.

Life-Prolonging Treatments. Every state's health care form asks about preferences for life-prolonging treatments or procedures. A life-prolonging treatment is one that would only briefly lengthen the process of dying or sustain a condition of permanent unconsciousness. In other words, the patient would die soon—or die without regaining meaningful consciousness—whether or not the treatment was administered. Common life-prolonging treatments include a respirator, cardiopulmonary resuscitation (CPR), dialysis, surgery, and antibiotic drugs.

You can use your living will to state that you want to receive all life-prolonging procedures or none at all. You can also pick and choose among procedures, naming those you'd like to receive and specifically rejecting others.

Artificially Administered Food and Water. If you are close to death from a serious illness or permanently unconscious, you may not be able to survive without the administration of food and water (often called nutrition and hydration.) Unless you indicate that treatment should be withheld, doctors will provide you with a mix of nutrients and fluids through tubes inserted in a vein, into your stomach through your nose, or directly into your stomach through a surgical incision, depending on your condition.

Permanently unconscious patients can sometimes live for years with artificial feeding and hydration without regaining consciousness. If food and water are removed, death will occur in a relatively short time due to dehydration, rather than starvation. Such a course of action generally includes a plan of medication to keep the patient comfortable.

When you make your living will, you can choose whether you want artificially administered food and water withheld or provided. This decision is difficult for many people. Keep in mind that as long as you are able to communicate your wishes, by whatever means, you will not be denied food and water if you want it.

Duty of Medical Personnel to Honor Your Health Care Directives

Health care providers are generally required to comply with the wishes you set out in your health care documents—and to honor your health care agent's authority as long as the agent's directions are a reasonable interpretation of your wishes. In some situations, however, a health care provider is permitted to reject a medical decision made by you or your agent. For example, this may be true if:

- The decision goes against the conscience of the individual health care provider.
- The decision goes against a policy of a health care institution that is based on reasons of conscience.
- The decision would lead to medically ineffective health care or health care that violates generally accepted health care standards applied by the health care provider or institution.

But this doesn't mean that your health care instructions can be ignored. A health care provider who refuses to comply with your wishes or the directions of your health care agent must promptly inform you or your agent. And if you or your agent wishes, the provider must immediately take steps to transfer you to another provider or institution that will honor your directive. In some states, a health care provider who intentionally violates these rules may be legally liable for damages.

In an Emergency: DNR Orders and POLST Forms

Some people who do not wish to receive life-prolonging treatment when close to death—most often those who are quite elderly or already critically ill—may also want to prepare a DNR order or POLST form.

If a medical emergency occurs, a Do Not Resuscitate (DNR) form alerts emergency personnel that you do not wish to receive cardiopulmonary resuscitation (CPR). The form can be prominently posted in your home, either near the front door or next to your bed. In addition to preparing and posting this form, you can also obtain an easily identifiable Medic Alert bracelet, anklet, or necklace.

Additionally, many states are starting to use a form that is similar to a DNR order, usually called a Physician's Orders for Life-Sustaining Treatment (POLST), a Clinician's Orders for Life-Sustaining Treatment (COLST), or Medical Orders for Scope of Treatment (MOST). Unlike a DNR order, a POLST form includes directions about life-sustaining measures—such as intubation, antibiotic use, and feeding tubes—in addition to CPR. This form helps to ensure that medical providers will understand your wishes at a glance. (But it is not a substitute for a thorough and properly prepared health care directive.) A POLST form may be used in addition to—or instead of—a DNR order.

If you think you might want to make a DNR order or POLST form, talk to your doctor or a hospital representative, or one of the staff if you live in a senior residence or long-term care facility.

Relief From Pain and Discomfort, Known as "Palliative Care" or "Comfort Care." If you want death to occur naturally—without life-prolonging intervention—it does not mean you must forgo treatment to alleviate pain or keep you comfortable. In fact, the health care documents for all states assume that you wish to receive any care that is necessary to keep you pain free, unless you specifically state otherwise.

This type of care is most often called palliative care. Rather than focusing on a cure or prolonging life, palliative care emphasizes quality of life and dignity by helping a patient to remain comfortable and free from pain until life ends naturally. Palliative care may be administered at home, at a hospice facility, or in a hospital.

Not all health care professionals are well educated about palliative care, so if it is important to you, you may want to spend some time learning about your options and discussing your wishes with your health care agent and your treatment providers. For more information, see the resources below. (You can also turn to Chapter 6 of this book to learn more about hospice care.)

For More Information About Health Care Choices

When completing your health care documents, you may find that you want more information about your options. If you have a regular physician, he or she may be able to explain medical procedures more fully and help you explore your options. You will also discover whether your doctor has any medical or moral objections to following your wishes. If your doctor does object and will not agree to follow your wishes, you may want to consider changing doctors.

If you don't have a regular doctor or you find that even your doctor does not have the information you need, you can do some research on your own. Here are two websites that can get you started:

- www.growthhouse.org, and
- www.pbs.org/wnet/onourownterms.

Your Durable Power of Attorney for Health Care

When you make a durable power of attorney for health care, you can give your health care agent as much or as little power as feels comfortable to you. Most people give their agent comprehensive power to supervise their care. Recognizing this, the power of attorney forms for most states give the person you name the authority to make all health care decisions for you unless you specifically place limits on that authority in the document. This means that your agent will normally be permitted to:

- consent or refuse consent to any medical treatment that affects your physical or mental health (though your agent is not permitted to authorize any act that violates the wishes you've stated in your living will)

- hire or fire medical personnel

- make decisions about the best medical facilities for you

- visit you in the hospital or other facility even when other visiting is restricted

- gain access to your medical records and other heath-care-related personal information, and

- get court authorization, if it is required, to obtain or withhold medical treatment, if for any reason a hospital or doctor does not honor your living will or the authority of your health care agent.

As long as you are able to understand and communicate your own wishes in a legal power of attorney document, your agent cannot override them. And, as mentioned, you are permitted in the document to restrict your agent's authority in any way that you like. For example, some people give their health care agents only the authority to carry out the health care wishes specified in their living wills, and not to make other medical decisions for them.

Think carefully, however, before you add limiting language to your power of attorney. One of the most important reasons for appointing a health care agent is so that someone will be there to respond to the needs of your situation as it develops. Your medical needs may change in ways that you cannot now foresee, and an agent who has full power can act for you no matter what the circumstances. Also, if your agent does not have full power, medical decisions about your care might be made only after difficult struggles among family members and health care providers.

Choosing Your Health Care Agent

There are a number of things to consider when choosing your health care agent. Most important, your agent should be someone you trust absolutely—and someone with whom you feel completely comfortable discussing your wishes for medical care. Your agent need not agree with all of your preferences, but must fully respect your right to get the kind of treatment you want. In addition, make sure the person you appoint:

- can be present when decisions need to be made (most often this means naming someone who lives nearby or who is willing to travel to be at your side for long periods of time), and
- would not easily be bullied or intimidated by doctors or family members who disagree with your wishes.

If you make a durable power of attorney for finances to name someone to manage your finances in case you become incapacitated (see "Financial Decisions," below), it's usually wise to name the same person as both your agent for health care and your agent for finances. If you feel that you must name different people, be very sure you name agents who get along well and will be able to work together. You wouldn't, for example, want your agent for finances to interfere with your health care wishes by stalling or resisting payment of medical or insurance bills, two things over which your agent for finances will most likely have control.

Finally, it's a good idea to appoint someone to act as a backup or replacement agent if your first choice is unable to serve. Make it clear, however, that the second person is an alternate. It is not wise to appoint coagents: Two decision makers may complicate the process and interfere with your ability to get the care that you want.

State Restrictions on Who Can Serve as Your Agent

A number of states have rules about who can serve as your agent. Attending physicians and other health care providers are commonly prohibited from serving. Some states presume that the motivations of such people may be clouded by self-interest. For example, a doctor may be motivated to provide every medical procedure available—to try every heroic or experimental treatment—even if that goes against a patient's wishes. On the other side, treatments may sometimes be withheld because of concerns about time or cost.

Before you select an agent, be sure to learn your state's requirements and restrictions.

When Your Documents Take Effect

Your health care documents take effect if your doctor determines that you lack the ability or capacity to make your own health care decisions. The definition of incapacity varies from state to state, but lacking capacity usually means that:

- You can't understand the nature and consequences of the health care choices that are available to you.

- You are unable to communicate your own wishes for care, either orally, in writing, or through gestures.

Practically speaking, this means that if you are so ill or injured that you cannot express your health care wishes in any way, your documents will spring immediately into effect. If, however, there is some question about your ability to understand your treatment choices and communicate clearly, your doctor (with the input of your health care agent or close relatives) will decide whether it is time for your health care documents to become operative.

In some states, it is possible to give your health care agent the authority to manage your medical care immediately—that is, as soon as you sign your documents. If your state allows this option, you may prefer to make an immediately effective document so that your agent can step in to act for you at any time, without the need to involve a doctor in the question of whether or not your health care documents should take effect.

Making your document effective immediately will not give your agent the authority to override what you want in terms of treatment; you will always be able to dictate your own medical care if you have the ability to do so. And even when you are no longer capable of making your own decisions, your health care agent must always act in your best interests and diligently try to follow any health care wishes you've expressed in your living will or otherwise.

Making Your Documents Legal

Every state requires that you sign your health care documents. If you are physically unable to sign them yourself, you can direct another person to sign them for you.

You must sign your documents, or have them signed for you, in the presence of witnesses or a notary public—sometimes both, depending on your state law. The purpose of this additional formality is to ensure that there is at least one other person who can confirm that you were of sound mind when you made the documents.

Each state's witness requirements are slightly different. In many states, for example, a spouse, other close relative, or any person who would inherit property from you under your state's law is not allowed to act as a witness. In others, the person you name as agent can't be a witness. The purpose of these laws is to avoid any appearance or possibility that another person was acting against your wishes when encouraging specific medical choices.

It's important that you understand and follow the witnessing and notarization requirements for your state; they should be listed with the instructions that accompany your state's form.

What to Do With Your Completed Documents

After you have completed your health care directives, there are a couple of additional steps you should take.

Make and Distribute Copies. Keep your signed, original health care documents where your agent can easily find them if the need arises, and give your agent a copy of the documents for reference. Also, give copies to:

- any doctor you regularly consult
- the office of the hospital or any other care facility where you are likely to receive treatment
- the patient representative of your HMO or insurance plan
- the administrator of the senior residence or long-term care facility where you live
- close relatives, particularly immediate family members—your spouse or partner, children, or siblings
- trusted friends, and
- your cleric or lawyer, particularly if you don't have a family member who lives nearby.

Make a list of all the people and places that get copies of your documents. It will make things easier if you later need to change or revoke your wishes.

Keep Your Documents Up to Date. Review your health care documents every couple of years, to make sure they still accurately reflect your wishes. Advances in technology or changes in your health may prompt you to change your mind about the kind of care you want.

In addition, consider making new documents if:

• You move to a new state.

• You get married or divorced (some states will automatically revoke your health care agent's authority, so it's best to make a new document).

• You made and finalized a document many years ago.

• Your health care agent becomes unable to serve, or you want to appoint a different person as your agent.

Revoking a Document

If you want to change or cancel your health care documents, you can do so at any time.

To revoke the appointment of your health care agent (or an alternate agent), most states require that you either deliver a written notice to your agent and health care providers, or personally inform your doctor that you no longer want your agent to serve. You may revoke other health care choices simply by informing or demonstrating to your health care providers and others who know about your wishes that you want to cancel or change them.

Nevertheless, if you are well enough to do so, the best practice is to revoke an out-of-date document in writing and prepare a new document that reflects your current wishes. When revoking a document, you should tear up the original and ask anyone who has a copy to return it to you to be destroyed.

As a practical matter, even if you prepare a written notice of revocation and tear up your old document, it is important to tell everyone who knows about the document that you have revoked it.

Where to Get Health Care Directive Forms

There are a number of ways to find the proper health care documents for your state. You don't need to consult a lawyer to obtain or prepare them, though you can certainly have a lawyer draw them up if that's more comfortable for you. If you want to prepare your own forms, here are some likely sources:

- local senior centers
- local hospitals (ask to speak with the patient representative; by law, any hospital that receives federal funds must provide patients with appropriate forms for directing health care)
- your regular physician
- your state's medical association
- the National Hospice and Palliative Care Organization's website "Caring Connections," at www.caringinfo.org, 800-658-8898, that provides free health care directive forms for every state
- *Quicken® WillMaker Plus* (software from Nolo) that contains forms for all states except Louisiana, and thorough instructions to help you complete them, and
- *Living Wills & Powers of Attorney for California*, by Shae Irving (Nolo), a book that provides complete forms and instructions to help California residents prepare health care directives.

Financial Decisions

Wills and probate will take care of distributing your income and assets after you're gone, but they do not kick in until your death. If you are incapacitated and unable to make financial decisions, you will need another document, called a durable power of attorney for finances, to make sure your finances are handled as you wish.

A durable power of attorney for finances allows you to name someone (called your "agent" or, in some states, your "attorney-in-fact") to handle your finances if you become incapacitated. Every state recognizes this type of document. Preparing a durable power of attorney is simple and inexpensive—and will help those closest to you handle your financial affairs, should the need ever arise. If you don't prepare a power of attorney before you become incapacitated, your loved ones will have to ask a court to grant them authority over your financial affairs in a conservatorship or guardianship proceeding—which can be a time-consuming and expensive process. (See "Guardianships and Conservatorships," below.)

Granting Authority to Your Agent

The success of any power of attorney arrangement depends on the trust and understanding between you and the person you appoint as your agent. You can help make this relationship work by putting specific instructions in your document about the particular financial actions you do and do not want the agent to take. Your agent has only the financial authority you grant in your document. You can tailor the document to your specific financial situation, granting your agent the authority to pay routine bills, make bank deposits, handle Social Security, insurance, and other paperwork, make investments, operate your business, or even sell your home.

You may want to define and limit your agent's authority over certain financial matters. But keep in mind that you can't predict every financial issue that might arise in the future. To make sure that even unexpected financial matters are handled as you would want them to be, you must choose someone you trust, and who has sound financial judgment, to be your agent. As mentioned earlier, it usually makes sense to name the same person you choose as your agent for health care decisions, unless that person isn't good with money. If you name two different people for these jobs, make sure they can—and will—work together.

How to Find the Forms You Need

You can use *Quicken® WillMaker Plus* software from Nolo to prepare a durable power of attorney for finances that is valid in your state.

Deciding When Your Durable Power of Attorney Should Take Effect

There are two types of durable powers of attorney for finances: those that take effect immediately, and those that don't go into effect unless and until a doctor certifies that you are incapacitated. Which one you should use depends on when you want your agent to start handling your financial affairs—and on the relationship you have with your agent.

If you want someone to take over some or all of your financial tasks now, you should make your document effective as soon as you sign it. Your agent can start helping you right away and can continue to do so if you later are unable to make decisions for yourself.

If you want to make all of your own financial decisions unless and until you become incapacitated, you have two options. If you trust your agent not to take over until it's absolutely necessary, you can make your power of attorney effective immediately. This gives your agent the legal authority to act on your behalf should the need arise, but you can still handle your finances yourself.

If you don't want to make your document effective immediately, you can execute a "springing" power of attorney—a document that gives your agent the power to act only if you are declared incapacitated, in writing, by a doctor.

Springing powers of attorney are attractive to many people; they allow people to keep maximum authority over their own affairs and permit others to step in only if absolutely necessary. However, there are a few drawbacks to springing powers of attorney. First, your agent will have to go through the potentially time-consuming and complicated process of getting one or more doctors to declare you incapacitated. Second, some people and institutions are reluctant to accept a springing power of attorney, even though the document is perfectly legal. An institution might insist on proof that you are really incapacitated, for example, or might hold up a transaction while it satisfies itself that the document is valid. Although these hassles don't come up often, they can cause delays and disruptions.

Finalizing and Changing Your Documents

After you've completed your durable power of attorney for finances, you must observe a few formalities to make it legal. You must sign your power of attorney in the presence of a notary public for your state. In some states, notarization is legally required to make the document valid. But even if it isn't legally required, signing before a notary will make life easier for your agent. People and institutions often expect to see a notarized document—and may not accept one that isn't notarized, even though it's valid.

Some states also require you to sign your document in front of witnesses. Your witnesses must be mentally competent adults, and your agent may not act as a witness. A few states impose additional witness requirements—and some require your agent to sign the power of attorney or a separate consent form before taking action on your behalf.

If your document grants your agent power over real estate, you must file a copy of your document with the land records office of any county where you own real estate. This process is called "recording" or "registration." In two states, North Carolina and South Carolina, you must record your durable power of attorney in order for it to remain in effect if you become incapacitated. For details about how to record a document in your state, contact your county's recorder's office. This information is often available online.

Once you have finalized your document, you should give the original to your agent, if the document takes effect immediately. If you created a springing power of attorney, keep the original yourself, in a safe, convenient place that your agent can reach quickly, if necessary. Your agent will need the original document to act on your behalf. You may also want to give copies of the document to the people and institutions your agent will have to deal with—banks, government offices, or insurance companies, for example.

You can change the agent or other terms of the document at any time, as long as you are legally competent.

Powers of Attorney and Medicaid

As explained in Chapter 8, there are several ways to protect your assets from the reach of a long-term care facility while still qualifying for Medicaid. Several of these methods, however, might require you to transfer assets after you are no longer capable of doing so. If you create a durable power of attorney for finances, you may want to include the power to transfer title of property and other assets to a spouse, children, or other specifically named people—the same people to whom you would want the property to pass after your death.

Estate Planning Resources From Nolo

When the time comes to consider long-term care, it is also time to plan for the disposition of your estate. Nolo offers many resources to help you with estate planning tasks, including wills, living trusts, and other tools for probate avoidance and estate tax savings.

You may want to start by visiting Nolo's website at www.nolo.com, where you'll find lots of helpful (and free) information about estate planning. For more, you can turn to the following tools:

Quicken® WillMaker Plus (software for Windows), allows you to use your computer to prepare a will, health care directive, and durable power of attorney for finances. It can also help you make a document setting out your wishes for your final arrangements.

Nolo's Online Will and *Nolo's Online Living Trust* let you make your will or living trust online, quickly and easily. The program asks you a series of straightforward questions and offers detailed help along the way. When you're done, you just print and sign your documents.

Plan Your Estate (book) by Denis Clifford, offers in-depth coverage of all significant elements of estate planning, from simple wills to probate avoidance and complex tax-saving trusts.

Estate Planning Basics (book) by Denis Clifford, is a short course in estate planning, providing simple and straightforward explanations that help you learn what you need to know to complete your estate plan.

Quick & Legal Will Book (book with eforms) by Denis Clifford, shows you how to prepare a will that meets your needs, including basic trusts for minor children or grandchildren. Will forms are provided as tear-outs and as downloadable eforms.

Make Your Own Living Trust (book with eforms) by Denis Clifford, provides a complete explanation of how to prepare a living trust. The book contains forms allowing you to create a probate-avoiding living trust and, for married couples, a tax-saving AB trust.

8 Ways to Avoid Probate (book) by Mary Randolph, offers a thorough discussion of all the major ways to avoid probate by transferring property at death outside of a will.

Guardianships and Conservatorships

Much of the advice so far in this chapter may not apply to you if the elder you are concerned about is already incapacitated and unable to make decisions. At that point, the elder can no longer enter into legal arrangements or delegate responsibility for decisions to others. Yet, there is a danger that without these prior legal arrangements, financial institutions, government agencies, health care providers, and bureaucrats of every variety will either refuse to take action regarding the elder's affairs or will take actions without regard for your wishes or for what you know the elder would want.

In this situation, you may have to go to court and ask a judge to appoint you or another friend or relative to act on the elder's behalf. There are procedures in every state to do this. Some states have only one legal category, usually called guardianship, while others have a second category, usually called conservatorship and often limited to financial matters.

In general guardianship proceedings, the legal question is whether or not the elder has become "incompetent" to handle any of his or her own affairs. In about half the states, you will have to present medical evidence of incompetence to the court. In more limited proceedings to establish a financial conservatorship or guardianship only (see below), the court can act if it finds that the elder is unable to handle financial affairs, even though he or she is not completely legally incompetent.

In conservatorship or guardianship proceedings, an elder has a right to appear in court with an attorney and to consent or object to the proposed arrangement. In many states, if the elder does not have an attorney, the court may appoint one. Similarly, changing the conservator or guardian's authority requires an additional court order to which the elder can consent or object. The conservator or guardian is held responsible for any mismanagement of the elder's property.

In some states, you can handle conservatorship proceedings without the assistance of a lawyer if no one challenges the need for the conservatorship and its scope. More complicated guardianship procedures, however, will require a lawyer's help, particularly if the elder or anyone else does not agree that the guardianship is necessary or that the person seeking to be guardian is the right person for the job.

Financial Conservatorship or Guardianship

A conservator or guardian can be appointed by a court solely to protect an elder's property—savings, real estate, and investments, for example. He or she can also conduct daily financial affairs, such as paying bills, or arrange for services when the elder is unable to do so. This type of limited management assistance is appropriate when the elder is still capable of caring for himself or herself, but is unable to carry out personal business affairs efficiently because of disorientation or disability. In this situation, the conservator or guardian does not have power over the elder's personal conduct, but has authority over financial or other affairs as the court orders.

One advantage of a limited conservatorship or guardianship is that it leaves an elder free to make many important decisions independently: where to live, with whom to associate, what medical care to receive, and how to handle property, for example. Nonetheless, it is still a court process in which a judge makes a ruling, occasionally against the elder's will, that gives another person authority over some parts of the elder's life. It is, therefore, a procedure to be used only if no other solution seems feasible.

Full Guardianship

Full guardianship is an extreme measure that severely restricts the legal rights of an elder based on a court's finding of legal incompetence. It reduces one's legal status to that of a minor, with no control over one's own money or property, decisions about medical care, or institutionalization. A person under guardianship even loses the right to vote.

If an elder retains some degree of orientation and capability, a court's decision that he or she is incompetent can be emotionally devastating and, in fact, self-fulfilling. The person deemed legally incompetent may well give up the will to care for himself or herself and become much less competent than before. Obviously, full guardianship is a very serious step, to be taken only when a person's mental condition leaves no other choice.

Conservatorships, Guardianships, and Medicaid

A conservator or guardian is under a legal obligation to act only in the best interests of the elder. There are times when those best interests may require transferring assets to a spouse, child, or other person so the elder can qualify for Medicaid. Taken at face value, giving away someone's property does not appear to be in that person's best interests. Therefore, a conservator or guardian who wants to transfer an elder's property for Medicaid purposes should first go to court, explain the proposed transfer, and get the court's approval.

Elder Fraud

Older Americans are targets for a wide variety of professional con artists. They are also frequently tricked or pressured by unscrupulous relatives, neighbors, and companions. And, they are sometimes preyed upon by paid caretakers or staff in organized residences whose close contact with vulnerable elders may offer troublesome temptation.

Fraud and excessive pressure tactics strike not just well-to-do older people but those with modest and very limited assets as well. The results can be devastating, in money and even a home lost and in emotional damage. These scams and looting may also directly affect an elder's adult children. An estate children would have received from a parent may be severely diminished, if not lost altogether. And, because these assets are gone, the adult children may wind up having to pay for much of the parent's long-term care as well.

This chapter covers some common types of fraud committed by professional con artists. It also discusses the ways in which family, companions, acquaintances, and paid caretakers sometimes use their frequent contact and positions of trust to unduly influence older persons. It explains how to spot such frauds and undue pressure, and where to get help if an elder is being victimized.

Why Elders Are Targets

National crime statistics show that people over 60 are *twice* as likely to be victims of fraud and undue influence as are younger people. In fact, the number is probably quite a bit higher, because many elders are too embarrassed or frightened by, or uncertain about, deceptions to report them. There are a number of reasons why seniors are defrauded and pressured at such an alarmingly high rate.

Concentrated assets. Older people tend to have most of their financial assets concentrated in two or three large blocks—for example, a bank account, a few major stocks, and the home they live in. Because these assets can be easily tapped into for large amounts, they are very attractive to con artists.

Long life, limited funds. It is now common for people to live a long time. And the cost of long-term care can be staggeringly high. Many seniors are afraid that their savings will not be enough to support their lifetime needs. As a result, they may be too quick to respond when someone offers a scheme promising to dramatically increase their assets.

Isolation. Retirement, physical problems, and fear of the streets mean that many older people spend most of their time at home. Therefore, they are likely to be there when telemarketers or door-to-door scam artists call. Also, the very thing that provides the easiest contact with the outside world—the telephone—is the source of much fraud (see "Telemarketing," below). And, because most elders are not out in the world of work and commerce, they tend not to have many people with whom to discuss the shady proposals that come their way.

Physical and emotional vulnerability. Many elders are alone and often lonely much of the time—spouse deceased, family scattered, network of friends dwindling. They are, therefore, more likely to be receptive when anyone—con artist, scheming relative—pays attention to them. Elders also may need help, both physical and organizational, with their daily and long-term personal and financial affairs. These helpers, unfortunately, can too easily help themselves.

Because of their disconnection from the workaday world, many elders believe that there are both financial opportunities and risks "out there," but do not know exactly what they are. As a result, they are susceptible when someone comes along claiming to explain things to them. This problem is often made worse by the mild forgetfulness and lack of mental sharpness that often accompanies advanced age.

Group Living Doesn't End the Risk

If you are responsible for a parent or another elder's financial well-being, do not let down your guard simply because the elder is now "safely" living in an organized senior residence.

Although most professional frauds are perpetrated against elders who live at home alone or as a couple, living in a group setting, such as senior housing, assisted living, or a long-term care facility, does not entirely insulate them from con artists or schemes.

Whenever an elder has access to a telephone or the Internet, he or she is prey to telemarketers and scam artists. Also, in group living situations, sophisticated financial scammers can spread their schemes from person to person like a virus. And, as people in assisted living situations become increasingly frail and dependent, they become more vulnerable to the quiet pressures of family members and paid caretakers. The staff who run senior and assisted living facilities have too much on their plates already to effectively screen against financial schemes or unscrupulous relatives.

Who Commits Elder Fraud

There are a variety of common scams and pressure tactics used against elders. They include professional con artists who use telemarketing, email, postal mail, and door-to-door solicitations and seminars and other group meetings to ensnare and defraud seniors. But they also include neighbors, acquaintances, paid caregivers, and family members who take advantage of their positions of trust with vulnerable elders.

Con Artists

Con artists come in many shapes and sizes—old and young, friendly helpers and professional advisors, financial wizards and beefy ditch-diggers. Here are some common methods they use to separate elders from their money. (Specific scams and pressure tactics are described at the end of this chapter.)

Telemarketing

The telephone is a lifeline for many elders. It helps them keep in touch with distant friends and family. And it helps them communicate with shops and service providers when physical frailty or disability makes venturing out difficult. But the phone also allows con artists to get in touch with elders who are often at home. An elder's telephone may offer a line of least resistance, as older people may be more willing to speak to a stranger on the phone than in person and may be more easily persuaded by a pitch made on the phone than through the mail.

Telemarketing scams come in many varieties. They include phony solicitations for charities, "free" prizes that cost you to collect, get-rich-quick investment "opportunities," sweepstakes, holiday packages, health products, magazine sales, and work-at-home kits. There are even "recovery" scams—false promises to help previously hoodwinked people recover their losses.

To avoid being caught in one of these frauds, here are some tips on when to be suspicious and rules to follow to protect yourself or an elder. Certain practices commonly used by telemarketing con artists can serve as red flags—warning that you may be the target of a scam.

"Free" prizes or gifts. Be extremely wary if someone tells you "You have won!" A telemarketer may tell you that your name was randomly selected to receive a "free" gift, prize, or trip. This may be part of a supposed sweepstakes, or a "complimentary" gift. In order to claim this prize or gift, however, you "only" have to pay postage, shipping, handling, taxes, or other supposed costs or order a small amount of some other product. The problem is that regardless of how wonderful the prize or gift sounds on the phone, it always turns out to be worth far less than the money you must send to claim it.

Limited time only. "Act now," a telemarketer may tell you—"this is a one-time-only offer." "This limited-time offer will expire tomorrow." Or, "You have to hurry; there are only a few of these left." Any of these phrases should ring the alarm bell. They are a classic pressure tactic that tricks people into forgetting about all the usual standards they would apply when buying something. Jumping at such a telephone offer without having seen the actual item often means committing yourself to a shoddy product. You can always find legitimate products offered at reduced prices somewhere, so comparison shopping among different retailers will bring you the best price, not a one-time-only phone deal.

Don't Give Out Personal Information

Identity theft is the use of another person's credit card, Social Security number, bank numbers, or other information to pose as that person and illegally make purchases or withdraw money. Fraudulent telemarketers sometimes engage in identity theft by asking for personal or financial information for "identification purposes only" or to "verify" that you are the winner of a gift or prize.

Companies with which you already are doing business may properly ask for information to verify your identity *if you call them*. But you should never give out such information to a company that has contacted you on the phone and with which you have not previously done business.

Available only by phone. Before agreeing to anything or giving any information over the phone, you should always ask to have written materials sent to you. This will allow you to study the details of the offer without the pressure and possibly misleading tactics of the telemarketer or telephone salesperson. You should also ask for the company's contact information—name, address, and phone number. This information will allow you to check the company's reliability with a government agency or consumer protection organization before you commit yourself to anything.

Con artists often try to get people to skip these sensible precautions by claiming that the offer is available "only by phone." Or, the salesperson may say there is no printed material because the company is "new" or the offer is only "for a limited time." Whatever the reason, unless you have written materials and contact information, you should immediately end any conversation with the telemarketer—after saying that you don't want to be called again.

No risk. Any offer that claims to be "risk free" is likely to be bogus. You should immediately end the conversation if you hear these claims, particularly with offers for investment or other money-making schemes. There is no such thing as a risk-free investment. These telemarketers are in business to make money, and the money they are after is yours. One way or another, if you send them or give them access to your money, they will find a way to keep at least some—and, too often, all—of it.

National "Do Not Call" Registry

One way you can protect against unwanted calls is to register your telephone number on the federal government's national Do Not Call list. Once your number is on this list, you can't be called by any company soliciting business, unless you already do business with them. (There are a few other exceptions discussed below.)

Registration is free—simply dial toll-free 888-382-1222 (TTY 866-290-4326) from the phone number you want to protect. Or, you can register online at www.donotcall.gov, if you have an email address (yours or a friend or relative's) to which the Registry can send a confirmation. Within 72 hours of registering online, you will get a confirmation email with simple instructions for completing the registration process.

Another way to limit the number of unwanted calls you get is to have your name removed from the telephone directory. Unwanted callers can still obtain your number from marketing lists, but it can cut down on calls from some shady operations. Call your local phone company to have your name removed from the directory.

Lawful telemarketers. It may take up to 12 weeks to get the full benefit of registering on the Do Not Call Registry because companies are only required to check the registry every three months. However, anytime a company does call, you may tell them that you have signed onto the registry and ask them not to call you again; they are legally required to honor your request.

Your registration on the Do Not Call list is permanent for each phone number. However, if you change your phone number or add another phone line, you will need to register that number separately.

National "Do Not Call" Registry (cont'd)

The Do Not Call Registry does not cover every potential lawful telemarketer. The registry does not apply to nonprofit groups, survey companies, political organizations, or charities (though if a charity calls you and you ask not to be called again, they must honor your request). The registry also does not apply to any company with whom you have done business—bought something, signed up for service, made a payment—within the previous 18 months. That means you will continue to get calls from your local phone company, cable company, bank, credit card company, and the like. However, you may tell any such company not to call you again, and they are required to follow your request.

Telephone con artists. If telemarketing con artists are ready to commit fraud and other crimes while preying on the elderly, how can the Do Not Call Registry protect against them? Registering on the Do Not Call list can help in two ways. First, some large-scale telemarket scam operations use the registry to cut down on wasted calls. Although they don't care about violating the registry law, they do not want to waste time and energy making calls to people who are registered and, therefore, less likely to respond to their telephone pitches.

The other way registering can help protect you is to raise an alarm for you when you get a call from a company with which you have not previously done business. Because legitimate companies do not normally violate the Do Not Call Registry, you should immediately suspect that such a call is coming from a fly-by-night or downright illegal operation.

Door-to-Door

Elders are particularly vulnerable to door-to-door con artists for the simple reason that they are often alone at home during the day. Also, the convenience of someone making a "house call" can be very attractive to elders. And door-to-door salespeople are often very persuasive—friendly, convincing, and honestseeming—to people who are home alone.

Many door-to-door sales frauds have to do with the house itself—home repair, home improvement, painting, gardening or landscaping, and kitchen or other homemaking gadgets. Magazine and book club sales are also common, as are solicitations for charity.

Some of the tricks most often used by door-to-door scam artists, and ways to avoid them, are described below.

"I'm in the neighborhood ..." Con artists often say that they have come to your door because they were already working for others in the neighborhood. If you are interested in what someone has to sell, ask for references—the names and addresses or phone numbers of the neighbors the salesperson has supposedly done work for. If the salesperson can't give you references, don't do business with them. If you do get names, tell the salesperson that you will contact the references first, and then get in touch with them. Check with the references about the quality of the work performed or products sold before agreeing to anything yourself. Also, make sure—by getting addresses—that the people you talk to actually had the work done or bought the product and are not merely accomplices.

"Hi, you're Rosie Jones, aren't you?" Many con artists are extremely smooth talkers. One of the ways they try to gain your confidence is by addressing you by name when you answer the door. This gives you a first impression that they already "know" you from friends or neighbors. In fact, it probably means nothing more than they have seen your name on your mail or in the phone book.

CHAPTER 11 | ELDER FRAUD | 321

"We can talk better inside." Con artists often say that they can talk more comfortably, or can show pictures or papers better, or simply that it is more polite, to continue a conversation inside the house. They know that once they are inside a home, it is much easier to pressure someone into buying something. Elders, in particular, can become nervous when a stranger is in the house. Sometimes an elder will agree to buy something in the hope that doing so will get the person to leave.

The answer to this problem is simple—never let someone you don't know into your house. Conduct all initial discussions either outside or through your door, with the other person outside. If the initial information you get from people makes you want to consider doing business with them, set up an appointment for them to return on another day. And, have a friend, relative, or adviser present during that later appointment.

"Don't worry about paperwork." Many door-to-door hucksters tell people that part of what's so great about what they're offering is that they are ready to get right down to work without any paperwork "nonsense." They do this to conceal their lack of legitimate credentials. Of course, some small jobs—a little garden work, washing windows—can be done very well and properly without the workers having any official license or permit and without any written contract. But for almost anything else, you should have a copy of the following paperwork:

- **Business card or brochure.** Get a copy of the salesperson's business card or brochure. It should have complete identification information on it, including an actual address (not just a post office box) and phone number.

- **License or permit.** Many cities and counties require all door-to-door salespeople to have a special business license. And if the salesperson is proposing home repair or improvement, he or she should have a contractor's license. When you get the number, check with your city, county, or state consumer protection agency or Better Business

Your Right to Cancel

If you buy any product from a door-to-door salesperson, a Federal Trade Commission (FTC) rule permits you to cancel your purchase, without giving any reason and without penalty, within three days. This Cooling-Off Rule, as it is known, recognizes that people often buy things not because they really want to but because they give in to the pressure tactics of door-to-door salespeople.

In general, the Cooling-Off Rule applies to anything you buy from a salesperson at your home for $25 or more. It does *not* apply, however, to the purchase of services such as home repair, home improvement, cleaning, painting, gardening, or the like. Under this rule, salespeople are required to tell you about your cancellation rights when they make a sale. And they are supposed to give you a preprinted cancellation form, to use if you want to exercise your right to cancel during the three-day cooling-off period. If they do not provide you with a cancellation form, you may cancel by writing a letter identifying the date, price, and item of purchase and stating that you are canceling the purchase under the FTC's Cooling-Off Rule. If you cancel your purchase in writing within three days, the seller has ten days to refund any money you have paid.

For more information about the Cooling-Off Rule, you can call the FTC toll-free at 877-382-4357 or look at "Facts for Consumers—The Cooling-Off Rule: When and How to Cancel a Sale" on the FTC website at www.ftc.gov/bcp/edu/pubs/consumer/products/pro03.shtm.

Bureau to make sure that the permit or license is legitimate. (See "Where to Get Help," below.)

- **Written offer/bid with details.** If you decide to do business with a door-to-door salesperson, make sure the transaction is spelled out in detail in a written contract. The contract should describe exactly and completely the work to be done or the product to be purchased, including warranties and conditions for return or refund. It should state the full and final price and exactly what that price includes (materials, labor, hauling, shipping, "handling," installation). It should also provide dates by which the work is to begin and finish, or the product is to be delivered. Anything you agree on with the salesperson should be included in the written contract: Never rely on something you are told or promised that is not put in writing. Do not leave any blank terms on the contract for the salesperson or company to "fill in" later. And make sure that the salesperson signs and dates the contract before you do.

"It's now or never." Con artists often pressure people into buying something or agreeing to do home repair or improvement work immediately. They say that the "great deal" that is available is about to end, or that work can only be done cheaply while they are still in the neighborhood. The pressure is meant to keep you from checking their credentials and references. It is also intended to keep you from getting a second and third opinion about whether work really needs to be done and from getting other bids or prices by shopping around. Just because someone at your door tells you that certain work must be done—a roof repaired, new windows installed, a driveway repaved—doesn't necessarily mean it's true. Before agreeing to anything, talk to established businesses that do the same work. And if the work does actually need to be done, get several bids or estimates. Similarly, if a salesperson at your door offers a product, shop around—by phone, in stores, online—for the best price and quality before buying.

Seminars

It may seem that anyone who has gone to the trouble and expense of setting up a formal seminar, or has had a brochure or prospectus printed, is likely to be a legitimate businessperson. In fact, it may only mean that the scam they are running is after bigger chunks of your money than a small-time operation.

Seminars and printed brochures and prospectuses are frequently used in financial schemes—investments, insurance, annuities, supposed tax-savings plans, trusts, home equity loans. They often begin by circulating a flyer advertising the seminar at a place where seniors congregate—a senior residential complex, senior center, or church. The seminar itself may be held at the same place or at a nearby hotel or office building meeting room. Part of the scam may be to charge money for attending the seminar. However, many of the seminars are free, trying to lure people toward the bigger scam offered convincingly during the seminar itself.

The first thing to realize is that you should not put any trust in a seminar just because a legitimate senior center, residential complex, or church has given permission for it to be held there. Those places usually do not research the qualifications and business records of people who want to use their meeting space.

Likewise, you should not trust a seminar sales pitch just because it is given by a lawyer, accountant, mortgage broker, or other licensed financial adviser. These people may have legal credentials, and they may have products to sell that in some cases are legitimate. The problem is that they often try to get you to buy or invest in something that you already have, that you do not need, or that cannot meet the sparkling promises they make for it. Or, they get you to pay far too high a price for something you could get elsewhere.

The other common element in seminar scams is to get you into a seminar, then have you pay for "special" or "confidential" materials, then pay again for a "bonus" or "super" seminar, then pay for "personalized" advice. The total can run into hundreds or thousands of dollars, even though ultimately you might get nothing useful from it all.

Family Villains, Neighbors, and So-Called Friends

Professional con artists are not the only ones who take advantage of vulnerable elders. Unscrupulous family members, friends, and neighbors, all of whom are already in positions of trust, can be a source of great danger. Similarly, a new love interest may be looking more for a sweetheart scam than for companionship. One of these seemingly trustworthy people can develop a relationship in which the elder slowly falls prey to undue influence and pressure and from which it is difficult to escape.

The risk these family members and acquaintances pose can be even greater than that of a con artist. A professional con artist may take a single chunk of money from an elder for a phony or shoddy product or service. But a family member or new companion might gain access to, or even control over, all of an elder's assets, ultimately leaving the elder with nothing.

Older people who live alone and do not have frequent contact with many family members are the most vulnerable to such undue influence and pressure. This is particularly true if they are physically frail. Their loneliness is often compounded by a lack of confidence in dealing with the world and an attitude of not wanting to be seen as "bothering" adult children or other family members. In this situation, an elder is more likely to fall prey to the influence of some "new" person in their life. It may be a relative who has not previously had much to do with the elder but suddenly becomes involved. It may be neighbors who take the elder under their wing. Or, it may be a new friend or love interest who begins to spend a lot of time around the elder, providing first companionship, then assistance, and ending up controlling an elder's every move.

The pattern of control. There is a familiar pattern to this kind of undue influence by a manipulative family member or friend. It usually begins with a "new" person—someone who has not previously been involved in the elder's life—suddenly spending a lot of time with the elder. At first, the elder welcomes the advice, assistance, and companionship of the new person. But, slowly, the elder becomes dependent on that person, and begins to feel that this other person is now "the boss." This feeling is often compounded when the other person convinces the elder that the two of them are alone against the world—that other family and friends are all against them. This creates new fear and a sense of vulnerability in the elder, who cedes more and more information and control to the exploiting new friend. Ultimately, this exploiter may be so successful in isolating the elder that the elder comes to believe that this person is the elder's only hope for survival. At that point, this person can do almost anything without even so much as a protest by the elder, eventually controlling and looting all of the elder's assets. The specific ways in which some family and friends loot an elder's finances are discussed later in this chapter.

Warning Signs of Undue Influence or Control

There are several common warning signs that can alert you to the financial abuse of an elder by a family member, acquaintance, caregiver, or residence staff member. None of these signs necessarily means that financial shenanigans are occurring. But, they should at least alert you to pay close attention to what is going on and to investigate the state of the elder's financial affairs.

Changes in Behavior. A change in an elder's behavior may be the result of something in the elder's physical or emotional condition that has nothing to do with any outsider's influence. However, the following changes are common to undue influence situations. If an elder begins to exhibit some of these behavioral changes, a red flag should go up to find out what is going on, and to address the problem, whatever its source.

- withdrawal from people with whom the elder is usually in touch; failing to make or return phone calls; refusing visitors; being withdrawn, secretive, hesitant; avoiding discussing certain subjects, particularly relating to where the elder has gone and who has been visiting

Warning Signs of Undue Influence or Control (cont'd)

- frequent appearance of a "new" person in the elder's life. This is particularly worrisome if this person restricts other people's access to the elder or is always present when others visit the elder or if the elder defers to this person when speaking with others, especially regarding financial matters.
- frequent reference by the elder to one specific person who has not previously figured greatly in the elder's life, particularly if the elder seems to show great deference or respect for this person's ideas or suggestions
- change in habits, such as going frequently to the bank, doing lots of shopping, or having many new items at home. Conversely, if the elder or the elder's residence seems to be poorly cared for, this may be a sign that someone is siphoning off funds that should be used for the elder's care and well-being.

Changes in Financial Patterns. If there are changes in an elder's patterns of spending or in documents related to financial affairs, family members should check thoroughly to see that no one person is gaining control over the elder's finances. Warning signs of these changes include:

- sudden, unexplained changes in, disappearance of, or addition of someone's name to legal or financial documents, such as a will, power of attorney, bank account papers, ATM cards, credit cards, checkbooks, or the like
- extra and unusual financial activity, such as large or frequent bank or stock withdrawals, disappearance of funds, or transfers of assets
- disappearance of valuable possessions
- a new or suspicious version of the elder's signature, on checks, credit card receipts, or other documents
- services or items (or receipts or credit card records for their purchase) that the elder does not need or cannot use, or
- unpaid bills or lack of sufficient food and personal amenities.

Paid Caretakers and Residential Staff

Paid caretakers are often a wonderful source of comfort and relief to elders. And, they take a tremendous burden off family members. Despite low wages, long hours, and difficult working conditions, most paid caretakers provide dedicated service to physically and emotionally vulnerable elders. Similarly, the staff of senior housing, assisted living, and long-term care facilities are usually committed to the well-being of the elders who live there.

However, the amount of time a caretaker or residential staff member spends alone with an elder can also present tremendous temptation. Caretakers often help elders go shopping, pay bills, and do banking. This can be a great help to any elder. But the handling of an elder's money also presents an opportunity for misbehavior that a few caretakers can't resist. Also, because caretakers, staff members, and the elders in their care often get to know each other intimately, an elder may be vulnerable to all sorts of financial requests and schemes. The range of ways in which caretakers sometimes financially take advantage of elders is discussed in the next section. For a list of signs that indicate that a caretaker might be abusing a position of confidence, see "Warning Signs of Undue Influence or Control," above.

Types of Elder Fraud

This section discusses common types of elder fraud. It explains how particular types of fraud are perpetrated and the warning signs that can help you spot them.

Home Repair, Improvement, or Maintenance

Home repair and improvement is an extremely lucrative area of fraud upon the elderly. Many older people are unable to do any heavy work for themselves in and around their homes, yet at the same, time they know how important it is to properly maintain their home—often their only major asset. And home repair and improvement is expensive, so con artists and unscrupulous contractors can pry large amounts of money out of people in just one scam.

Home repair and improvement scams range from small-scale yard work and housecleaning to painting, pest control, major landscaping, roof and window replacement, siding, paving, kitchen and bathroom renovation, and even the construction of entirely new rooms. Sometimes scam artists will promise work, take a down payment, and never show up again. Sometimes they will make a small beginning but fail to complete the work. Or, they will do a cheap, slipshod job with shoddy materials, sometimes on repairs that were unnecessary in the first place.

Of course, you need not take the same kind of care with someone who wants to mow the grass compared with a contractor who wants to put on a new roof. But the principles are the same. Here are some things to do to protect yourself:

- Always investigate the individual or company who wants to do work before signing anything or permitting any work to be done. Ask for references to others for whom work has been done and then actually speak with those people, go see the work for yourself, or have someone you trust do that for you. If the work involves actual repair or construction, ask for the number of the company's contractor's license and insurance certificate, then check the status of both with the state or local licensing board. If you are unsure about whether a license is required or about whom to contact, call your local building inspection office or Better Business Bureau.

- If the proposed work is for some sort of repair, find out if the repair is really necessary. Have two or three other companies who do similar work examine the property and give estimates of what work truly needs to be done, if any, and how much it would cost if they did it.

- Never jump at an offer simply because someone has come to the house in person. Always comparison shop before buying. A legitimate contractor or worker will not mind returning another time after you have found out more about the proposed work.

• Be suspicious of any offer to do work at a "special price" for cash. Except for someone who does small jobs like mowing the lawn, washing the windows, or doing an occasional housecleaning, anyone in business should be willing to accept payment by check or credit card. And, while contractors may be entitled to some portion of payment in advance, they never should be paid in full until the work is properly completed.

• Get all agreements, guarantees, and warranties in writing and signed. All documents should have the company's name, address, phone number, and (if applicable) contractor's license number. And the papers should include every aspect of the job—timing, exact work to be done, and *total* cost including all labor, materials, and taxes. Nothing about the job should be left undecided when you sign a contract, and anything agreed upon should be included in the written agreement. If some term needs to be added by hand, make sure the salesperson signs next to that handwritten addition.

Watch Out for Liens

If you sign a home repair or improvement contract, you may be giving the contractor a lien against your property. Some of these liens are included in the contracts. In other situations, the contractor is automatically given a lien—often called a "mechanic's lien"—by operation of law.

In either case, the contractor can register this lien against your property if the job is not fully paid for. And as long as the lien remains, it can prevent the sale or refinancing of your property. This is an extra incentive to hire only a legitimate contractor and to have a solid agreement with the contractor about what the job is and how much it will cost.

Financial Planning and Estate Planning

One of the most extensive fields for defrauding elders is in the complicated and confusing world of estate and tax planning. Life insurance, supplemental health insurance, and annuities are also full of scam artists. It is not that these unscrupulous characters do not sometimes have legitimate trusts, annuities, and insurance policies to sell. Rather, they give false impressions about what these products and arrangements can do. And they sell them for far too much money to people who do not need them.

Perhaps the most common of these scams is the "living trust seminar." A living trust can be a valuable tool for transferring your assets upon your death without the formalities and expense of probate. But scam artists often get elders to pay for a living trust by giving them the false idea that the trust will save on their income or estate taxes. Similarly, con artists often convince elders to buy annuities to put into trusts, sometimes with the false suggestion that this will help them qualify for government assistance for long-term care. In truth, however, such annuities provide the con artist with a commission but do nothing to save on the elder's taxes or otherwise protect assets.

Con artists also get people to pay for new living trusts or other planning devices when they have perfectly good existing ones. Similarly, con artists get elders to sell their existing life insurance policies or annuities in order to purchase "better" ones. This replacement process often results in high penalties or tax losses for the elder and helps only the con artist seller who makes a fat commission.

Get Independent Advice on Any Loan, Trust, Insurance, or Estate Plan

Before you pay for any kind of trust, annuity, insurance, or other estate planning device or take out a loan or mortgage on your home, you should take several steps. First, get complete written information about the plan or loan and take it home so that you and people whose opinion you value can study it carefully. Any legitimate finance company or seller of estate or financial planning devices will have a printed description of the product and should expect you to take the written material home to study.

Then, consult with someone who is familiar with the legal device or loan to determine (1) exactly what its terms provide, (2) whether it can do what you think it can, (3) whether it should replace arrangements you already have, and (4) whether the cost is a fair price for what you get. This could be a friend or family member who works in the field of financial planning or lending. Or, it could be a trusted accountant, lawyer, or financial adviser. Paying a fee, if necessary, to get independent advice is probably well worth it. It may save you a lot of money in the long run and perhaps even prevent the fraudulent loss of your home.

Finally, if you still believe that the planning device or loan is a good idea for you, shop around to see if you can get better terms somewhere else.

Nolo Estate Planning Resources. Before you start paying for expensive estate and tax planning devices offered through a seminar, and even before you hire an independent adviser to look over a particular plan, you may want to do a little quick and inexpensive research on your own to learn what these devices can and cannot do for you. Nolo has an extensive list of books and software to help you get up to speed before—and perhaps instead of—blindly buying an expensive trust or other estate planning device. And, if ultimately you decide that you do want one of these planning devices, with the help of some Nolo resources you may be able to prepare the documents yourself, without having to pay a large fee to a lawyer, accountant, or other financial planner. For a discussion of these Nolo resources, see "Estate Planning Resources From Nolo," in Chapter 10. And go to www.nolo.com for lots of free information.

Refinancing, Home Equity Loans, and Reverse Mortgages

Unscrupulous finance companies and their pitchmen know that many elders have most of their life's savings tied up in their homes, but have very limited incomes. So, they pitch a variety of schemes to elders in which they convince elders to use their homes as collateral for loans. Of course, mortgage refinancing, home equity loans, and reverse mortgages are legitimate ways for people to use the value of their homes to get much-needed income. But these shady finance companies structure the loans and mortgages in such a way that elders unknowingly pay far too high a price for the income. And in some cases, the loans are set up in such a way that an elder is likely to default and wind up losing the property altogether.

Lenders engage in several types of deceptive practices to separate older homeowners from their money. One is called "loan flipping." In this scheme, the lender encourages what seems like a low-cost, long-term loan to replace an existing mortgage, with delayed payment on fees and points and interest. The lender calls again after a few months and offers a new loan, with more cash up front, to be paid over a longer time. Servicing this new loan eventually becomes a problem, so the lender offers another loan, and then another, until the borrower is plowing all of his borrowed money back into servicing the loan.

Another of these schemes is called "equity stripping." The lender offers a loan with repayment terms that eventually rise or balloon and which the lender knows will put a strain on the elder's income. This leads to a new loan with even worse terms, which eventually leads to default and foreclosure on the elder's home.

There are a variety of other deceptive loan practices that involve false figures or hidden charges. Lenders sometimes change the terms of a loan at the last minute, when you actually sit down to sign the papers. Under pressure to take it or leave it, many people sign. Another scam is to add unnecessary or overpriced "credit insurance" or various unexplained "fees" on top of the costs you have already agreed on. And some fraudulent lenders even go so far as to send you incomplete or inaccurate account statements so that you cannot keep track of what you actually owe.

Quick-Buck Investments

Remember that there is no such thing as a free lunch. Elders who are no longer working seem to be particularly vulnerable to fraudulent investment schemes that promise a fast, big payoff with no risk. These investment offers often come over the phone or by email, though they may also be part of a seminar scam.

Private Placements. This is a term that is applied to a very few legitimate but very high-risk investments that need not be registered with the Securities and Exchange Commission or a state securities agency. They are investments that only very sophisticated and wealthy investors should consider. Because such investments are off the government protection radar, many scam artists use this term when referring to their own fraudulent schemes, as an excuse for why an investor cannot check the investment's legitimacy with another broker or a securities agency.

Treasury Bills. Scam artists use the sense of legitimacy offered by the words U.S. Treasury to con investors. These supposed Treasury bill investments are sometimes called "Limited Edition" securities. Or, the offer is to "lease" an existing Treasury security. Sometimes the offer will include a picture of the supposed Treasury bond, which is actually a picture of a worthless retired bond. Be extremely suspicious anytime you are offered an investment in a Treasury security from an individual or company you do not know.

High-Yield Investment Programs (HYIPs). In HYIPs, con artists offer investments in "off-balance-sheet" trading, "deep-discount" notes, or "offshore bonds" and the like. These supposedly guarantee a risk-free return of some phenomenal interest rate, usually over 50%.

FOREX and Commodities Trading. Foreign currency (FOREX) and commodities trading are mystery worlds to most investors, so anything a con artist says may seem plausible. Investment in commodities like precious metals, gems, coins, and oil rights are often bolstered with the false promise that the values of such "hard" commodities never fall. The fact is, both types of investments are notorious for both rising and falling unpredictably. Neither type of investment should be entered except with a trader registered with the Securities and Exchange Commission.

Viaticals Fraud. Viaticals are another type of investment in which frauds are prevalent. A viatical is an investment in someone else's life insurance policy. You are offered at a discount the life insurance policy of someone who is seriously ill, providing you with a future profit in exchange for providing the insured person with some immediate money to help with medical care. If you are offered a viatical investment and hear that the return is going to be huge and the payoff quick, you should be very suspicious. Legitimate viatical investment should only be made through a licensed viaticals company or broker.

"Frozen Funds" and Other "Guaranteed" Investment Scams. An entire world of fraud exists around letters or emails from supposed lawyers, brokers, and other "professionals" overseas. For a long time, Nigeria has been a source of many of these scams, though they may come from anywhere around the globe. These messages offer huge returns in exchange for help getting large funds released after they have been supposedly "frozen" or otherwise blocked by a bank, insurance company, or court somewhere. Sometimes these funds are claimed to have arisen out of a traffic accident, legal case, or an estate battle. The con artist may even identify the person receiving the letters as somehow distantly related or connected to a deceased person whose money it was. At first, these messages may ask for identification information, then for money for expenses to get the funds released.

Whatever the specifics of an investment fraud, all of them offer some version of a very high return that is "guaranteed." Here are some of the things you can do to protect yourself against these fraudulent schemes:

- If an investment is offered as having a guaranteed return or having "no risk," forget about it. All investments have risk, and rates of return cannot be guaranteed. If you hear either term, it is a good bet that everything else about the investment is as false as that promise.

- "Offshore" is another word that should set off alarm bells. It is an all-purpose term con artists use to falsely explain why an investment is not registered with the SEC or state agencies and to pretend that you would not be liable for taxes on any income you receive.

- Beware of promises of high returns. If an investment could really guarantee a high return (over 10%), everyone in the world would be putting their money in it. In truth, the potential for a high return usually means a very high risk of losing everything.

- Beware of promises of a quick payoff. Investments are unpredictable, and the promise of a fast return on your money is usually the sign of a scam.

- Find out whether the seller is registered with your state securities commission or the National Association of Securities Dealers. Don't settle for registration with some "new" and probably phony online securities exchange or a supposed foreign securities exchange.

- Never invest under pressure. If someone tells you that you have to act immediately or lose the investment opportunity, the only thing you should do immediately is to end the conversation.

- Get all details of the offer in writing. Never invest through emails or phone conversations alone.

- When you have received all the written terms of the offer, take the papers to a financial adviser for independent advice.

Questions to Ask About Any Investment

If you have considered all the warning signs in this section but are still interested in pursuing an investment, the Securities and Exchange Commission strongly suggests that you first get satisfactory answers to the following questions:

- Is this investment product registered with the SEC and my state securities agency?
- How will this investment make money? (Dividends? Interest? Capital gains?) Specifically, what must happen for this investment to increase in value? (For example, increase in interest rates, real estate values, or market share?)
- What are the total fees to purchase, maintain, and sell this investment? After all the fees are paid, how much does this investment have to increase in value before I break even?
- How liquid is this investment? How easy would it be to sell if I needed my money right away?
- What are the specific risks associated with this investment? What is the maximum I could lose? (For example, what will be the effect of changing interest rates, economic recession, high competition, or stock market ups and downs?)
- How long has the company been in business? Is its management experienced? Has management been successful in the past? Have they ever made money for investors before?
- Is the company making money? How are they doing compared to their competitors?
- Where can I get more information about this investment? Can I get the latest reports filed by the company with the SEC: a prospectus or offering circular, or the latest annual report and financial statements?

Sweepstakes and Contests

All sweepstakes and contests are huge gambles with little chance of winning. But many of them do worse than just tempting you to take a longshot. Many phone or mail sweepstakes scams tell you that you have already won a prize, but that you must pay a shipping, handling, or "redemption" fee, postage, or some sort of "tax" in order for you to collect it. Other sweepstakes suggest that you have to buy something else—a magazine subscription, or one of a selection of grooming products, for example—in order for you to win the prize. Both of these set-ups are illegal. You should never pay anything to claim a prize.

The other common scam is to promise you a very attractive "bonus" prize if you purchase something. But the bonus prize turns out to be a flimsy, shoddy, or fake version of what you thought you were getting—a "boat" turns out to be a child's inflatable raft, a "fine chef's carving knife" turns out to be a floppy, plastic-handled toy that couldn't cut butter.

Some sweepstakes and contest frauds also seek a prize of their own that's bigger than just the money they can get you to send them. Some sweepstakes con artists try to get you to give them personal information—credit card, bank account, Social Security numbers—to claim your prize. Then, they use that information to defraud you in a big way, by charging huge amounts to your accounts.

"Recovery" Schemes

Unfortunately, the old expression "Once bitten, twice shy" does not always apply to victims of fraud. Elders seem particularly vulnerable to a second scam in which someone calls saying they can recover the elder's losses from an earlier fraud.

Sometimes these people identify themselves as attorneys or investigators. Others claim to be from law enforcement or some government agency with a vaguely familiar name. In order to gain the elder's confidence, they describe accurately the scam that the elder suffered before. (Of course they can describe it accurately—they are the same people who operated that earlier scam.) They then claim that they have been "tracking" these scams for lots of victims and have been recovering the victims' losses. All a victim has to do is pay them a fee and they will recover those losses, too. The truth, however, is that the recovery fee goes down the same fraud hole as the original loss did, and the elder is a victim once again.

Exploitive Control Over Finances and Decision Making

Probably the most devastating of all frauds upon elders is committed not by professional con artists but by opportunistic family members, companions, and caretakers. These exploiters usually work gradually, so that the elder does not fully realize the extent to which they are taking over control of the elder's finances and life. And they operate secretively, so that the elder's family does not realize what is happening until it is too late. The process by which these exploiters gain an elder's confidence and then take control over the elder's decision making and finances is described earlier in this chapter.

The specific steps a family member, caretaker, or companion takes to gain control and ultimately to loot an elder's resources often start small. These may include doing the shopping, paying the bills, and getting spending cash for the elder. Each of these things involves handling the elder's money, in one form or another, and allows small-scale siphoning of the elder's funds. At the same time, the exploiter often takes and reads the elder's mail.

The next step is to convince the elder that "for convenience" the exploiter should be able to write and sign the elder's checks, sign for the elder's credit card charges, or keep the elder's ATM card and PIN number. This may soon escalate into having the exploiting person's name added to the elder's bank account and to having a bank and credit card issued in his or her name. If the exploiter is already doing the bill paying and handling related paperwork, it becomes easy to rack up large debts on the elder's accounts, without the elder or anyone else realizing it. The longer this control of daily finances goes undetected, the more extensive and difficult it becomes to trace the looting.

A relative, companion, or caretaker may also try to take an elder's money in big chunks. They may do this by convincing the elder to invest in some business or money-making project. This may be a long-odds scheme the exploiter truly hopes will pay off. Or, it may be a completely bogus scheme, designed simply to separate money from the elder: The exploiter pockets the money, then later reports that the scheme did not pan out and that both lost their money.

Exploiters also loot assets by convincing elders, with one sort of sob story or another, that they need a loan—for school, for medical care, for a sick relative, to save a troubled business, or the like. Not only is this loan never paid back, but it is often followed up by a second or third loan when the exploiter reports that the first one did not do the trick.

The biggest looting of all takes place when a relative, companion, or caretaker convinces an elder to execute legal documents handing over authority or deciding the future of the elder's estate. This may include a power of attorney over the elder's person and finances, the deeding of property, the execution of a trust with the exploiter as the trustee or beneficiary, buying life insurance with the exploiter as beneficiary, or having the elder change his or her will.

Internet and Email Scams

An increasing number of seniors regularly use the Internet to connect with loved ones and conduct the business of their daily lives. Using the Internet, however, also exposes elders to a relentless world of scammers.

Types of Internet and Email Scams

Internet and email scams come in a variety of forms – from the obviously fake and ridiculous, to elaborate and sophisticated schemes. Here are some of the key dangers to be aware of.

Classic Fraud via Email. Scammers often use familiar yet tempting tricks to fool you into giving them money. For example, you receive an email that offers you an amazing deal—discount medicines or software, easy money for working at home, investment opportunities, guaranteed loans or credit, and so on. You respond to the offer and pay your money, but receive nothing in return.

To avoid these schemes, adhere to a strict policy of not responding to any email offers that you have not requested. If you receive an offer from what you believe to be a valid business, perhaps because you've done business with them before, do not respond via email or through links in the email offer. Instead, go to the business's regular website —if the business is legit, it'll have one—and, if the offer is repeated there, contact them directly through that site.

Don't Try to Give Help Through Email

Internet scammers have become experts at preying on those with a desire to help others. In some scams, they send urgent emails pleading for your help. Often they say they're trying to access a large amount of cash and claim that if you send them a little money, they will reward your kindness by splitting the pot with you. This type of fraud has a reputation for originating in Nigeria, but these emails can come from anywhere in the world, and they are always a scam.

Additionally, scammers have taken to profiting from natural disasters. After a flood, fire, earthquake, tsunami, or other devastating event, they send emails soliciting donations for relief efforts—but the money goes straight into the scammers' pockets.

If you wish to help those in need, do not respond to unsolicited emails. Instead, use a charity that you know and trust from previous experience.

Phishing. Phishing refers to emails that *appear* to be from a familiar business, but are actually from a scammer. They often look exactly like legitimate emails you would receive from your bank, credit card company, social networking site, or some other business you regularly deal with. They may even appear to use that business's logo and website address. Usually the emails tell you that you need to log into your account or do something else on the business's website. However, if you use the links in the email, you're sent to a bogus website which looks almost identical to the authentic website. Once there, you're asked to enter your personal information—which they then use to steal from you and businesses—or you unsuspectingly download malicious software onto your computer.

The best way to avoid phishing is never use links within an email. If a business legitimately needs you to access your account, you will always be able to do that by going to the website on your own, not through links in the email. Even if you find yourself absolutely sure that you received an email from a business you trust, before you click on any link, always double-check the Web address you land on, to make sure it is the legitimate address of that business.

Malicious software. A great Internet danger today is viruses that put malicious software on your computer. You may not even know they're there, and yet they can cause serious damage while you use your computer.

Sometimes called "trojan horses," these programs come disguised as an attachment to an otherwise friendly-looking email. The email may contain a joke, a kind note, or an advertisement. When you open the attachment, a virus is downloaded to your computer. It may allow the attacker to track your activity on the Internet—including logins and passwords to secure sites—or give the attacker access to the files on your computer. It could also install an electronic "bug" onto your computer that can send spam or viruses from your email account. Any of these can cause severe damage to you or others.

To avoid downloading malicious software, treat all email attachments with extreme caution. One red flag about dangerous attachments is the file's extension, which is the last few letters of the file name after the period. Most safe files will have extensions you recognize, like .doc for Word documents or .jpg for photos. If you see an extension you don't recognize, do not open the file. Finally, get good antivirus software to protect you in case you do mistakenly open an infected file.

How to Avoid Email and Internet Scams

Here is a summary of what you need to do to protect yourself or an elder from email and Internet scams.

Use a good spam filter. The best way to avoid nasty emails is to never receive them. Most reliable email programs have pretty good spam filters that keep out most of the junk.

Don't trust unsolicited email. Follow a general rule of ignoring and deleting emails from unfamiliar senders, assuming they're bogus. If you come across an unsolicited email that you think might be legit, access its website directly through your browser (*not* through an email link) and investigate the company before you give them any of your personal information.

Avoid opening email attachments. If you decide to open an attachment, be sure you recognize the file extension first (see above). If you receive an attachment from a friend that you're not sure about, email the friend and ask if them if it's the real deal.

Don't click links in emails. Instead of clicking links in emails, contact the business through what you know to be its legitimate website.

Install antivirus software and a personal fire wall. These will help you avoid receiving viruses and will also help isolate and destroy any that do find their way onto your computer. Be sure to keep these programs up-to-date so that they are ready to catch the latest scams.

Stay mindful of new ploys. There are many sites dedicated to tracking scams and educating consumers about using the Internet safely. A few that can help you keep up to date on the latest dangers are:

- FBI Cyber Investigations: www.fbi.gov/scams-safety/e-scams
- Hoax Slayer: www.hoax-slayer.com, and
- Scamdex: www.scamdex.com.

How to Report a Cyber Crime

If you or an elder are a victim of a crime perpetrated through email or the Internet, you may want to report the crime to the authorities. Although actually catching and punishing the perpetrators may be unlikely, reporting such crimes is a necessary step toward identifying the scams and keeping them from happening again. You can report a cyber crime on the website of the The Internet Crime Complaint Center (IC3)—a partnership between the Federal Bureau of Investigation (FBI), the National White Collar Crime Center (NW3C), and the Bureau of Justice Assistance (BJA). The Web address is www.ic3.gov.

Other Common Crime Scenes

Finally, here are some of the other common devices used by con artists to steal smaller, but nonetheless substantial, amounts of money, especially from elders. If you or a loved one is considering spending money on any of these, pay extra attention to the credentials of the people asking for that money.

Package Holidays. Elders often have extensive leisure time, but are not usually comfortable setting out on vacations on their own. Instead, they tend to sign up for package holidays. Knowing this, con artists offer all kinds of attractive deals—including airfare or cruise ship accommodations, hotels, and tours. These all too often wind up being either completely false promises or shabby, disorganized, wildly overpriced versions of what was offered. Whenever considering a package holiday, always make sure you are dealing with a reputable company by speaking with others who have used their services and by checking with the local Better Business Bureau.

Charities. Telephone solicitations for charities are always risky business. Scam charities are plentiful, especially after natural disasters. If you are interested in giving to a charity, ask to have written materials sent to you that explain exactly what the organization is and does, and what percentage of donations actually goes to the charitable work. Never agree to a charity donation in an initial phone call. And never give out credit card or bank information over the phone. To check on the legitimacy of a charity, you can contact the Better Business Bureau's Wise Giving Alliance at www.bbb.org/us/charity or at 703-276-0100.

Health and Comfort Products. Understandably, older people tend to be very concerned about their health and the physical difficulties of aging. As a result, they are often interested in products that claim to make life healthier, more comfortable, or safer. Newspapers, magazines, and the Internet are full of advertisements for vitamins, herbs, protein powders, sleep aids, home safety devices, and exercise equipment. Unfortunately, most of these products are either useless or so poorly made that they quickly fall apart. And some of them are even dangerous. So, always check with a doctor about effectiveness and safety before ingesting any mail-order health products. And beware of any equipment or device unless you have actually seen the product used repeatedly by a friend or neighbor.

Work-at-Home Kits. Many elders feel financially pinched but can no longer, or no longer want to, work outside their homes. There are many schemes that promise the chance to earn good money from home. But most of these so-called work-at-home jobs are scams. They require you to pay for materials, training, or a "license." And they never deliver any real money-making work.

Where to Get Help

If you believe that you or a loved one may be the victim of a fraud or of improper influence or control, there are a number of places you can turn for help. This section identifies some sources of information and government protection for victims of specific types of fraud.

Home Repair or Improvement

When considering a contractor, check with the Better Business Bureau to find out if it has any record of complaints against the company. They can also help you find out whether the company is properly licensed. The Bureau office closest to you will be listed in the business portion of the telephone book, or you can find them by going online at www.bbb.org. You can also find good information from the National Consumer Law Center, a nonprofit legal group that helps enforce consumer protection laws. You can find them at www.nclc.org.

If you believe you have been the victim of a scam, you can contact your local district attorney or county counsel's office. Most offices have a special consumer protection or consumer fraud division. Or, you can contact your state government consumer protection agency. You can find both numbers in the Government section of the phone book white pages. The Federal Trade Commission also maintains a Bureau of Consumer Protection (BCP) where you may file a complaint. Contact the BCP at www.ftc.gov/bcp or at 877-382-4357.

Investment Fraud

If you are suspicious about a potential investment, or if you are having trouble getting information about an investment you have already made, you may want to contact one or more of these resources to discuss your options:

- **The National Fraud Information Center.** The National Fraud Information Center is a service of the nonprofit National Consumers League. You can file a complaint and read about many types of investment fraud at www.fraud.org.

- **The Securities and Exchange Commission.** 800-732-0330 or www.sec.gov

- **North American Securities Administrators Association.** 202-737-0900 or www.nasaa.org, and

- **National Futures Association.** For problems or questions regarding investments in commodities; 800-621-3570 or www.nfa.futures.org.

Deceptive Sales or Advertising Practices

Fraudulent sales and advertising tactics range from large matters, such as home mortgages, to relatively small things like a mail-order kitchen gadget. Whatever the size of the scam and the scope of your loss, a good place to start finding out about your rights and your chances of recovery is the Better Business Bureau. Go to www.bbb.org to find the number of the office nearest you. Or, you can find the nearest office in the white pages of your phone directory.

Another place to turn is the consumer fraud unit of your local or state prosecuting attorney's office. Most county district attorney offices and all state attorney general offices maintain separate consumer fraud or consumer protection units that specializes in keeping track of con artists working in their local areas and helping consumers recover their losses. You can find the phone number for your local district attorney's office and your state attorney general's office in the Government pages of the phone book—there is usually a separate phone listing for the consumer fraud or consumer protection unit.

You can get assistance from the nonprofit National Fraud Information Center at www.fraud.org. You may also find good information and referrals from the National Consumer Law Center, a nonprofit legal group that helps enforce consumer protection laws. You can find them at www.nclc.org.

If your loss is large enough, it may also be worth it to hire your own private attorney. If the loss is large and the chances of recovery are good, an attorney may be willing to take your case on what is called a contingency fee basis. That means the lawyer gets paid a percentage of the money he or she recovers for you. And if there is no recovery, you do not have to pay the lawyer. The National Consumer Law Center may have referrals to lawyers in your area who specialize in consumer fraud cases.

Finding and Working With a Lawyer

If you or a loved one has been the victim of a large-scale fraud, you may want or need to hire a private attorney to help you prove the fraud and recover your money. An attorney may also be needed to help an elder escape the clutches of a controlling and exploiting individual. And, an attorney may be needed to fight a battle for you after the elder has died, against someone who had managed to siphon off the elder's assets or to manipulate themselves into the position of receiving the bulk of the elder's estate.

If you are considering hiring a lawyer to represent you in such a matter, be aware that not just any lawyer will do. You should find a lawyer with experience in the specific legal issue that pertains to your situation.

- If you or a loved one has been the victim of fraud, you need to find a lawyer with experience representing individual claimants in litigation—meaning going to court for people with personal legal issues.

- If the problem involves an elder being controlled or manipulated by an exploiting relative or other individual, you may need a lawyer experienced in conservatorship, guardianship, and other matters which fall under the general heading of "elder law."

- If the dispute is over the assets of an elder who has died, you may need someone experienced in probate.

There are several ways to find a lawyer with the experience you need. If you or a relative or friend have had a satisfactory experience with a lawyer on another matter, contact that lawyer as a place to start—lawyers usually know or can find out for you about other lawyers in a particular legal specialty. Also, almost every county's local bar association—the lawyers' professional organization—maintains a referral service. You describe your legal problem, and then they direct you to several local lawyers in that field. Be aware, however, that these referral services do not guarantee the quality or limit the charges of the lawyers they connect you with. Finally, you may be able to get a referral to a local lawyer who specializes in matters pertaining to seniors by contacting the various national organizations listed in the appendix of this book under "Legal Assistance."

Undue Influence and Control Over an Elder

Getting help for an elder who has fallen under someone's manipulative influence or control can be difficult because, in these circumstances, the elder may not want or be able to cooperate. But it is just such circumstances in which getting help is most important.

The first step is to try to speak with the elder without the exploiting person present, asking the elder if he or she realizes what is happening and would like help getting out of the person's clutches. If possible, more than one person should attend such a meeting. This gives the elder the idea that there will be substantial support. And if you get a positive response from the elder, having more than one witness to the elder's complaints can provide stronger evidence when you report the problem and try to take steps to remedy it. If the elder is in an organized residential setting or long-term care facility, also report the problem to the facility administrators and seek their support and assistance.

If you cannot see the elder alone or cannot get the elder to recognize or respond to the problem, you will need outside assistance. You and other family members may want to hire a private attorney to respond to the problem. (See "Finding and Working With a Lawyer," above.) But there are also public agencies that are experienced in elder exploitation problems and that are set up to intervene when a family cannot solve the problem alone. The primary public agency for such intervention is called Adult Protective Services (APS). An APS office will investigate your complaint and has the authority to take all legal steps necessary to free an elder from someone's undue influence and control, and to recover any funds that person has improperly siphoned from the elder's assets. This includes having someone appointed conservator or guardian of the elder's person or finances. If there is no trustworthy family member or other person living close to the elder, APS can arrange to have a court appoint a public guardian instead.

Local APS offices operate as part of county social services departments, county counsel's offices, or other city or county departments. You can find a listing for your local office by looking under Adult Protective Services in the Government pages of your phone directory. If you have trouble locating the office or otherwise getting assistance, you can get help from the nationwide free government service called Eldercare Locator at www.eldercare.gov or at 800-677-1116.

Every state also maintains a toll-free telephone hot line where elder abuse, including financial exploitation, can be reported. These hot line services will then put you in touch with the local agency that can best respond to the elder's problem. Two sets of hot lines are maintained, one for elders living on their own or in senior residences, the other for elders living in long-term care facilities. You can find the number for your state's elder abuse hot line at the website of the National Center on Elder Abuse at www.ncea.aoa.gov. Or, you can get the number by calling the Eldercare Locator at 800-677-1116. ●

Resource Directory

Area and State Agencies on Aging

The federal government and every state government operate Area Agencies on Aging, which are central clearinghouses of information for people seeking services for elders:

- To find the federal government-sponsored Area Agency on Aging nearest you, go to www.n4a.org/about-n4a click on "About AAA/Title VI," and then find your state and local area.
- To find the state agency on aging for your state, go to www.aoa.gov and click "SUA/AAA Finder" to use the interactive state agency finder.

Alzheimer's Disease Organizations

Two national organizations focus exclusively on Alzheimer's disease. Both provide information on the disease, on medical and nonmedical care, and on assistance for those who provide care to those with Alzheimer's.

Alzheimer's Association

800-272-3900

www.alz.org

Alzheimer's Disease Education and Referral Center

800-438-4380

www.nia.nih.gov/alzheimers

Caregiver Support Groups

Children of Aging Parents
800-227-7294

www.caps4caregivers.org

National Family Caregivers Association
800-896-3650

www.nfcacares.org

Family Caregiver Alliance
800-445-8106

www.caregiver.org

National Alliance for Caregiving
www.caregiving.org

info@caregiving.org

Home Care, Community Programs, and Senior Residences

The following organizations provide information about home care agencies, community senior services, and nonnursing-home senior residences. Some provide referrals to specific providers and facilities. They can also put you in touch with state and local organizations, which can, in turn, provide you with even more detailed information and referrals.

National Organizations for Home Care, Community Programs, and Senior Residences

Alliance for Children and Families
414-359-1040
www.alliance1.org
Offers senior referrals as well as other family services

The Eldercare Locator
800-677-1116
www.eldercare.gov
Open Monday through Friday, 9 a.m. to 11 p.m. (EST), this hot line refers people to elder care services in communities across the country

National Association for Home Care & Hospice
202-547-7424
www.nahc.org
Maintains a list of home care agencies and offers a guide on choosing the right one

National Association of Professional Geriatric Care Managers
520-881-8008
www.caremanager.org

National Council on Aging
202-479-1200
800-424-9046
www.ncoa.org

National Health Information Center
Department of Health and Human Services
Referral Specialist
800-336-4797
www.health.gov/nhic

National Hispanic Council on Aging
202-347-9733
www.nhcoa.org
Provides information on topics related to Hispanics and aging, and provides assistance for Spanish-speaking seniors

Visiting Nurse Associations of America
202-384-1420
www.vnaa.org

Hospice Organizations

To find a hospice, palliative care, or other end-of-life care agency near you, contact any of the following.

National Hospice and Palliative Care Organization (NHPCO)

www.n4a.org/about-n4a (click on "About AAA/Title VI")

800-658-8898

877-658-8896 (for languages other than English)

The Hospice Association of America

www.nahc.org/haa

202-546-4759

The Hospice Directory of the Hospice Foundation of America

www.hospicedirectory.org

800-854-3402

Insurance—Long-Term Care

State Departments of Insurance

Each state has a government agency that regulates the sale of insurance. There should be a listing for an insurance department in the Government section of the telephone directory. Or, search online using the name of your state and the term "state department of insurance." These agencies can provide you with a list of companies authorized to sell long-term insurance in your state.

State Agencies on Aging

Like the Department of Insurance, the Office on Aging in your state should have a current list of long-term care policies authorized for sale in your state. See "Area and State Agencies on Aging," earlier in this appendix for information about how to find an agency near you.

Legal Assistance

The following groups either provide, or give referrals for, legal assistance for elders. Some provide information on government programs and legislation affecting the elderly. Others will refer you to lawyers in your area who specialize in legal matters affecting elders, such as reviewing the terms of a reverse mortgage, preparing powers of attorney, and planning your estate.

National Academy of Elder Law Attorneys, Inc.
703-942-5711
www.naela.com

National Caucus and Center on Black Aged, Inc.
202-637-8400
www.ncba-aged.org

National Senior Citizens Law Center
202-289-6976
www.nsclc.org/index.php/consumers

Medicaid Assistance

Qualifying for Medicaid (Medi-Cal in California) coverage can be complicated and confusing. However, every state has a State Health Insurance Assistance Program (SHIP), which provides free assistance for people seeking Medicaid coverage. The state program may go by one of several different names—SHIP, Health Insurance Counseling and Advocacy Program (HICAP), Senior Health Insurance Benefits Advisors (SHIBA), or the like. There is a SHIP office in most metropolitan areas. To find the SHIP office nearest you, visit the website of the National SHIP Resource Center at www.shiptalk.org or phone the Eldercare Locator at 800-677-1116.

Nursing Facility and Alternative Residence Organizations

The following organizations monitor nursing facilities and other elder residences across the country. They can direct you to information, organizations, and state agencies that list and refer consumers to specific nursing homes and other residences in your area. They can also give you contact information to the state agency that issues licenses and monitors complaints against nursing facilities in your state.

American Association of Homes and Services for the Aging

202-783-2242

www.aahsa.org

A nonprofit national association of nursing facilities and senior independent living and assisted living residences. It will provide a list of all member facilities in your state, including level of facility, type of sponsorship, number of living units or beds, and services offered.

American Health Care Association

202-842-4444

www.ahca.org

A national association of accredited nursing facilities. It will provide a list of its member facilities in your state.

The National Consumer Voice for Quality Long-Term Care

202-332-2275

www.theconsumervoice.org

Monitors enforcement of state and federal laws regarding conditions and practices in nursing facilities and other facilities for the elderly. Although it does not provide referrals to nursing facilities or other residences, it can refer you to local organizations that have information about specific facilities.

Ombudsman Offices

Each state has a central office that can refer you to the long-term care ombudsman responsible for any nursing facility that you are considering or in which you already reside. Long-term care ombudsmen respond to complaints about long-term care facilities and mediate disputes between residents and the facilities. They are in a unique position to know whether a facility has frequent complaints, and whether the facility responds well to them. There is no charge for their services. For information on local and state ombudsman programs in your state, check the National Long-Term Care Ombudsman Resource Center:

National LTC Ombudsman Resource Center
202-332-2275
http://ltcombudsman.org/ombudsman

Reverse Mortgage and Home Equity Conversion Assistance

The Department of Housing and Urban Development (HUD) monitors and approves the counseling agencies that can provide free help finding lenders who offer reverse mortgages in your area. Finding a counselor through the HUD referral system also will help you avoid reverse mortgage scam artists. For a referral to free counseling, call HUD at 800-569-4287 or go to www.hud.gov and enter "talk to a counselor" in the search box.

Life Insurance Settlement Assistance

The following organizations may give you leads to reputable life insurance settlement companies in your area. They may also provide you with some general information about the terms offered in life settlement plans. However, they do not answer specific questions about the advisability of entering into a life settlement or about the terms of any specific settlement offer. That is still entirely up to you, with the help of an accountant, lawyer, or other financial adviser.

Life Insurance Settlement Association

407-894-3797

www.lisassociation.org

Your state's Department of Insurance

Look online or in the "Government Listings" section of the white pages of your telephone book.

Index

A

O

Go to Nolo.com/newsletters to sign up for free newsletters and discounts on Nolo products.

- **Nolo's Special Offer.** A monthly newsletter with the biggest Nolo discounts around.

- **Landlord's Quarterly.** Deals and free tips for landlords and property managers.

 Don't forget to check for updates. Find this book at **Nolo.com** and click "Legal Updates."

Let Us Hear From You

3 Register your Nolo product and give us your feedback at Nolo.com/customer-support/ productregistration.

- Once you've registered, you qualify for technical support if you have any trouble with a download (though most folks don't).

- We'll send you a coupon for 15% off your next Nolo.com order!

ELD9

NOLO and USA TODAY

Cutting-Edge Content, Unparalleled Expertise

The Busy Family's Guide to Money
by Sandra Block, Kathy Chu & John Waggoner • $19.99

The Work From Home Handbook
Flex Your Time, Improve Your Life
by Diana Fitzpatrick & Stephen Fishman • $19.99

Retire Happy
What You Can Do NOW to Guarantee a Great Retirement
by Richard Stim & Ralph Warner • $19.99

The Essential Guide for First-Time Homeowners
Maximize Your Investment & Enjoy Your New Home
by Ilona Bray & Alayna Schroeder • $19.99

Easy Ways to Lower Your Taxes
Simple Strategies Every Taxpayer Should Know
by Sandra Block & Stephen Fishman • $19.99

First-Time Landlord
Your Guide to Renting Out a Single-Family Home
by Attorney Janet Portman, Marcia Stewart & Michael Molinski • $19.99

Stopping Identity Theft
10 Easy Steps to Security
by Scott Mitic, CEO, TrustedID, Inc. • $19.99

The Mom's Guide to Wills & Estate Planning
by Attorney Liza Hanks • $21.99

Running a Side Business
How to Create a Second Income
by Attorneys Richard Stim & Lisa Guerin • $21.99

Nannies and Au Pairs
Hiring In-Home Child Care
by Ilona Bray, J.D. • $19.99

The Judge Who Hated Red Nail Polish
& Other Crazy But True Stories of Law and Lawyers
by Ilona Bray, Richard Stim & the Editors of Nolo • $19.99

⚖ NOLO | *Online Legal Forms*

Nolo offers a large library of legal solutions and forms, created by Nolo's in-house legal staff. These reliable documents can be prepared in minutes.

Create a Document

- **Incorporation.** Incorporate your business in any state.
- **LLC Formations.** Gain asset protection and pass-through tax status in any state.
- **Wills.** Nolo has helped people make over 2 million wills. Is it time to make or revise yours?
- **Living Trust (avoid probate).** Plan now to save your family the cost, delays, and hassle of probate.
- **Trademark.** Protect the name of your business or product.
- **Provisional Patent.** Preserve your rights under patent law and claim "patent pending" status.

Download a Legal Form

Nolo.com has hundreds of top quality legal forms available for download—bills of sale, promissory notes, nondisclosure agreements, LLC operating agreements, corporate minutes, commercial lease and sublease, motor vehicle bill of sale, consignment agreements and many more.

Review Your Documents

Many lawyers in Nolo's consumer-friendly lawyer directory will review Nolo documents for a very reasonable fee. Check their detailed profiles at **Nolo.com/lawyers**.